Practical Home

DRESSMAKING

Illustrated

This smart suit, semi-tailored with a high button front, and the simple shirt-waist frock, which has slimming lines, are only two of the garments which you can make from the detailed instructions given in these pages. There are clear, diagrammatic drawings to show you how to cut the patterns correctly to your own measurements.

Practical Home
DRESSMAKING
Illustrated

+

Complete instructions in the
art of dressmaking for the beginner and
more experienced worker. Profusely illustrated
with easy to follow diagrammatic drawings
and photographs

By LYNN HILLSON

Odhams Press Limited · Long Acre · London

CONTENTS

Here you see a corner of a kitchen which has been fitted to make a sewing room. Note the cupboards and shelves, the table with a drawer for odds and ends, the good light from the window and electric light, a chair correct in height, and the iron and board near by.

6

EQUIPMENT

SEWING ROOM

There is not much joy in dressmaking if the work has to be packed up every time there are other things to do. The ideal is to have somewhere to leave it untouched.

If you have a small room which is not much used, or even a corner in the kitchen or dining-room, turn it into a sewing room, where you can dressmake in comfort. You will find this a great help and time saver; the work can be left where it is if you are called away to make a meal or entertain a friend. The materials and sewing equipment are kept neat and clean in their own corner. The furniture for a sewing room should be carefully chosen.

Have a small chest of drawers in which to keep the materials before making up. Paper patterns, notebooks, pressing cloths and other odds and ends can be kept in the spare drawers. Save a corner in a small drawer for the scraps of material left over from garments after making, which will be found useful for mending, alterations and trimmings.

If the sewing machine has no stand, a small table will be needed. Choose a table with a leaf on the left-hand side to hold the material during stitching.

If you have an electric sewing machine it will be necessary to have a point from which to work it. If there is no alternative use a two-bulb socket in the light, and secure any surplus flex neatly out of the way.

You will also need a larger table with a smooth surface, on which to lay out the work. Make sure that you can sit at it comfortably with your knees under-neath. A small drawer is useful to keep scissors, pins and needles close at hand when working. This table should be large enough for a cutting-out surface.

Keep an old cloth to spread beneath the table while working. This will serve the double purpose of keeping clean any part of the work which falls to the ground, and collecting cotton threads and snippings, which can then be gathered up easily afterwards.

The chair should be carefully chosen to get the right height and comfort when sitting at the machine, or at the table hand sewing.

There should be a dress stand, for fitting, and an old sheet or cloth to cover it and keep it clean.

The garments in making should be kept hung to avoid creasing. Have a small cupboard fitted with hooks and coat hangers, or put hooks behind the door, on the wall or in one corner of the room, and arrange a curtain to cover the hanging garments.

A full-length mirror is an asset when fitting has to be done. Fasten this to the wall or on the inside of the cupboard door.

In cold weather the room must be heated so have a small gas fire or electric stove. Either will be more convenient than a coal fire which is dusty and makes extra work.

If you have the spare space keep the pressing outfit in the sewing room, too. The electric point fitted for the machine can be used for the iron.

Drawing materials and other equipment can be kept in one of the drawers of the chest or on a cupboard shelf,

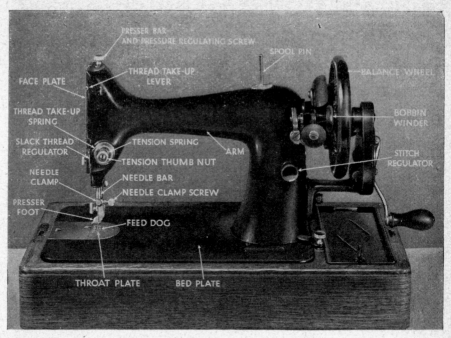

PRESSER BAR
AND PRESSURE REGULATING SCREW
SPOOL PIN
THREAD TAKE-UP
LEVER
BALANCE WHEEL
FACE PLATE
THREAD TAKE-UP
SPRING
BOBBIN
WINDER
SLACK THREAD
REGULATOR
TENSION SPRING
ARM
STITCH
REGULATOR
TENSION THUMB NUT
NEEDLE
CLAMP
NEEDLE BAR
NEEDLE CLAMP SCREW
PRESSER
FOOT
FEED DOG
THROAT PLATE
BED PLATE

A photograph of a popular sewing machine with each individual part named for easy reference; it is necessary to be acquainted with the different parts, for assistance in sewing.

THE SEWING MACHINE

The most essential item of equipment is the sewing machine; choose one of reliable make. A machine will, if well cared for, last a lifetime, so treat this purchase as an investment rather than an extravagance.

If you are setting up your workroom for the first time and will do a large amount of dressmaking, an electric machine is the best choice. The portable model is neat and compact and will fit into a corner when not in use. An electric machine on a stand is more practicable for general use, the stand, which is fitted with small drawers to hold scissors, pins and cottons, will take the place of an extra table.

The motor is controlled by the knee or the foot, leaving both hands free.

If you possess a hand or treadle machine in good order it is possible to have a small electric motor fitted with little expense and trouble. The small electric light can be fitted at the same time.

The uses of the principal parts of a sewing machine are:—

The Presser Foot.—Rests upon the fabric, prevents it rising with the needle and holds it in contact with the feed dog. The section of the foot which presses on the cloth is slotted so that the view of the stitching may not be obstructed.

The Presser Bar Lifter.—A lever at the back of the machine which raises the presser foot to release the material when machining is finished.

Spool Pin.—A spindle which holds the bobbin of cotton feeding the needle.

Pressure Regulating Thumb Screw. —A screw fitted to the top of the presser bar which regulates the pressure of the presser foot on the cloth; it is regulated according to the thickness of material being sewn to ensure an even line of stitching.

Clamp Stop Motion Screw.—A large nut on the driving wheel which is released, whilst the bobbin is being filled, to stop the motion of the needle of the machine.

Bobbin Winder Friction Ring.—The little rubber wheel which runs against the balance wheel when filling the bobbin.

Thread Take-up Spring.—A small wire spring fitted to the tension disks, which holds the needle cotton and helps keep the correct tension throughout the work.

Tension Spring.—A flat spring which keeps the tension disk tight and holds the cotton taut, and keeps the stitches neat.

Presser Foot Screw.—The small screw, at the side of the presser foot, which is released when the foot is to be removed.

Tension Thumb Nut.—The nut which holds the tension spring and tension disk in place. It can be released or tightened to regulate the tension of the cotton.

Needle Clamp.—A small clamp which fits on to the needle bar and holds the needle in place.

Needle Clamp Screw.—Fits into the needle clamp, holds it in place and keeps the needle rigid.

Slack Thread Regulator.—A solid hook fitted behind the face plate under which the cotton passes. It prevents the needle thread from looping whilst stitching.

The clamp stop motion screw is released when the bobbin is being wound to allow the winder to operate without the needle moving. The screw is found at the side of the balance wheel, it is turned left to loosen and right to tighten.

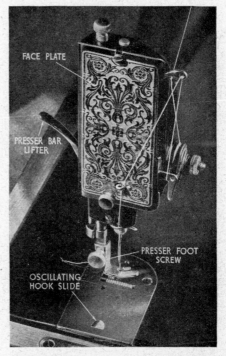

The face plate, a vertical plate at the end of the arm, can be removed to give access to the needle-bar mechanism for oiling.

CARE OF THE MACHINE

The mechanism of a sewing machine varies slightly with each different type.

The way in which machines are used and cared for is similar in each case, the main difference between them being the shape of the shuttle or bobbin. Some types have a long-shaped shuttle and others a round bobbin.

The detailed drawings on page 11 show a machine with a round bobbin, and on page 12 the long-shuttle type is illustrated. The oiling points differ slightly but the two drawings give a clear illustration of where they are placed.

Any sewing machine that is not well cared for will not give good service. It should be cleaned and oiled at least once a week, or daily if it is in constant use. If the oil is allowed to become dry and stiff the machine will run hard and not sew properly. Special sewing machine oil is available and should be used for this purpose. Do not use household or other kinds of lubricating oil.

Remove all dust, fluff and loose threads from the mechanism of the machine before oiling. Use a small bottle-brush or pipe-cleaner for this purpose and pay special attention to the bobbin case.

Use the oil sparingly. One drop of oil applied to each contact point is sufficient. Turn the head of the machine back on its hinges to get at the oiling points underneath. Lower the machine back into the upright position to oil the points in the main part of the machine.

When oiling the bobbin winder take care to prevent the oil from coming into contact with the rubber ring, as it will cause deterioration of the rubber and also make the wheel slip on the hub of the balance wheel.

The stand of a treadle machine must be oiled and kept free from dust in the same way as the working parts.

After oiling make sure that all the surplus oil is wiped away from the machine with a soft rag. If this is neglected the fabric of the garment may be ruined. Finally, get rid of the superfluous oil by running the machine, unthreaded, over a small piece of old material.

When the machine has been out of use for some time, and had little or no attention, you may find that it will run hard when you come to use it again. This bad running is usually caused by the oil having become dried up and sticky. To cure this complaint drop a little paraffin into each of the oiling points and run the machine rapidly for a few minutes. The machine should then be wiped thoroughly with a soft duster. Oil all the working parts after using paraffin, and it is also advisable to oil a second time after a few hours use.

Here are a few points to remember in the care of a machine, whichever type is being used.

When setting the needle into the machine turn the balance wheel towards you until the needle bar is at its highest position, and loosen the thumb screw. Insert the needle into the groove, with the flat side towards the needle bar, as far as it will go. Tighten the thumb screw.

Most machines are threaded from left to right, but a few are threaded the reverse way. The point to remember is that the cotton is passed through the hole on the side of the needle which has the long groove. This groove is always the reverse side to the flat side, and it is this which determines which side of the needle bar the needle is set.

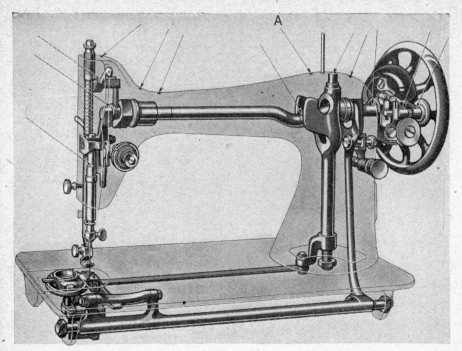

A

The sewing machine must be oiled at least once a week. All the moving parts must be covered with a film of oil and not allowed to become dry. Oil should be applied at all the points indicated by arrows; a drop of oil in each is sufficient. The take-up lever must be at the lowest point when oil is applied at A. Wipe away all surplus oil.

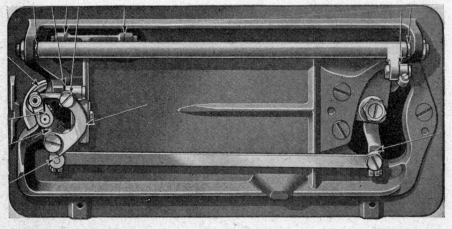

Turn the head of the machine back on the hinges to get at the oiling points underneath. These parts must be kept lubricated as often as those in the head of the machine. If there is a circle of felt in the bobbin case a drop of oil is applied to it ; this lubricates the important movable parts of the shuttle mechanism. Remove all fluff, cottons and dirt from the movable parts before applying the oil, where shown by the arrows.

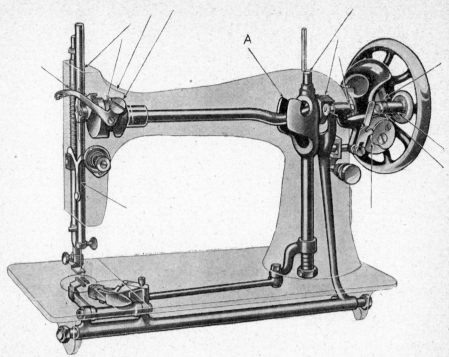

A

The oiling of a sewing machine with the long type spool is similar to the round-bobbin type, shown on the previous page. When cleaning and oiling remove the slide plate, shuttle, needle and presser foot. The under part of shuttle can then be cleaned and oiled.

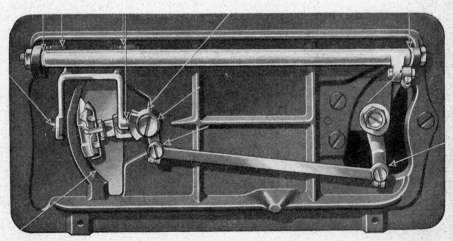

Use only high-grade oils for a sewing machine, other kinds will tend to clog the mechanism and may necessitate a complete overhaul of the machine. Insert the oil-can spout well into the oil holes. Lower the head back into the upright position and run the machine for a few minutes to distribute the oil. Wipe away all surplus oil with a soft duster.

When threading the machine, turn the balance wheel over towards you until the take-up lever is raised to its highest point, place the cotton on the reel pin and pass the cotton through the notch at the top of the machine, between the tension disks, and into the take-up spring. The exact details of threading must be followed to suit the particular type of machine being used.

Draw two or three inches of the thread through the needle before commencing to sew.

The under thread must be drawn to the top before sewing is started. To do this hold the end of the needle thread in the left hand, leaving it slack between the hand and the needle. Turn the balance wheel over towards you so that the needle moves down and up again to its highest point. The under thread will be caught up in a loop and can be pulled through to the top with a pair of scissors.

The shuttle or bobbin must be wound smoothly and evenly, and not over full. Learn how to insert it into the bobbin case correctly, otherwise the cotton will break whilst machining.

When running the machine for any purpose, always have a piece of material between the presser foot and the feed dog.

Practise straight stitching on a piece of paper, without thread, before doing any actual sewing.

Keep the tension regular and even. Always keep the machine covered when not in use, to prevent dust and dirt harming it.

Use the machine carefully and it will seldom go wrong. If little faults or difficulties do arise rectify them immediately. It is so simple and will save wear, tear and strain.

Some of the more common faults are:

Top Thread too Tight.—The cause can be that the needle is wrongly threaded or the tension is too tight. Regulate the top tension with the tension thumb nut, turn it to the left to loosen the tension and to the right to make it tighter.

A bent needle or one that is wrongly set or has a broken point can also be the cause of trouble. When inserting the needle take care to get it in the correct position. Push it up as far as it will go before tightening the screw.

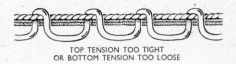

TOP TENSION TOO TIGHT
OR BOTTOM TENSION TOO LOOSE

Under Thread too Tight.—The cause can be that the bobbin is too tightly wound or filled too full. Take great care when filling the bobbin and make sure that it is being fed smoothly and evenly during winding.

TOP TENSION TOO LOOSE
OR BOTTOM TENSION TOO TIGHT

A bottom tension that is too tight may be the cause of trouble. This tension is regulated by the small screw under which the thread passes on the shuttle or bobbin case. This is always correctly adjusted before the machine leaves the factory so should seldom require altering. If you find it is necessary to do so turn the screw very

CORRECT TENSION

slightly to the left to loosen and to the right to tighten.

For correct stitching the tension of the two threads should be equal.

Needles Breaking.—Caused by the use of incorrect size and type of needle for the thread and material being sewn.

The presser foot, or attachment, may be insecurely fastened to the presser bar.

Do not try to remove the work from the machine until the thread take-up lever is at its highest point.

Stitches Missing.—Missing stitches may be caused by the needle being blunt, incorrectly set, or bent. A needle that is too fine for the cotton being used is another cause of this fault.

Looping.—Is usually caused by loose tensions. Incorrect upper and lower threading, or a badly wound bobbin.

Machine not Feeding Correctly.—This is usually caused by too tight tension, too light pressure on the material, or wrong adjustment of the stitch regulator.

Puckered Seams.—The stitch may be too long for the type of material being sewn, or the tension may be set too tight.

The Machine Working Heavily.—The oil may have gummed with standing and lack of use, or the belt of the treadle may be too tight.

The bobbin winder may have been snapped down into the operative position, thus putting pressure on the balance wheel, which prevents it turning freely.

USE OF THE MACHINE

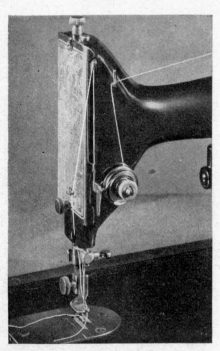

Make sure the needle is threaded correctly before use, or cotton and needle will break.

The performance of a sewing machine depends largely on having it threaded correctly. The method of threading varies slightly with each type of machine, so the instructions given with it must be read carefully first.

Winding the bobbin is another operation that needs great care. Make sure that the thread is wound smoothly and evenly, and do not fill the bobbin too full. Have a sufficient number of bobbins for the colours being used so that it will not be necessary to wind thread on a bobbin that is partly wound. If this is done the ends may become entangled and cause trouble in the bobbin case.

Always release the clamp stop motion screw before winding the bobbin then push the winder back into position, or it will press on the balance wheel.

To complete the threading of the machine drop the bobbin into the case. Here again it will be necessary to consult the instruction book given with the machine as they all differ slightly. If the bobbin is incorrectly placed it can cause no end of trouble. Pull the under thread through to the top before commencing to sew.

Great care in the choice of needles and cotton is needed. Make sure that you have a number of appropriate sizes to use with the various materials. Never use a fine needle with heavy material, it might break. A thick needle on fine material will make ugly holes.

Remember, too, that a fine material needs a light tension and heavy materials must have a stronger tension to make a perfect stitch.

A round bobbin in place.

Here are some important points to notice whilst machining:—

1. When stitching very fine material place a layer of paper underneath it and stitch the two together. The paper easily tears away afterwards leaving a good, evenly stitched seam.

2. If a straight edge is being sewn to a bias edge the bias piece must be placed underneath so that it will not stretch.

3. There are three ways in which seams may be finished off:

(*a*) After machining raise the presser foot leaving the needle still piercing the work. Turn the work right round and stitch along the machining for about one inch.

(*b*) Pull the top thread to the wrong side, and tie the two threads in a firm knot.

(*c*) Invisibly darn each thread separately into the material, after the sewing has been completed.

Wind the bobbin evenly and smoothly to avoid a too tight tension on the under thread.

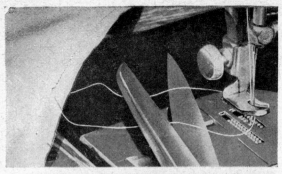

4. Do not attempt to remove work from the machine until the thread take-up lever is at its highest point. Lift the presser bar and pull garment to the back and to the left of the machine. Cut the threads, leaving ends for fastening.

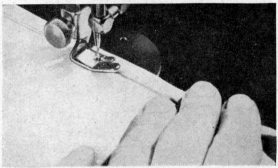

5. Keep the work flat on the bed plate of the machine, hold it firmly with the left hand but never pull it away from the needle. Only when the edge is crossway cut should it be eased under the needle. Arrange the bulk of the work on the left of the needle, and not bunched up under the arm.

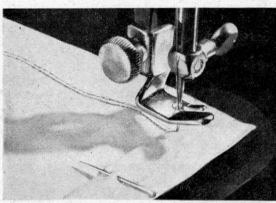

6. To turn corners when sewing hems or bindings, sew as far as the corner and stop with the needle piercing the material right in the corner of the hem. Lift the presser foot and turn the work round on the needle until the second side is in the right position for sewing. Drop the foot and continue stitching in the normal way in this direction.

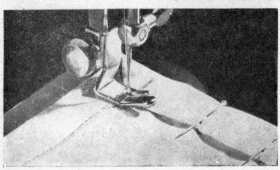

Note the position of the foot after turning the corner. Use the inside edge of the wider side of the presser foot as a guide to straight stitching when sewing hems and such edges. If sewing over tacking stitches try to stitch to one side of the tacking or the threads will be difficult to remove.

7. If the hem being sewn is not tacked the pins should be inserted at right angles to the hem so that they can be easily removed. When sewing a seam that is pinned have the pin heads towards you so that they can be easily removed. Avoid stitching over pins as this will blunt the needle.

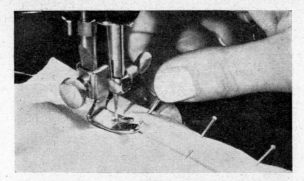

8. When making rows of parallel lines of machine stitching keep the lines straight and gauge the width between by using the edge of the presser foot as a guide. The first line is kept parallel with the edge of material. Use the left side of the foot for wide spaces and right for narrow ones.

9. Awkward corners and sudden thicknesses are sometimes difficult to machine over. Take these slowly and ease the bulk under the presser foot with a screwdriver or the closed points of scissors. If the machine being used is fitted with a hinged presser foot it will pass over additional thicknesses without further aid.

10. With a few exceptions gathers should be machined with the fulness laid flat to the feed dog. This prevents the presser foot from catching in the full material. When sewing with the gathers at the top ease the fulness under the presser foot with the points of scissors or a screwdriver as described in 9 above.

SEWING MACHINE ATTACHMENTS
and How To Use Them

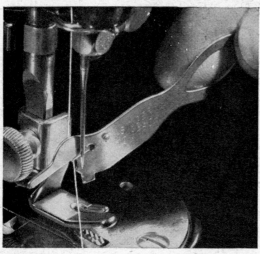

The hook of the needle threader is run down the groove of the needle until it finds the eye. Push the hook through the eye and pass the cotton under the long arm of the threader and then under the hook. Hold the cotton with left hand.

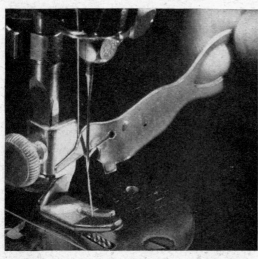

The hook is pulled through the eye of the needle whilst the cotton is still held with the left hand; release the cotton and then pull the thread right through the eye and the needle is threaded. Use of this gadget saves the strain of eyes and nerves.

There are a number of attachments supplied with every machine, which can be used for special types of work. The more complicated attachments, such as the darner and the ruffler, are not supplied with the machine but can be bought separately. These gadgets vary slightly with each make of machine, but the principles of use are similar. One point to remember—the attachments supplied with one make of machine will not work with another make.

Use the attachments intelligently and they will save you much labour and time. For instance, don't fix the hemmer to the machine to sew a short hem, it is quicker to turn the hem down by hand and tack it. On the other hand, if there are yards and yards of hem to be sewn the hemmer will save the extra work.

The illustrations in this chapter show gadgets being used on a well-known make of machine. From these you can gain an idea of the simplicity of use and the effective work that can be done. **The Needle Threader.** — A boon to all machinists as a time and patience saver. The threader is fitted with various sized hooks to fit the different needles. Press the gadget against the back of the needle and slide it gently down until the hook slips into the eye of the needle. Pass the cotton over the hook and pull it through the eye of the needle.

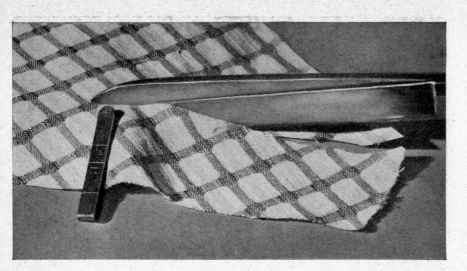

The Bias Cutting Gauge.—The gauge is fitted to the point of the scissors, the blue spring is set to the right width and the material is then inserted into the opening as far as the spring. It can be adjusted to three different widths —F for facings; B for bindings; and C is used for cords and pipings.

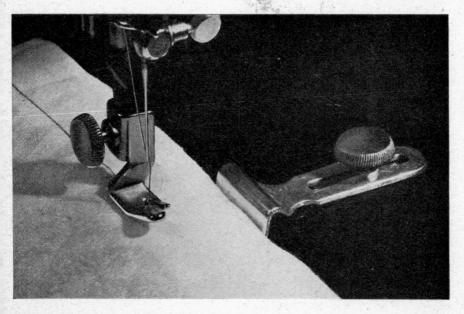

The Cloth Guide.—This gadget is fastened firmly to the bed plate of the machine with a thumb screw. The distances between the needle and guide should equal that between the material edge and the stitching. First fold the hem the correct width and tack it, then insert the work into the machine, keeping the folded edge of the hem just touching the cloth guide.

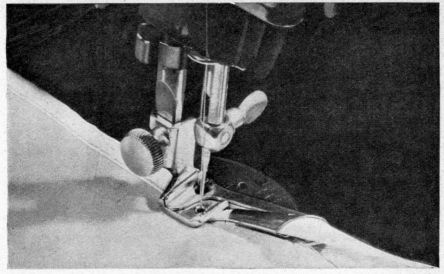

The raw edge of the binding is turned under whilst the line of machining is made.

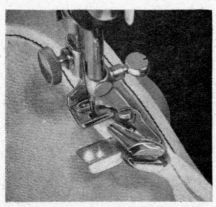

A french fold sewn in line with the binder.

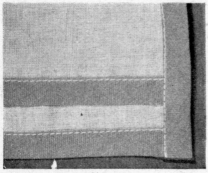

Binding and french fold machine sewn.

The Binder.—This gadget simplifies the binding of edges and the stitching of decorative bands for trimming blouses and children's tub frocks.

Remove the presser foot and attach the binder in its place. The bias strip, with the end cut to a point, is inserted in the slot of the binder scroll until it comes out at the lower end. The edge of the material to be bound is placed in the centre slot of the scroll. Pass this material and the binding under the presser foot of the binder. Drop the presser foot and stitch in the usual way. The edge of the binding will be turned under as it passes through the scroll.

When using bought bias binding, the edges of which are already turned under, insert it into the binder in the same way but thread it this time into the outside slot of the scroll. Braid or ribbon are used in this way.

To adjust the position of the line of stitching loosen the screw at the top and move the scroll to the right or to the left, as required for the work in hand.

If the edge of material is allowed to slip out of the scroll it will fall away from the fold of the binding when passing under the needle and the edge will not be caught into the stitching.

A decorative french fold can be applied by placing the material under the attachment, and not in the slot, after the binding has been inserted into the scroll. A chalk line drawn where the band is to be stitched will act as a guide to keeping the fold straight whilst the sewing is made.

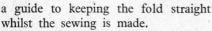

With practice you will soon become proficient in the use of this gadget for curves, corners and buttonhole loops. Remember to ease the binding round the outer edge of a corner and stretch it slightly at an inside curve, then the edge will lie perfectly flat.

The Edge Stitcher.—This attachment is invaluable for stitching two pieces of lace or ribbon together, or trimming on to the very edge of material. It is fitted on to the machine after the presser foot has been removed. Insert the material, or one piece of lace, through the first slot on the left of the gadget, and then under the edge stitcher itself. The lace is inserted under the second slot on the right and then under the foot but over the material. Drop the foot and stitch in the usual way. Care must be taken to keep the lace well over the material when stitching or it will slip away and the two edges will not be joined together.

Attractive striped effects can be obtained by joining several different coloured ribbons in this way.

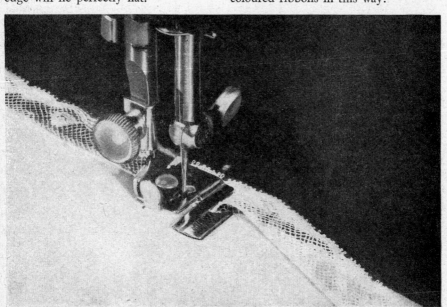

When applying lace to the edge of material, or joining two lengths of lace together, the edge stitcher is helpful. Keep the lace well over the material to obtain a good join.

The Adjustable Hemmer.—A gadget that will save hours of endless work when yards and yards of hem have to be made. It is especially useful in the making and mending of household linen.

This attachment is one which will make a hem of any width up to one inch and even wider than that with special adjustment. Remove the presser foot and attach the hemmer to the presser bar. Place the material in the hemmer, keeping it under the scale. Draw the work backwards and forwards

until the hem is formed. It will then be possible to determine the width and fold the end of the hem for the second turning. Draw the material forward until the end comes under the needle. Drop the presser bar and stitch in the usual way, guiding sufficient material carefully into the gadget to turn the hem properly.

Care should be taken to start the hem on the edge or it will run on the bias and become uneven at the other end. Practise using the hemmer with striped material. When you can match all the stripes exactly then you will be able to hem a garment properly.

To adjust the hemmer loosen the screw and move the guide to the right or to the left until the correct width is obtained.

When sewing soft materials slip a piece of thin paper under the hemmer next to the feed. This can be torn away after stitching, and it will help to prevent stretching and turn the hem more easily.

The Foot Hemmer.—This is especially useful for hemming the edges of

collars and frills in all soft materials, when a narrow hem is essential. When hemming flimsy fabrics such as georgette insert a piece of paper under the material and let it feed through with the work. Use a paper about the same weight and thickness as newspaper which can be torn away after stitching. This will help to turn the hem and prevent puckering.

When hemming a curved or bias edge insert paper under the

hemmer, to take up the fulness of the material.

To use the gadget remove the presser foot from the machine and replace it with the foot hemmer.

Start the hem at the very edge of the material; this is an important point to remember, if it is not started at the edge the material is pulled on the bias and the hem cannot be made.

Fold over one-sixteenth of an inch at the start and for a distance of one inch. Place the material in the hemmer just beyond the fold. Draw the material towards you through the hemmer, at the same time making the second fold at the very edge. When the edge of the hem is under the needle drop the presser foot and stitch in the usual way. To commence sewing pull the end of the hem gently away from the foot at the back.

The same width of material must be kept in the hemmer throughout the work. Guide the work with the thumb and forefinger.

This attachment is useful for making a hemmed seam, used on lingerie

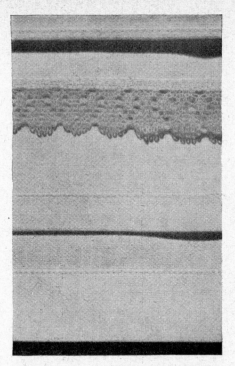

Use the adjustable hemmer for wide hems, and the foot hemmer for narrow ones. Lace is applied to a hem with the foot hemmer. Below, the foot hemmer in use.

and garments where a straight seam is made. Insert the two edges of the material into the foot together as previously described.

To attach lace or insertion to a narrow hem. Start the hem as before. Leave the needle in the hem and raise the presser bar, insert the lace under the foot hemmer and through the slot at the right. Catch the lace with the needle and stitch it along the edge of the hem whilst it is being made.

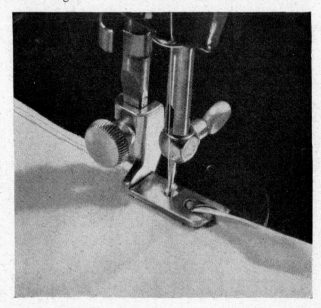

Insert the movable bar into the quilting foot as a guide to straight-line stitching. It can be used either side of the foot.

The Quilter.—This is very simple to use and invaluable in the making of quilted linings, bed jackets and other cosy garments.

The quilting foot is attached to the machine in place of the presser foot.

The quilter guide may be used either side of the needle. Slide the long rod into the quilting foot, and set the guide in the right position to gauge the width that is desired between the lines of stitching. The distance between the guide and the needle determines the width between the lines of stitching. Lower the foot on to the material and stitch in the normal way.

When making the first row of stitching let the guide follow the edge of the material, a crease or drawn line, to ensure that the sewing is straight. The subsequent rows of stitching are kept in line with the first by keeping the guide rigidly on the previous line of stitching.

If the quilting pattern is free in design, remove the rod from the slot so that it will not hamper you in any way whilst stitching.

The Under Braider.—Use this gadget when applying braid in decorative patterns, as an aid to keeping the stitching straight and in the centre of the braid. The quilting foot is used in place of the ordinary foot. If the design chosen is a geometric one the movable bar can be used in the same way as for quilting. When sewing scroll and other designs, use the foot alone. The under braider itself is a small plate which fits on to the bed of the machine. It is designed to hold corded braids in place when stitching. These plates vary slightly in the way they are fitted to the machine; some clip on to the edge of the throat plate, others are kept rigid by a screw.

When using this attachment all the machining is done on the wrong side of the garment.

Apply the design to be braided on to the under side of the material, or mark out the design on paper by stitching over the design with the machine unthreaded. This paper is then tacked on to the wrong side of the material. Stitch through the perforations and tear paper away after braiding is sewn.

Thread the braid through the tube in the plate, pass the design under the presser foot and hold the end of the braid in place with the point of the needle. Always commence stitching at one end of the design or where a join can be made conveniently without showing. The sewing is quite simple, but great care should be taken to see that the braid does not become twisted as it is being fed through the tube of the plate.

Trace the design on the wrong side of the material when using the braider. The braid should not become twisted and the line of stitching must be in the centre. Use the quilting foot for this work, with the under braider. The movable bar may be used for straight stitching.

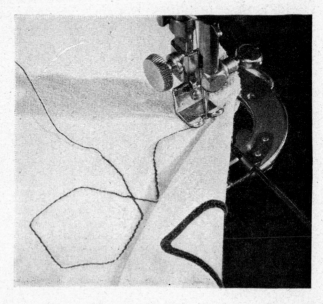

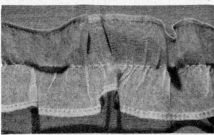

A narrow frill is gathered while it is being applied to the garment with the ruffler.

An edge can be gathered and neatened with a heading, by using the ruffler.

The Ruffler.—With this gadget the making of gathers and pleats is simplified to such an extent that you will never want to make them by hand again.

First remove the presser foot and attach the ruffler to the machine.

Gathers are made by placing the slot marked "1" on to the adjusting lever. The thumb nut in the middle of the gadget at the top regulates the fulness of the gathers. Screw it down tighter to increase the fulness, and release the screw to lessen the gathers. Always test the ruffler on a scrap of material before sewing the garment, and make the necessary adjustments until the gathers are the desired fulness.

Pass the material between the two blue blades. Pull the edge of the material away from you until it is slightly past the needle, keeping the edge to be gathered well between the blades. Drop the presser bar and sew in the usual way.

Narrow ruffles for trimming can be gathered and sewn on to the garment in one operation. Thread the piece to be ruffled between the two blue blades as before, taking care to have the needle over the line of stitching. The line to which the frill is to be sewn on the garment is passed under the separator blade, or under the ruffler itself. Guide the material lightly so that it will feed away from the heading guide.

Pleats.—Are made with same gadget but this time the slot "5" is placed on the adjusting lever, and the thumb nut is screwed right down as far as it will go. This will make the tiny pleats about one-eighth of an inch in width. To increase the distance between the pleats lengthen the stitch; decrease it in size to bring them closer together.

Evenly arranged pleats, or ones pleasantly grouped, are easily made with the ruffler.

Groups of pleats are made by simply lifting the adjusting lever on to the centre projection. While the lever is in this position plain sewing can be done for any length required. Readjust again to "5" to make the next group of pleats. The number of pleats in each group must be decided first so that they are uniform.

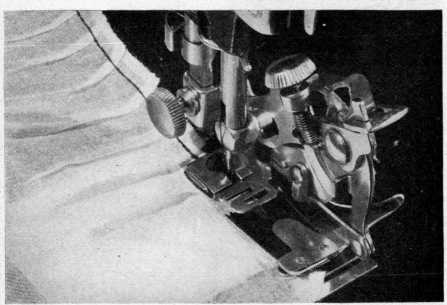

The ruffler is used for making pleats, equally spaced or in groups, as well as gathers.

27

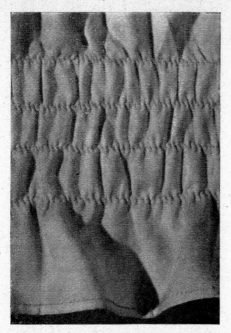

The Small Gathering Foot.—This

gadget will simplify the making of shirring; several rows of gathers worked in parallel lines, used as decoration and to introduce fulness into sleeves and skirts of children's frocks, blouses and dirndls.

The attachment is used in place of the presser foot. Place the material under the gathering foot and sew as if making a straight line of stitching. The gathers will be made by the machine and will be sewn in place at the same time. Use the edge of the foot as a guide to keeping the distance between the rows of gathers even, and the lines of stitching straight.

More fulness will be obtained by increasing the size of the stitch, likewise a shorter stitch will decrease the fulness.

It is sometimes necessary to finish the edge of shirring with a heading or binding, this can be attached at the time the first row of shirring is made.

Several rows of gathers, using the small gathering foot, for attractive ruching. A heading can be applied at the same time.

Slip the material for the heading between the slot in the foot. Make sure that it is under the needle when stitching, then sew as before.

A more decorative type of shirring can be worked by using embroidery cotton in the under bobbin, this will necessitate sewing the gathers with the wrong side uppermost.

This gadget can be used in the same way for making a single line of gathering. The method of working is exactly the same; the stitching is kept in line by allowing the edge of the gathering foot to follow the edge of the material.

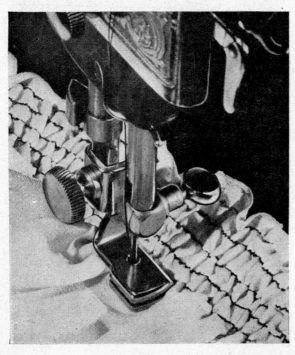

The Tucker.—This attachment gauges the width of the tuck being sewn and also marks the position of the next tuck. Attach the gadget to the machine in place of the presser foot, making sure that the needle clamp presses on the marking lever when sewing so that the position of the next tuck is marked. Set the scale to obtain the width of tuck required and also to get the correct distance between the tucks.

Fold the crease of the first tuck by hand. Insert the folded edge into the tucker from the left, placing it between the spur blade and the space scale, and between the two blades of the tuck scale. Make sure that the material when threaded into the tucker will feed against the tuck guide. Draw the material towards you until the edge is immediately under the needle. Lower the presser bar and sew.

Use the tucker to make decorative tucks for children's frocks, blouses and other garments.

When making tucks on silk or chiffon, materials which are hard to crease, slip a piece of paper under the tucker, and adjust the tension, before sewing.

Tucks of all widths can be made with the tucker, which not only gauges the width of the tuck being made, but marks the distance between each one. Make sure that the fold is on the straight of the material, or the tuck will pull badly out of line. Fold the first tuck by hand, keeping it straight by the edge of the material or a line of tacking stitches.

The Hemstitcher.—This gadget is one of the most simple to use. Attach it to the machine in place of the presser foot. Have two pieces of material, one under and one over the attachment, and make an ordinary line of stitching, sewing the two together. A fairly large stitch should be used so that the hemstitch bars are not too close together. After the line of stitching has been made, open the two pieces of material out flat, away from each other, and press them. Turn the raw edges back under the main fabric and fasten them down with a line of straight machine stitching, close to the edge.

One of the most attractive ways of fastening a hem to the edge of household linen or tailored collars and cuffs is by hemstitching; with this attachment it can be done quickly and easily. Cut a strip of material for the hem,

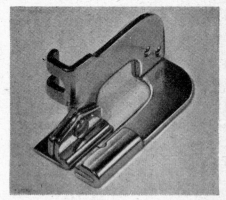

Hemstitching must be plain stitched each side to prevent the bars closing up, see top left. At top right, the hemstitching attachment in detail. At the bottom the gadget in use. A large stitch is used when hemstitching to keep the bars apart.

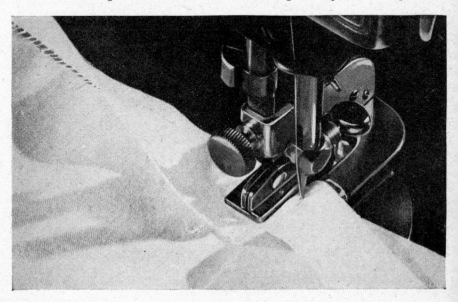

The hemstitcher is used for picot edging; draw out the top thread of machining, leaving a series of tiny loops along the edge of the material. Machine the edge on the right side.

twice the finished width plus half an inch for turnings. Fold this strip in half lengthwise and press the fold. Place the two raw edges level with the edge of the garment and sew them together in the normal way, using the hemstitcher. Finish with a line of plain stitching each side of the hemstitching as previously described.

When making hemstitching take care to have the correct tension, if it is too loose the bars will be untidy, if too tight they will pull out of shape.

Picot Edging.—Can be worked with this gadget, very satisfactorily, but it is not a suitable finish for the raw edge of material as it will not prevent the fabric from fraying, finish the edge with a tiny hem. The method used is exactly the same as for hemstitching. A small strip of material is sewn on to the garment, this need not be very wide or of a matching shade as it is removed after stitching. Always have this strip underneath whilst machining. When the line of sewing has been made, turn under the garment edge and fasten it down with a line of plain machining, close to the edge; this keeps the loops in place. Then draw out the under thread of machining, leaving tiny loops on the edge of the garment. The raw edge of the hem can be neatened on the wrong side with overcasting, page 154, or tiny running stitches.

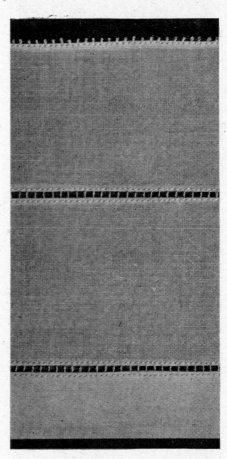

The hemstitcher can be used to attach a hem to a garment, to join two pieces of material together, and to finish an edge with picot. The method of using the gadget in all these cases is similar.

31

Corded piping when sewn in place with the cording foot.

The Cording Foot.—In appearance, this is similar to half an ordinary presser foot. It is designed in this way so that stitching can be made close up to a raised thickness, such as a corded piping. Have the needle next to the cord whilst machining. Remove the presser foot and fix the cording foot in its place. Then make a single line of stitching in the normal way.

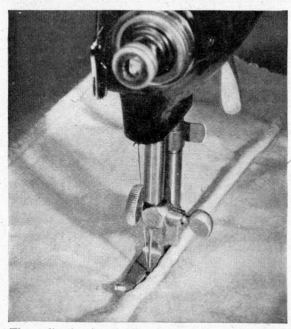

The cording foot in use. Note the needle close to the piping.

The Darner.—Darning of fabric can be done on the sewing machine as neatly as by hand, and in half the time. It requires a little patience and practice at first, but once you get used to handling the gadget everything will be plain sailing.

First remove the presser foot and the thumb screw which fastens it to the presser bar. Then remove the needle clamp and re-place it with the darning presser, still keeping the needle in the same place. Take care to keep the needle in the correct position and make sure that it is pushed up as far as it will go into the needle clamp.

Slide the shuttle cover back and clip the feed cover plate over the needle plate, making sure that the needle passes through the little hole in the centre. Close the shuttle plate again.

When threading for darning, pass the cotton through the hole in the slack thread regulator and not underneath. Use a fine needle and fine mer-cerized cotton.

The hole to be darned is stretched taut by fixing the material into a darning hoop. Pass the work under the needle and drop the presser bar so that the needle enters the material at one edge of the darn. Move the hoop backwards and forwards stitching all the time. When the darn has been covered with stitching one way, turn the work and sew in the other direction.

Move the hoop slowly to obtain a short stitch and quickly for a long one.

The darn, when finished, should be round or oval in shape, thus avoiding too much strain on any one thread. Take the lines of stitching half an inch beyond the hole each side, this will strengthen the material round the hole. Endeavour to match the darn to the texture of the material.

General Notes.—A few hints on the use of all these attachments. If, after reading this chapter and studying the directions given with your machine, you would like further advice and help, go to your nearest machine shop. The assistants will willingly give you a demonstration of how to use the gadgets and the machine generally. Such a visit will be of interest as you will pick up many useful hints on the use and upkeep of the machine.

Household linen can be repaired as neatly on the machine as by hand, if the darner is used. Practice in using this gadget will be needed before a perfect darn can be made.

THE WORK BASKET AND ACCESSORIES

A well-stocked work basket is the first essential of every needlewoman. Nothing is more irritating than to sit down to do a job of mending or sewing and to find that there are no buttons, no cotton of the right colour, or that some other small item is missing.

The woman with a family and husband to care for should stock her basket with a selection of shirt buttons, pearl and linen buttons of all sizes for underclothing, tape in varying widths, black and white press fasteners and hooks and eyes, ribbon for shoulder straps, black and white cotton of different grades and coloured cottons in popular shades, needles in all sizes, pins, a thimble, scissors of different shapes and a good strong tape measure.

Such things as bias binding, fancy buttons and trimmings, can be saved as they are collected for various garments. It is not advisable to buy these unless they are needed for a particular purpose; the colour or texture may be wrong when they are required.

It is always worth while to select tools and materials of the best quality which will last for ever. There is a lot of hard wear on sewing tools.

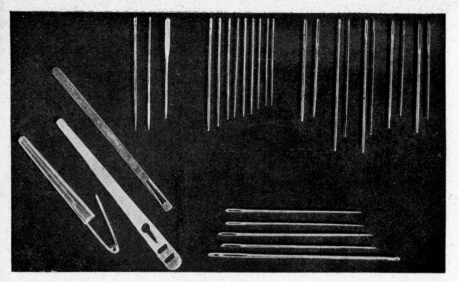

The top row shows: a sewing needle with a split eye, for easy threading; a three-sided needle; machine needle; all sizes of sewing needles; wool, straw, darning, crewel and tapestry needles. Larger darning needles, a bodkin and ribbon threaders at the bottom.

Needles.—Choose good quality needles of different kinds and in varying sizes. Keep them in the black paper cases, in a tin. Each package is marked with the size it contains and the paper prevents tarnishing.

The size of the needle should suit the weight of material being sewn, and should carry the sewing thread easily.

Study the table given below for a guide to the correct size.

Ribbon Threaders and Bodkins.—Three different kinds of ribbon threaders are shown in the picture. The one with the safety pin is the most practical to use when threading elastic. The two other examples have slots at one end designed to hold the ribbon firm.

TABLE OF NEEDLE AND THREAD SIZES

MATERIALS	SEWING NEEDLES	MACHINE NEEDLES	THREADS		
			Cotton	Silk	Linen
Thin muslin, cambric and georgette	10/11	9	100 to 150	30	—
Very fine cottons and fine silks .	9/10	11	80 to 100	24 to 30	—
Sheeting and household materials	7/8	14	60 to 80	20	—
Heavy calico and silks, light woollens	6/7	16	40 to 60	16 to 18	—
Ticking, heavy woollens . .	5/6	18	30 to 40	10 to 12	—
Heavy woollens for coats . .	4/5	19	24 to 30	—	60 to 80
Coarse cloth	3/4	21	Very coarse	—	40 to 60

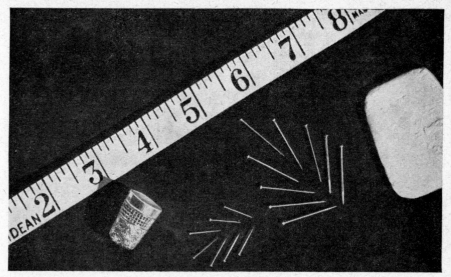

A tape measure that will not stretch, clearly marked in inches; a thimble; "lil" pins for fine work, steel pins for normal use and tailor's chalk for making fitting marks.

An example of a bodkin, used for threading ribbon and cords, is shown at the bottom of the picture.

Pins.—Pins should be carefully chosen, harsh blunted points will make black marks in the fabric causing it to be spoilt unnecessarily.

For normal use choose medium-sized thin steel pins, these are sharp and easy to use. Always avoid using brass pins as these are thick and clumsy and will mark the material badly.

For dainty work and when pinning chiffons the tiny "lil" pins are the most suitable, but they must be steel. These are not strong enough to use on the heavier materials.

Tacking Cotton.—It is possible to buy large reels of basting cotton, which is not so strong as ordinary sewing cotton but quite suitable for tacking. White is the best colour to use for normal sewing, but if you are working white or light-coloured fabrics a darker colour should be used as a contrast. Avoid, if possible, black or very dark colours as these will stain the material.

Tape Measure.—The waxed variety is the best as it is strong and will not stretch. Make sure the measure is clearly marked and easy to read. Choose a tape sixty inches long.

The Thimble.—Select one that is comfortable and not too heavy. Brass thimbles are not good as they tend to mark the materials in the same way that they soil the fingers. The main thing to aim at is a good fit.

Hem Guide.—A measure on a stand which is used for marking the correct position of hems. A metal peg, which holds a piece of chalk, fits into a hole at the required height for the hem line. Stand close to the guide, turn round gradually, and have someone mark the hem line with the chalk.

Yard Stick.—No description is required here as the name describes the measure. It will, however, be found invaluable for marking hem lengths if there is no hem guide available.

It can also be used to measure lengths of material. Use it, too, when cutting out or when pattern drawing.

36

Tailor's Chalk.—This is a soft chalk made in white for use on dark materials and in many shades for light fabrics. It is preferable to other kinds of chalk as it will rub off the material easily.

Use chalk to mark the outline of the pattern on material, the position of tucks, darts, gathers, other fitting marks. Use it, too, when making alterations during fitting.

Button Box.—Save buttons from worn out garments, and keep them with other loose buttons of all kinds in a little box. Keep hooks and eyes and press fasteners in a box of their own.

Pin Cushion.—Pins are more easily picked from a pin cushion; have this handy when fitting garments, it will save time and irritation. It is a good idea to make one that will pin on to your frock, or have one sewn on to a piece of elastic so that it can be slipped on to the wrist.

Small Ruler. — Choose one that is transparent and washable, it will be easier to use and to keep clean. Use this ruler when measuring the width of hems, the position of buttons and buttonholes and other fastenings. It is more accurate for these purposes than a tape measure, as it will stay flat and not stretch.

Fuller's Earth Powder. —Dust the hands with the fuller's earth powder whilst sewing, this will keep them soft and dry and prevent the garment from becoming soiled.

French Chalk.—If a spot of oil from the sewing machine gets on to the work it can be removed with french chalk. Sprinkle a little of the chalk on the spot and leave it some time to let it penetrate well into the material and absorb the grease.

Then shake the powder off the fabric gently.

In a loosely woven fabric the chalk will fall between the fibres, brush it out with a very soft brush.

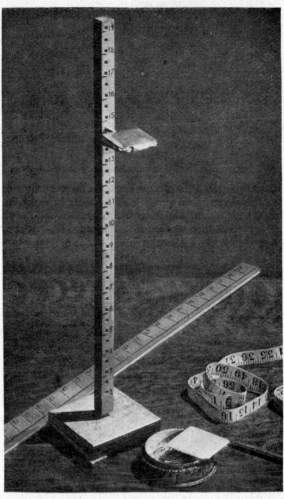

A measure on a stand and a yard stick for measuring hems. Note the chalk in the metal peg which fits into the holes.

37

SCISSORS AND SHEARS

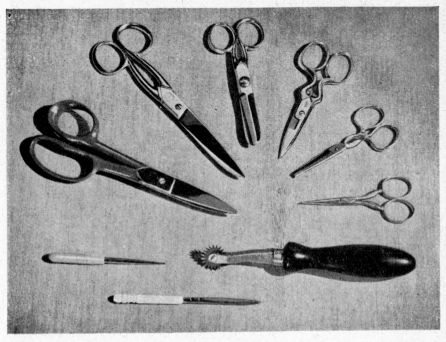

Starting at the left of the semicircle are large cutting out shears for heavy materials, next smaller shears which çan be used on lightweight fabrics and for cutting patterns. Then pinking shears, adjustable buttonhole scissors, ball end scissors, and small pointed scissors for cutting cottons and snicking corners. Across the bottom of the picture at the left, a round stiletto, a flat stiletto, and a tracing wheel for marking fitting features.

Small, sharp pointed scissors are invaluable for snipping tacking threads and ends of cotton. Use them for cutting into the points of corners and the ends of darts, and any difficulties which the points will fit.

These are some of the most important items of equipment in the work basket. It is essential to have scissors of the very best quality; the cut of a garment can be completely ruined if blunt or too small scissors are used. Varying sizes for different purposes will be needed. **Trimming Scissors.**—These should be pointed and very sharp. They are used for trimming the edges of seams, snipping tacking cottons and for general purposes.

A tiny pair of scissors will be found of use, too, for cutting machine cottons, snicking into corners, unpicking and all fine work.

Cutting-out Shears.—Choose a pair of shears that you find easy to handle.

One blade of shears is usually wider than the other, keep this to the table when cutting.

Do not have them too small, especially if heavy materials are to be cut. Shears should have large holes for the thumb and fingers; otherwise, with a large amount of cutting, the hand will become very tired. Never use these scissors for cutting paper or they will be ruined. Keep a lighter and not so good pair for rough purposes.

Shears, if in constant use, should be ground and reset frequently by an expert.

Ball End Scissors.—These scissors are used for cutting one layer of two thicknesses of material. One of the blades has a blunt end, so there is no fear of snicking the under layer.

Buttonhole Scissors.—Can be adjusted to cut any size of buttonhole without damaging the edge of the garment. The size is regulated as required by the screw in the centre of the scissors. Test the scissors for size on a scrap of material before cutting the buttonhole in the garment.

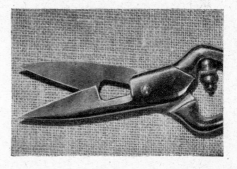

The blunted blade of ball end scissors, above, prevents the under fabric being cut. Below, details of buttonhole scissors with the size adjusting knob are shown.

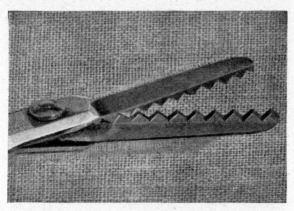

The die-cut blades of the pinking scissors, above, pink the material into a serrated edge with normal cutting. A quick way of neating seam edges.

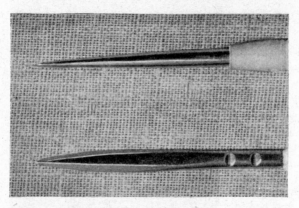

Above, two kinds of stiletto points, at the top the round type, at the bottom a flat point. Below, the pointed wheel used for tracing is shown.

Pinking Scissors.—The blades of these scissors are die-cut in a zigzag so that when they cut the material it is pinked at the same time. If used to trim edges of seams on non-fraying materials no other kind of neatening is required. It is sometimes possible to cut out the garment with the pinking scissors and so eliminate any further work on the seam edges.

Stiletto. — These vary slightly in shape, they can be perfectly round, or with a point flattened on two sides. The latter type makes larger holes. Stilettos are used for making eyelet holes and for any other purpose where the material is to be punched without breaking the threads.

Tracing Wheel. — The name describes this tool and its use. It is a small wheel of sharp spikes, mounted on to a handle. It is used to trace the position of darts and fitting marks; it is also used for tracing round the edges of patterns. The advantage over other methods of marking is that it will trace through several thicknesses of paper or material at the same time. It is much quicker than tacking. Always take the precaution of having a piece of board under the material when tracing, or the table top will be ruined.

PRESSING OUTFIT

Having fitted your work basket out with the best possible equipment, turn your attention to the pressing outfit which is just as important.

To obtain the best results in dressmaking it is essential to press each seam, dart and every little detail during the process of making. So many amateur dressmakers neglect to do this and leave all the pressing until the garment is completed; consequently, the finished result has a permanent "homemade unpressed" look. It is a good plan, therefore, to keep the pressing tools handy in the sewing room, and so save time and energy.

This chapter describes in detail some of the most essential pressing needs. Choose the best quality that you can afford and they will last a lifetime.

The Iron.—This is the most important pressing tool and should be treated as a treasured possession. Choose one that is heavy and with a smooth surface. Electric irons are the most popular as they are easy to use. If there is no electricity available a gas iron will be a good substitute; these are heated by a small gas jet during use. If a flat iron has to be used care should be taken to ensure that it is clean after heating to prevent the work from becoming soiled.

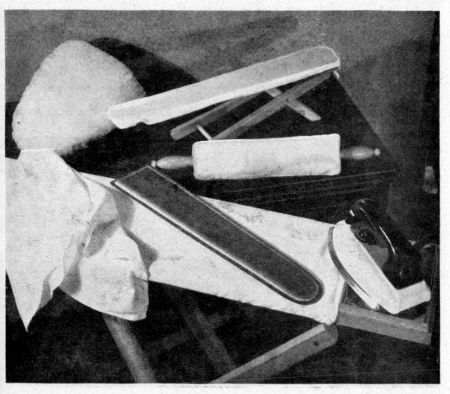

The main requirements of a pressing outfit: a tailor's cushion; sleeve board and roller for pressing seams; the iron; needle board and damp cloths; and the ironing board.

The Ironing Board.—Choose a board that is solid and firm on the legs, nothing is more annoying than an ironing board that rocks like a baby's cradle during the pressing. The board itself should be evenly padded all over with thick felt or blanket. Make a removable cover out of old white linen or cotton sheeting that fits the board exactly without wrinkles or creases. At one end there is a triangular shaped pocket which fits over the point of the ironing board. Tapes are fastened to both sides and are tied under the board.

A board with a fireproof iron stand at one end will eliminate the possibility of fire. If the iron is left standing upright it is liable to get knocked over and damage will be caused to the iron or surrounding furniture.

Pressing Cloths.—Use old material for these, preferably linen as this will absorb the moisture evenly without being too wet. Failing linen use cotton, but it must be material that has been washed and with the dressing taken out. A sponge is useful, too, for damping odd corners.

Sleeve Board.—This is a small version of an ironing board with a stand of its own. It should be about four inches wide at one end tapering to half the width at the other. When

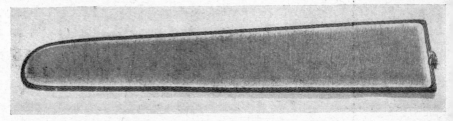

The needle board is used when velvets and other pile materials are being pressed.

The sleeve board is a miniature ironing board and it is used for the pressing of seams, tops of sleeves and other awkward corners. Make a detachable linen cover to fit.

padded and covered in the same way as the ironing board it is invaluable for pressing sleeve seams, armhole seams and awkward corners.

Needle Board.—This is used when pressing velvet and other pile fabrics. It consists of a board to which is attached a strip of canvas very finely studded with tiny wires, which prevent the surface from being flattened.

Ironing Pad.—A very useful pressing pad with flannel on one side and wire gauze on the other. When this pad is used there is no fear of scorch or shine.

Having dealt with the routine equipment which you can buy, there are now two simple little gadgets which you can make for yourself, quickly and easily, and with little cost.

The Tailor's Cushion.—This is a useful addition to the pressing outfit. It is used when pressing darts, curved seams, the tops of sleeves; in fact any part of a garment which cannot be pressed satisfactorily on a flat board, or roller.

Use stout cotton sheeting or other material that is strong in texture for making this cushion. Cut out two pear-shaped pieces, fifteen by eleven inches. Machine stitch these two pieces together round the edges, with two lines of stitching for strength, leaving an opening at one side. Turn this bag inside out and stuff it tightly with fine sawdust, cotton wool or rags and sew the opening. The diagram at the top of the page gives the measurements for the cushion. It is advisable to keep to the egg shape illustrated as the pointed end is useful for pressing smaller curves.

Pack the cushion as tightly as possible so that it will not sag. If the cushion becomes soft with constant use, or through the sawdust drying, unpick the opening and add more stuffing until it is hard again.

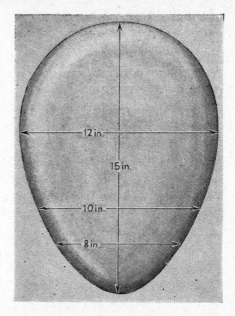

The tailor's cushion is egg shaped; two pieces of strong linen are sewn together and stuffed tightly with sawdust until quite hard.

Pressing Roller.—If seams are pressed on a rounded surface the finished result is much cleaner and sharper than if a flat board is used. This also prevents the edge of the seam turnings making a mark on the right side of the garment, particularly if thin material is being pressed. Any rounded surface will do providing it is well padded, but here is a way to use an ordinary rolling pin.

Have a slice sawn off the rolling pin to give it a flat side, this will prevent it from rolling about during pressing. Fold a double thickness of old blanket round the roller and then a piece of linen ; stitch these firmly in place.

To make a longer roller use a stout broom handle.

THE DRESS FORM

The home dressmaker who has to do her own fitting will find a dress form, made to her own measurements, an immense help. It will save much time and discouragement as faults can be corrected whilst the work progresses. Details can be studied from every angle,

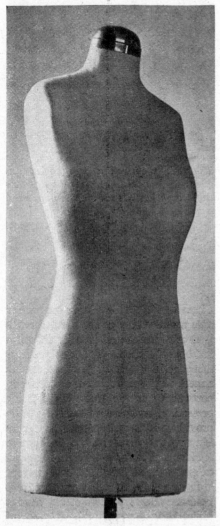

The solid form can be made to given measurements but can only be altered by the addition of padding.

awkward seams and fitting darts can be adjusted, and the hang and length of the hem may be corrected with ease.

When preparing a garment for fitting on the dress form, remember that this is a solid figure which has no give or movement. It will be necessary, therefore, to allow a larger opening than normally; the garment can then be slipped over the shoulders without ripping the seams.

The dress form must of course be the exact measurement of the person for whom the garment is being made, otherwise all the fitting will be incorrect. It is sometimes necessary to adjust the size of the dress form so that it will conform to the altered measurements of your own figure. Details of how to do this are given in this chapter.

Choose a form that is fixed on a firm stand; never have castors fitted to the feet or the form will run about whilst the fitting is being carried out. Most dress forms are fixed to the stand in such a way that they can be turned round easily without having to be moved on the floor; this is a point to look for In these stands there is a screw which, when tightened, will hold the body of the form in a fixed position.

Another most important point to look for is that the height can be adjusted. There is nothing more back aching than to have to bend down all the time when fitting a garment; on the other hand if the shoulders are too high it will not be possible to see how they fit.

It is sometimes found helpful if a tacking thread is sewn into the form down the centre back and front. Other useful points to mark in this way are —the shoulder darts, the natural waist line, the hip line and the armhole level. These parts of the garment are matched with the tacks.

ADJUSTING THE DRESS FORM

There are several kinds of dress forms from which to choose, each one having merits which the others have not. It is really a matter of personal choice which is the one selected.

The Solid Form.—This is the best-known dress form, and it can be obtained in various sizes. It is easy to work on as it is fitted on to a stand, and it is firm and solid. It is possible to have a solid form made to your own measurements, but this is not advisable as there may be slight changes in your figure. The best way is to buy a solid form near to your own measurements but slightly smaller, and pad it.

Adjusting a Solid Form.—A solid dress form which is slightly smaller than your figure can be padded to fit your own measurements. Make a plain cotton slip which fits you exactly.

To make the bodice you will need the following measurements:—

Centre Front—from base of neck to waist plus fifteen inches to allow for the depth of the stand.

Bust—round the fullest part of bust taking the tape measure high at back.

Waist—round natural waist line.

Hips—round fullest part of hips.

Centre Back—from the base of neck to the waist plus fifteen inches as for the front length.

Across Back—across shoulder blades.

Make a paper pattern from these measurements in the same way as described for cutting a block pattern, see page 69. When cutting the bodice in the material allow good turnings all round, including the centre front which should be left open, the centre back should be placed to a fold.

Tack all the seams and fit it to your figure. If possible, have someone to do the fitting and make darts where

necessary to get a perfect fit. See the chapter on fitting, page 127. Mark the centre front with a row of pins or tacking both sides of the bodice.

Machine the shoulder and side seams, cut away the surplus turnings and press the seams. Bind the armhole and neck edges after they have been trimmed to the right size.

Now put the slip on to the dress form and pad where necessary to obtain the right size. This padding needs to be done with very great care as it must be made solid and firm, at the same time a good shape must be retained or there will be bumps in the wrong places.

When all the padding has been completed turn in the front edges so that the two rows of pins meet, and sew the two edges together.

Turn under the edges round the bottom and fasten it to the dress form with drawing pins.

Check the measurements of the dress form constantly with your own and make any adjustments that may be necessary. This will necessitate removing the bodice from the form and refitting it to the figure. Sew the seams and darts again on the new fitting line and press them.

Replace the bodice on the form again and pad it as already described.

Make the most of this opportunity and launder the loose cover whilst it is off the form. It is advisable to wash the cover before refitting, especially if made of new material; it may shrink.

The solid form can only be made larger by adding a loose bodice. If your measurements have become smaller the figure will be of no further use.

Always keep the dress form covered with an old sheet when not in use, otherwise it will become soiled.

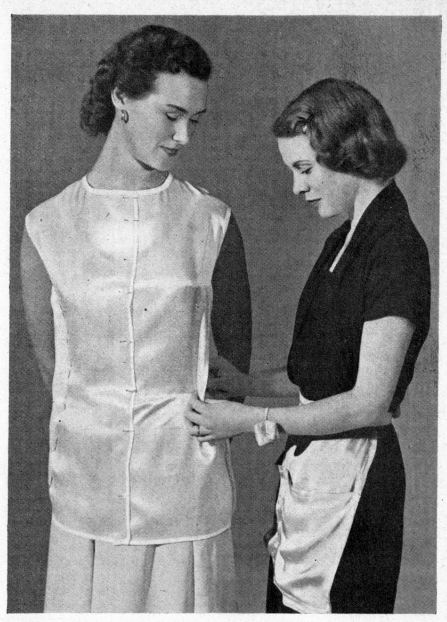

To adjust the size of a solid form, make a bodice in strong calico or linen. Cut out the pattern to your own measurements and tack the seams, fit this to the figure so that it is skin tight, making fitting darts and adjustments where necessary. Large turnings must be allowed on the seams and especially on the centre front, to allow for wrap over. Sew the seams, with two rows of machine stitching, making them quite firm and strong; hem the bottom edge and bind the armholes and neck edges. Cut away all surplus turnings and press the seams open and flat. Turn the bodice right side out when completed.

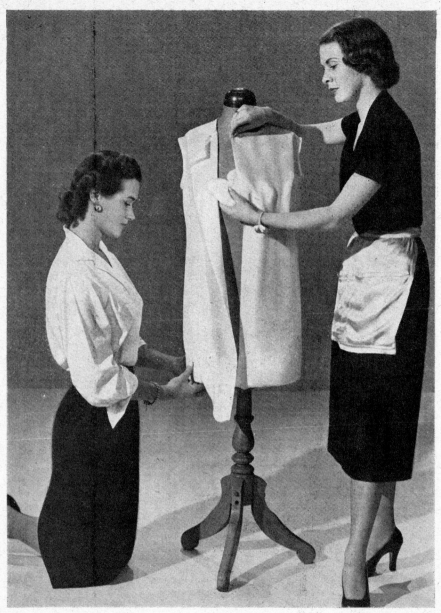

Place the bodice over the solid form. Pad all the hollows and places where there is space between the dummy and the bodice. Use cotton wool for this and make the padding quite firm so that it will not work flat and loose through the constant use of the form. Having made sure that the bodice is sufficiently well padded and as near to the figure as possible, match the pins at the front, turn under the edges and sew them all the way down. Turn the surplus material, at the bottom edge, underneath and fasten it neatly and securely with drawing pins or tacks. The bodice, thus made, is adjustable.

47

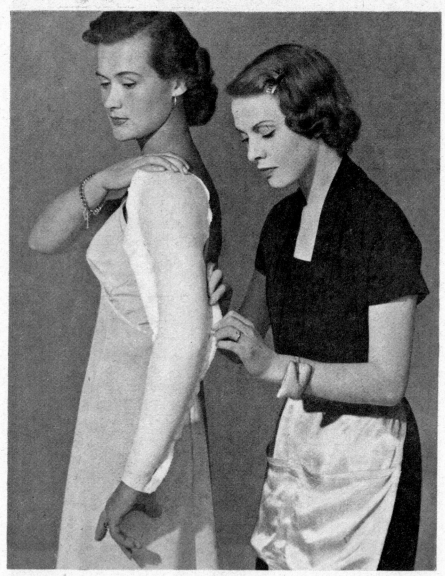

Use the normal sleeve pattern to make a padded arm, fit it skin tight to the arm for size.

The sleeve needs as much fitting and with the same amount of care as the rest of the garment. A badly set or twisted sleeve draws the eye more than any other part of the garment, with perhaps one exception, the collar.

Dress forms with arms attached are not easy to obtain, but there is a way of overcoming this difficulty. The padded arm is simply made from the ordinary sleeve pattern and can be attached to the ordinary dress form.

You will find this piece of equipment most helpful in the making and fitting of sleeves, the adjusting of darts and fulness at the top and the hang of the sleeve.

Two different kinds of arm can be made, but it is only necessary to have one arm as one sleeve may be fitted on the right side and the other on the wrong.

The Two-Piece Padded Arm.— This arm is made quite easily from the two-piece sleeve pattern, see page 72. Cut the sleeve out in firm material allowing turnings all round. Make a line of tacking round the edge of the pattern to indicate the fitting line, stage (1). Cut a third piece to fit the top part of the sleeve extending from the underarm curve to the top.

Now cut out the same pattern shapes in cotton wadding, without turnings.

Tack the cotton wadding pieces firmly to the wrong side of the material. The small shaped piece is arranged as a second layer at the top of the sleeve, stage (2).

Fit the sleeve to the arm to get the correct size. Machine the sleeve seams with a double row of stitching and press them open.

Stitch the curve of the small material piece to the top part of the sleeve, right sides facing. Turn it over so that it

When the padded arm has been stuffed tightly with sawdust, it can be fixed to the solid form for the fitting of sleeves. The semi-circular attachment is pinned over the shoulder.

covers the cotton wadding, and leave it for the time being, stage (3).

Close the opening at the wrist with an oval-shaped piece of the material. To get the size measure the wrist across the top and also take a rough measurement of the thickness. Using these two measurements draw a rectangle and round off the corners, stage (4). Cut this shape out in material with turnings, and stitch it into the end of the sleeve with small firm stitches. Cut away the surplus turnings, and turn the sleeve right side out.

Pack the sleeve tightly with dry sawdust up to the level of the underarm curve.

Now cut a piece of material the right shape and size to cover the sawdust. Sew one edge of this across the upper part of the sleeve just above the sawdust, thus forming a flap, stage (5). Tuck the edge of the flap in, between the filling and the cotton wadding all round,

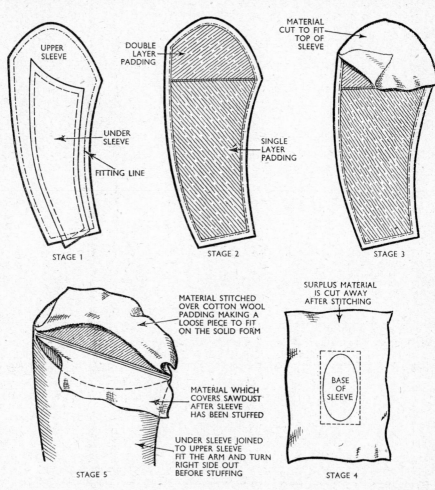

The two-piece padded arm is made from the two-piece sleeve pattern in such a way that it can be fastened to the solid form as an arm. The calico shapes are first padded firmly with sawdust and cotton wadding, before making up.

then stitch the edge of the under part of the sleeve to the flap as firmly as possible. Finally sew the loose piece of material over the cotton wool padding at the top of the arm.

You have now an arm fully padded as far as the underarm, with the top only partly padded so that it can be fastened to the shoulder of the dress form.

To fasten the padded arm to the dress form have a shaped strip at the top, made as follows: Cut a piece of material seven by five inches, and fold it in half lengthwise; curve the raw edges to a semicircular shape. Turn the raw edges in, stitch them together and press flat. Sew the centre of the folded edge to the top edge of the sleeve. The curved edge is then pinned to the dress form.

The One-Piece Padded Arm.—

This is made from the one-piece sleeve pattern described

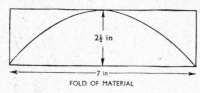

2½ in

7 in
FOLD OF MATERIAL

A semicircular piece of calico is attached to the top of the arm to enable it to be fastened to the dummy.

on page 74, cut out in firm material, with turnings all round. It should fit the arm snugly so that it is as near as possible to the shape and size. Machine along the seam and the back dart, trim the seams and press them open.

Cut a small circle of the same material to fit the wrist opening. The diameter of this circle is one-third the wrist measurement, plus turnings. Stitch this circle firmly to the end of the sleeve on the wrong side. Trim away the raw edges. Now cut a piece of material to fit the shape of the top part of the sleeve and stitch it neatly into place round the curved edge of the sleeve.

Turn the sleeve right side out, after pressing, and pack it tightly with clean sawdust. Close the remainder of the opening by hemming the material on to the under part of the armhole. Fasten this arm to dummy as for a two-piece arm.

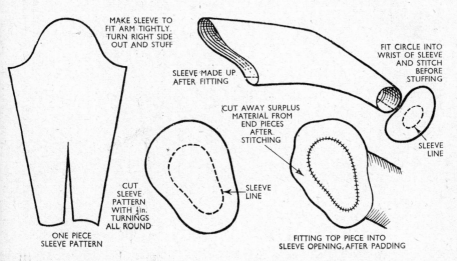

MAKE SLEEVE TO FIT ARM TIGHTLY. TURN RIGHT SIDE OUT AND STUFF

FIT CIRCLE INTO WRIST OF SLEEVE AND STITCH BEFORE STUFFING

SLEEVE MADE UP AFTER FITTING

CUT AWAY SURPLUS MATERIAL FROM END PIECES AFTER STITCHING

SLEEVE LINE

CUT SLEEVE PATTERN WITH ½in. TURNINGS ALL ROUND

SLEEVE LINE

ONE PIECE SLEEVE PATTERN

FITTING TOP PIECE INTO SLEEVE OPENING, AFTER PADDING

The one-piece sleeve is simple to make. Use strong calico and sew the seams with two rows of machining, for security. When all the seams have been sewn pad the arm very tightly with sawdust, so it is quite firm, and will not sag.

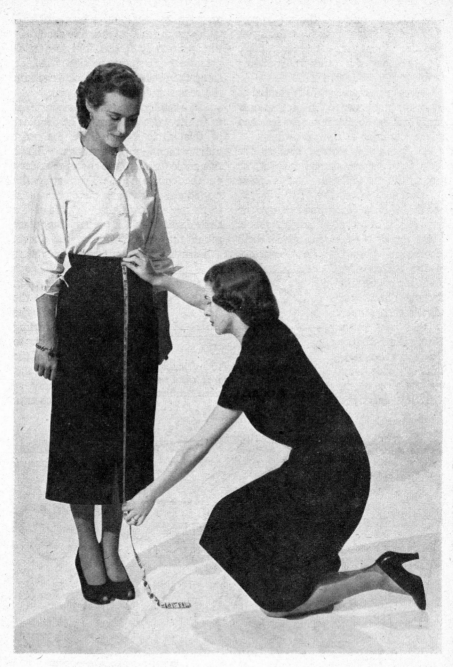

Accurate measurements are the first essentials of a smart and well-fitting garment. Stand naturally erect and do not slouch when being measured. Note how the edge of the skirt being worn can be used as a guide to measuring the correct length. The tape must be kept quite straight with the line of the figure and not slanted to left or right.

MEASUREMENTS
HOW TO TAKE THEM

The measurements you will need to cut your own patterns are described in detail in this chapter. They must be taken accurately and carefully.

If the style of garment chosen is plain then these measurements will be adequate. On the other hand, if an elaborate design is chosen it will be necessary to measure all details.

Get a friend to help you take your

own measurements exactly, and write them down in a note-book at the time. The same measurements will do for all time, but check them to see that no adjustment is required.

Remove any bulky clothing and pin an inch-wide tape round the waist line. Stand quite naturally and do not sag.

Measurements should be taken comfortably without pulling the tape too tight; do not have it loose.

LENGTH

1. Centre Back to Waist Line.—Measure from the bone at the nape of the neck to the lower edge of the tape round the waist, keeping the measuring tape straight down the spine.

2. Centre Back from Waist Line to Edge of Skirt.—For a skirt this measurement is taken from the top edge

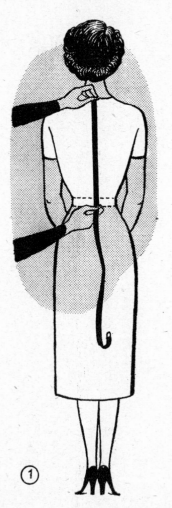

of the waist-line tape to the edge of the skirt, with the tape measure straight down the centre back.

When measuring the full length of a frock or long coat extend the measure from the lower edge of the waist tape to the hem edge, after the centre back length has been taken.

To obtain the length of a short coat or jumper continue the measure from the waist to the length required.

Whilst these measurements are being taken stand perfectly straight without being too rigid.

3. Centre Back from Nape to Armhole Level.—Place the tape measure round the neck with the ends, one long and one short, in front. Hold the short end, the long end passes under the arm, across the back, and under the other arm. Measure to bottom of this tape.

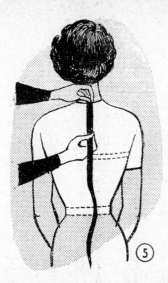

5. Middle Back between Nape and Armhole Level.—This is taken straight down the spine and should be half the measurement of No. 3.

4. Back Length. From Shoulder Line, Close to Neck, to Waist Line.—Measure to lower edge of waist tape.

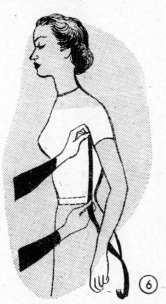

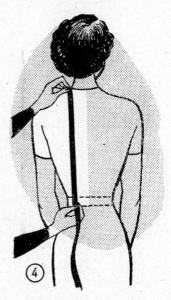

6. Side Seam from Under Arm to Waist (Lower Edge of Tape).—Do not lift the arm, as this pulls the garment up and lengthens the seam.

8. Inside Arm from Armpit to Wrist.—Do not bend the arm or the measurement will be short. Take the tape to the inside of the wrist.

9. Side Skirt Length from Waist Line.—The tape passes over the hip curve to allow for extra length needed on the side seam. Wear a skirt the correct length when taking this measurement, and measure from top of tape.

7. Front Length, from Shoulder Line Close to Neck, to Waist Line.— Keep the tape straight down the front and over the highest point of the bust, to allow for spring on the bodice front.

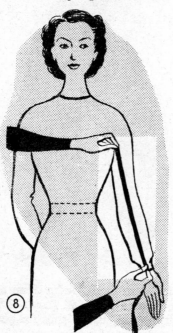

10. Skirt Length from Waist at Centre Front.—Measure from the top of the waist tape to the bottom of the hem. It is easier to gauge the right measurement if a skirt of the correct length is worn.

11 and 12. Outside Arm Length.—First measure from the top of the sleeve to the tip of the bent elbow. Hold the tape in this position and continue

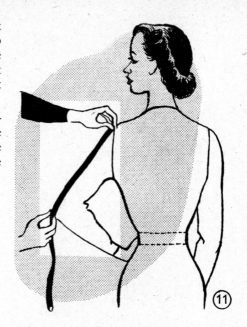

measuring round the bent elbow to the wrist. This measurement is taken with the elbow bent so as to get sufficient length on the back seam, to allow for movement, and to prevent the sleeve pulling up with arm movement.

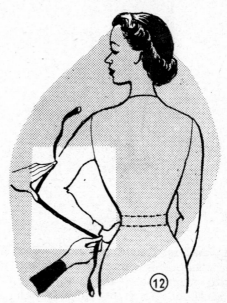

of the shoulder blades at the back. If the tape is allowed to drop at the back the size of the bodice will be too small. The measure should be taken comfortably, run the fingers round inside the tape to ensure there is enough room and that it is not too tight. It is a common fault to pull the tape tight for this measurement and so make the bodice much too small and uncomfortable.

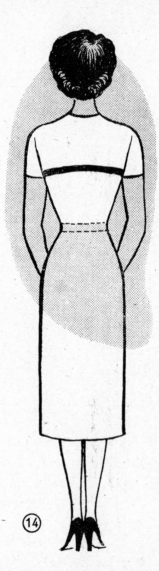

WIDTH

13 and 14. Round the Bust.—The tape measure is taken round the fullest part of the bust at the front, and it should be kept high over the lower part

15. Round the Waist.—This is a difficult measurement to take as the tape can easily be pulled too tightly. The guide waist tape will indicate where the measure should be taken.

16. Round the Hips at the Widest Part.—The natural hip line is usually judged to be seven inches below the waist. This general rule is, perhaps, more varied than any other normal

measurement. To check the position of the hip line measure down from the waist as far as the widest part of the hips. Measure round the hips comfortably at this point. If the widest part is much more than seven inches below the waist it is advisable to measure the hip at the seven-inch line and also round the seat, this will allow the extra room required for sitting.

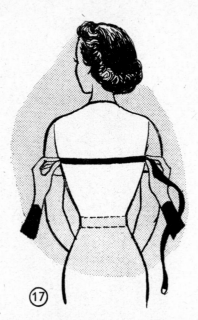

for the back, and plus one inch for the front. The two measurements added together equal the full bust size. If, however, the figure being measured is broad across the back and small in the bust, or the reverse way; this way of finding the size will not be accurate.

To check these lengths measure across the back, and across the front, over the fullest part of the bust, between the side seams and just below the armhole seam. To ensure an accurate measure, wear a garment that fits well.

17 and 18. Across Back and Across Fullest Part of Bust at Armhole Level.—Normally these measurements are—half the bust size less one inch,

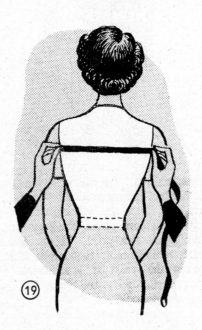

19. Across the Middle Back.—This measurement is taken from sleeve seam to sleeve seam half-way between the nape and underarm level. Keep the measuring tape at right angles to the spine.

Be generous with this measurement rather than the reverse; if the back is too wide it can be rectified in the fitting.

20. Across the Chest.—Take this measurement and No. 19 with care. A garment that is too narrow across the chest or across the shoulders is most uncomfortable, also this fault will pull the sleeves badly. Measure straight across the chest, half-way between the neck line and the armhole level.

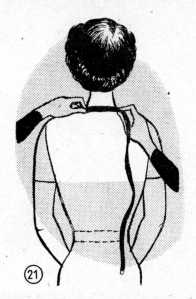

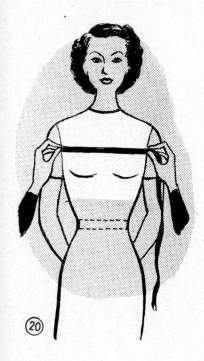

22. Width of Shoulder.—Take this measurement from the base of the neck, just behind the ear, to the edge of the shoulder, at the sleeve seam.

This is another measurement to be taken on the more generous side.

21. Across the Nape of Neck.—Accuracy is the keynote of this measurement; if there is any doubt about it take it on the small side. It is possible to make a neck bigger but when cut too big it is difficult to fill in the spaces; the garment will look ugly and untidy on the shoulders and pull away at the sides.

The measurement is taken from one shoulder seam to the other, keeping the tape above the bone at the nape. Wear a frock that has the right size of neck.

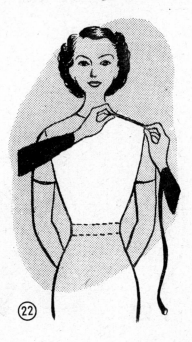

(23)

24. Round Armhole.—Place the tape measure under the arm and bring it round, easily, to meet at the top of the shoulder. The arm must not be lifted whilst this measurement is being taken, but kept straight down the side; otherwise the measure will be too small. Keep the tape well on to the shoulder, and make sure that it is slipped right under and up to the armpit.

23. Round the Neck.—The average neck tapers slightly towards the face; it is essential, therefore, that the tape measure should be kept as near to the base as possible. Do not measure too loosely, as the size of the garment neck is regulated by this measurement.

(24)

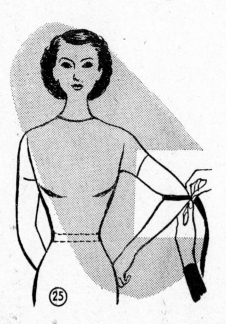

(25)

25. Round the Elbow.—This measurement is taken with the elbow bent so as to allow for plenty of elbow room in the sleeve. Place the tape round the crook of the elbow and bring it together to meet at the tip. Make sure that the elbow is well bent and have the measuring tape firm but not too tight, or the sleeve will pull and look very ugly. Alternatively if the tape is loose the sleeve will be baggy at the elbow and it will hang in an untidy way.

27. Round Upper Arm.—The main reason for taking this measurement is to get the cuff size for a short sleeve. It also ensures there will be enough room in the upper sleeve.

26. Round Forearm.—Take this measurement round the widest part of the forearm. It is required when cutting patterns for tight-fitting sleeves.

29. Round the Hand.—This measurement must be taken round the largest part of the hand, over the thumb joint.

28. Round Wrist.—Required for a long tight-fitting sleeve which is to fasten close at the wrist. Do not take this measurement too tightly.

MEASURING CORRECTLY

Points to Remember

The taking of measurements is the most important part of dressmaking. A whole garment can be ruined if the measurements are badly or incorrectly taken. The cut and style will be completely lost apart from the fit being wrong.

Having described each measurement in detail here are a few hints which should be remembered at all times.

1. **Length Measurements.**—(*a*) The tape must be kept absolutely straight, i.e. parallel with the spine or the centre front for the bodice. Straight down the centre front or back, or down the seam of a skirt. If the tape is allowed to slant even slightly to one side, the measurement will be too long and there will be endless trouble when the garment is fitted.

(*b*) Take great care to start and finish a measurement at the correct spots, i.e. when measuring the centre back of the bodice make sure that the tape is taken high enough into the neck, feel for the large bone at the nape. The measurement must extend right to the waist, but not farther.

(*c*) It is important that plenty of spring should be allowed on the front of a bodice, especially for full busted figures, otherwise the front will be too short and "pook" in the centre. This is a difficult fault to remedy.

(*d*) When measuring the outside length of a sleeve be sure the tape is taken high enough at the top, or the sleeve will pull and drag and be too short. Keep the elbow well bent to get the full length, and extend the tape well down over the wrist.

(*e*) The skirt length needs careful measuring, too. It is a good idea to wear a skirt that is the correct length and the same level all round whilst this measure is being taken. Pull it well down first. An uneven skirt is a difficult thing to remedy, and it can be very ugly.

2. **Width Measurements.**—(*a*) The bust measurement is, perhaps, the most difficult to take correctly. It is essential that the tape should be lifted up at the back so that it passes over the shoulder blades. If it is allowed to drop, the measurement will be too small, and the bodice, when finished, too tight. It is not easy to make a small bodice larger.

(*b*) The hips need very careful measuring. As well as taking the measurement round the hip line (seven inches below the waist) take a second one round the widest part, especially if the hips are rather large. This second measurement gives an idea of how much spring to leave on the skirt. If this is not allowed for, the skirt will pull badly across the front and will have an ugly hang.

(*c*) As for measuring the sleeve width, keep the elbow well bent when measuring round the elbow. If this width is not wide enough the sleeve will be too tight and ugly.

(*d*) When taking the armhole measurement the arm must be kept straight down the side, otherwise the armhole of the garment will be too small.

3. **Correct Standing Position.**—Finally, a short note on the correct position in which to stand while measurements are being taken. Hold yourself absolutely straight and naturally, without being rigid, but do not sag.

Do not measure over a badly fitting frock, it will probably lead to inaccuracies which cannot be rectified.

You may prefer to use ready-made patterns, in which case, study the list of sizes printed on the back of the pattern and compare them with your own. This will help you to choose the size most adaptable to your figure and save endless work afterwards.

The woman with the average figure will not have much difficulty in selecting a bought pattern. All she has to do is to buy the right bust size.

When the hips are larger than average it is best to buy a pattern with a larger bust to get the correct hip measurement and adjust it accordingly.

With equal hip and bust measurements again buy the size which gives the hips correctly and then enlarge the bust size as required.

The hints given in "altering the pattern," page 87, will be helpful when making these adjustments.

STOCK SIZES
Corresponding Measurements

There are about three types of figure which are the most usual in size. As ready-made garments are made to these proportions they are known as stock sizes.

The average figure has the hips about three inches bigger than the bust and the waist ten inches smaller than the hips.

The slender hipped figure has this measurement equal to the bust with a waist about eight inches smaller. This proportion generally applies to people who are rather stout, but many very slim figures have equal bust and hip sizes with a waist six inches smaller.

Finally there is the figure with very large hips, probably five or six inches bigger than the bust, and waist eleven or twelve inches smaller than the hips.

Of course there are other types of figure where the hip measurement is only one inch or one and a half inches larger than the bust, and occasionally we find the bust measurement slightly larger than the hip. Or people with large waists, when all three measurements are almost equal. But these are the exceptions and are not stock sizes.

Compare your own measurements carefully, so that you have a good impression of your type of figure. This will be useful knowledge when choosing a style or making your own design.

THE AVERAGE FIGURE

Bust	Waist	Hips
34	27	37
36	28	38
38	30	40
40	33	44
42	34	46

FIGURE WITH LARGE HIPS

Bust	Waist	Hips
34	28	39
36	30	41
38	32	43
40	34	45
42	36	47

FIGURE WITH FULL
BUST AND SLENDER HIPLINE

This type of figure, has equal bust and hip measurements.

Bust	Waist	Hips
40	32	40
42	34	42
44	37	44
46	39	46
48	41	48

All the above measurements are in inches.

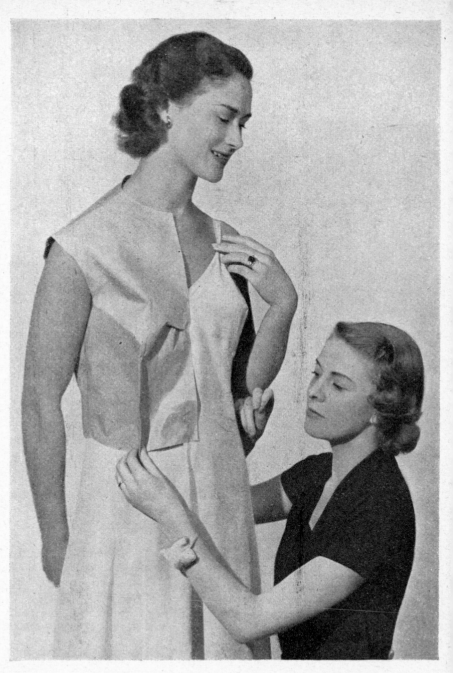

The paper pattern should be fitted to the figure, for checking, at all stages in the making. When the block has been drawn and cut out in paper it is fitted so that any necessary adjustments can be made, as can be seen in this picture; then re-cut the pattern in another sheet of paper, making allowances for any alterations that have been marked.

PATTERNS
IN DETAIL

When creating your own clothes it is far better to make them to measure rather than trust to a hit-and-miss method, by relying entirely on bought patterns. Truly, if more interest and trouble is taken to adapt ready made patterns, good results can be achieved.

Ready made patterns can be obtained in many sizes. As these are made to fit stock-size figures it is sometimes a little confusing; not everyone can boast these measurements. Whereas one person may be narrow chested with a rounded back, another may have a straight narrow back and full chest—yet both will measure thirty-six inches round the bust.

These patterns are not made to allow for the mistakes of amateurs. So, having painstakingly cut the garment according to the instructions, you may be horrified to find that it hangs in shapeless folds without any apparent relation to fit and form. When this happens it is a tragedy, not only is the material wasted but it takes a clever dressmaker to model a shapeless "sack" into a garment with good fit and line.

With experience you will soon learn how to measure these patterns and adjust them to your own measurements.

A more reliable way of cutting a garment is to use a pattern made to your own measurements. This is known as a block pattern and can be used as a base for any design of dress, blouse, skirt or coat. Having learnt, in the previous chapter, how to take measurements accurately you can now go ahead with making block patterns.

There is yet a third way of cutting garments. It is a method used by professional dressmakers and designers. Practical experience is required if the result is to be a success. Beginners are not advised to attempt this method.

The material itself, or a soft muslin, is draped on to the figure in the design of the frock. Armholes, neck and darts are marked and cut whilst the material is on the figure. If muslin is used this is then turned into the pattern for cutting the material. Drapery and folds can be designed in this way.

Whichever type of pattern is chosen the aim is always the same—to achieve the professional touch, obtained by good cut and a perfect fit.

When you have learnt to cut your own patterns you can then choose any style from fashion catalogue or journal; or you may be able to memorize the main details of models displayed in fashion windows or mannequin parades, and make patterns accordingly. The more you study pattern making, the quicker will you discover how to obtain style and finish. Also, when using ready made patterns, it is a great advantage to understand the cut.

The main points to remember in pattern making are:—

(1) Accurate measurements.
(2) Precision in detail.
(3) Careful cutting.

Lastly, fit the pattern to the figure before cutting the material, to ensure that it is correct and so avoid wastage.

MAKING PATTERNS

THE BLOCK PATTERN

First make the block, which is a basic pattern cut exactly to your own measurements. On this no allowance is made for turnings or fulness of any kind. It is, in fact, a tight fitting bodice on which to build garments of any style.

Accuracy of measurement and precision in drawing are the key to good pattern making. To obtain the perfect pattern it is necessary to have a few simple tools to aid the drawing, these are: a long ruler; a set square; soft pencils in two or three colours and a rubber; scissors; a note-book in which to keep measurements; compasses and a protractor are useful when curves are to be drawn; tracing paper for tracing designs. Graph paper will be a guide to the drawing, especially if marked up in inches as well as small squares.

Having made the block and cut it out in paper, fit it to the figure and make sure that it is a good fit, making any adjustments necessary. Then cut it out in cardboard or stiff paper to make a pattern that will keep for all time. Of course the measurements must be checked from time to time and any necessary adjustments made.

This is an instance where the tracing wheel will be found useful; place the pattern on the cardboard and mark round with the wheel, then cut along the perforated line.

Another good idea to get a permanent block pattern is to cut it out in soft muslin, this can then be fitted to the figure and adjusted easily.

BODICE BLOCK

When possible use graph paper for the drawing of block patterns. Allow one small square to one inch of the measurements.

Draw a rectangle—half bust measurement, lines A—B and C—D, by length from shoulder to waist, plus one inch, A—C and B—D, see Diagram.

Half back: draw the half back pattern as follows—from A, along line A—B mark half measurement across nape, and make this point E. Join E with a gradual curve to a point three-quarters of an inch below A, along A—C, for the neck curve.

F is a point two and a half inches from A—B and the shoulder length from E. Join E to F.

Find the middle back line by measuring this length from line A—B and drawing a dotted line. Make a dot on this line, at armhole edge, middle back width from A—C.

Draw another dotted line for the armhole level, measured from A—B. Along this line indicate quarter bust measurement plus half an inch with a dot, measuring from A—C. Draw a curve for the armhole from this point to F through the dot on middle chest line.

The side seam is drawn from the underarm point to G—half an inch inwards and one inch up from line C—D. To complete the bodice pattern join G to C with a line parallel with C—D.

Half front: this part of the pattern is

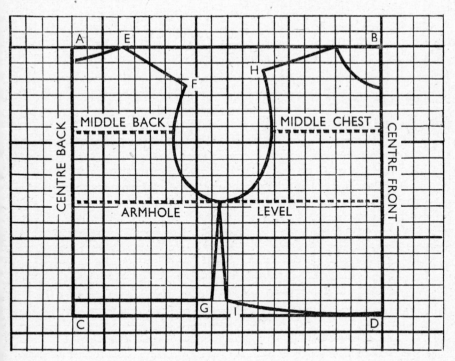

The pattern for the bodice block is cut in two pieces, the half front and the half back. Draw these side by side in a rectangle which is half the bust measurement in length. Each small square on the graph represents one inch of the measurement.

drawn in the remainder of the rectangle, side by side with the back.

From B measure three inches along A—B, and two and a half inches along B—D. Join these two points for the neck line curve.

The front shoulder length is the same as the back, it is drawn from the point of the neck line curve on A—B to H, a point one and a half inches below A—B.

Draw a dotted line for the middle chest, measured from line A—B. Along this dotted line indicate the required width with a dot.

Continue the dotted line at armhole level to B—D, and measure quarter bust width plus half an inch. This should join up with the back at the underarm point. Join this point to H through the dot at middle chest line, for the armhole curve.

The side seam is drawn from the

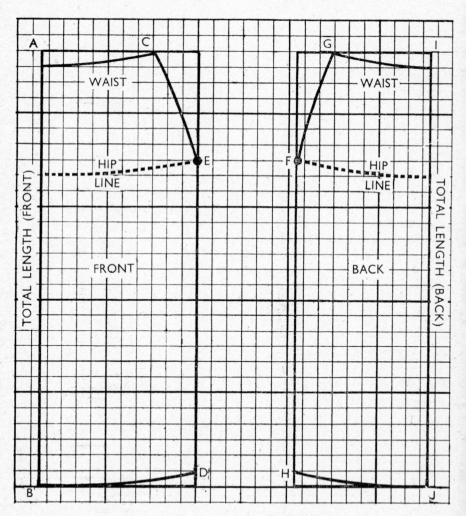

Add a half inch to each half of the front skirt pattern and take a half inch off the back so that the two half patterns equal the half waist measurement.

underarm point to I, half an inch inwards and one inch up from c—d. Join I to D in a gradual curve, leaving the extra inch at the centre front to allow for "bust rise."

Cut out each pattern separately and fit to the figure, making any adjustments necessary. Join the seams for this fitting with small strips of paper pinned across the joins.

The adjustments to the pattern should be made by pinning in darts, or slitting the paper where necessary, then lay the pattern out quite flat on a piece of paper and re-cut it to the amended shape.

TWO-PIECE SKIRT BLOCK

Draw two rectangles on graph paper, with A—B and I—J the longest length of the skirt plus one inch. The rectangle for front is half hip plus half inch, the back is half hip less half inch, see Diagram.

Half back: measure quarter waist size, less half an inch along line A—I and mark this point G. From a point one inch below I, along I—J, draw a gradual curve to G.

Indicate the hip line, measuring this length from I and from G, and draw with a dotted line in a gradual curve. Mark point F on this line measuring quarter hip width, less half an inch from I—J. Join G to F with a curve.

Drop a perpendicular from F to H, one inch above line J—B. Join J to H with a curve following waist line.

Half front: this part of the pattern is drawn side by side with the back in the second rectangle.

Mark point C at quarter waist size, plus half an inch, from A. Draw a gradual curve from C to one inch below A, along A—B.

Draw a dotted line for the hip line in a curve, following the waist line. Measure the required depth from A and from C. Indicate E on this line at quarter hip size, plus half an inch measuring from A—B. Join C to E with a slight curve.

Drop a perpendicular from E to D, one inch above line B—J and join D to B with a curved line to complete the pattern.

Cut out the patterns separately and fit, as described for the bodice block.

SLEEVE BLOCKS

Two-Piece Sleeve.—This pattern consists of two pieces, the upper sleeve, which is the wider, and the under sleeve. They are drawn quite separately.
The upper sleeve: draw a rectangle, the full length of the sleeve, outside arm measurement, by one-fifth bust size plus two inches. Mark the four corners of this rectangle A, B, C, D, see Diagram on page 72.

From D measure one inch along the line D—B and mark this point X.

Measure the underarm sleeve length from X, along D—B and mark this point F.

From A measure along A—C, one-third of the distance between B and F, mark this point G.

Indicate the centre of line A—B with a dot, then draw the curve for the top of the sleeve from G through this dot to F.

Halfway between X and F draw a dotted line at right angles to B—D and A—C, this is the elbow line. Measure one inch along this line from B—D and make a dot H.

Draw a curved line from F to E through H, E is half an inch from X.

For the wrist draw a straight line from E to within quarter of an inch of C—D. The length of this line should be half the complete cuff size, plus half an inch. The extra half inch is added to adjust the seam so that it will fall on the under side of the wrist. The complete cuff measurement is usually three-quarters the length round the elbow.

Measure one inch along elbow line from A—C and make a dot I. Draw a gradual curve from G through I to the end of wrist line.

The under sleeve : draw a rectangle the same size as for the upper sleeve and mark the four corners A, B, C, D in the same way, see Diagram.

From D measure one inch along D—B and mark this point X. Then measure one and a half inches from X, at right angles to D—B and make a dot E.

Along B—D measure, from X, the inside sleeve length and make point F one inch in from B—D.

Halfway between E and F make a dotted line for the elbow line. Measure two inches along this line from B—D and make point H. Join E to F with a curved line through H.

From E draw a line for the wrist;

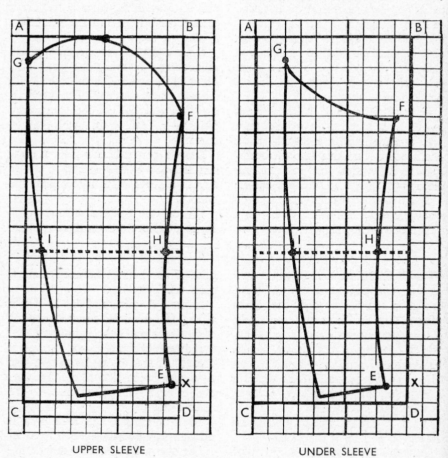

UPPER SLEEVE   UNDER SLEEVE

The two-piece sleeve pattern is used mainly on tailored garments. It is not a tight fitting sleeve, but the shaping of the back seam gives it a good hang and neat appearance. The gradual curves of the armhole edges must be carefully drawn.

this length should be half cuff size, less two inches, and it should reach a point quarter of an inch above line C—D.

From A measure along A—C, one-third of the distance between B and F and at this point make a dot G, two inches away from A—C.

Measure two and a half inches along the elbow line from A—C and make a dot I. Draw a slightly curved line from G to the end of wrist line, through I.

Finally, draw the curve for the under-arm between G and F. The lowest part of this curve should be quarter of an inch below a horizontal line drawn through F, no lower.

The One-Piece Sleeve Block.—As
the name of the pattern indicates this block is made in one complete piece. It is therefore better to draw the shape on folded graph paper.

First draw a rectangle two-fifths bust measurement by outside arm measurement. Fold this in half so that there are two rectangles, one-fifth bust size by arm length.

The top part of the sleeve pattern is drawn first and when doing this the fold should be to the left of the rectangle. Mark each corner of this rectangle A, B, C and D, see Diagram on page 74.

From D measure one inch along B—D and mark this point with a dot. Continue measuring along B—D for the inside arm length. This point should be about five inches from B. Halfway between these two dots make a dotted line for the elbow line and measure one inch along this from B—D. Draw a gradual curve joining these three dots, for the inside sleeve seam.

Draw the curve for the wrist line from the end of the sleeve seam to C at the folded edge.

Now draw the head of the sleeve in

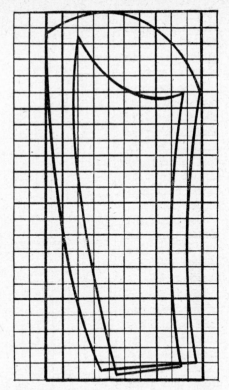

The seams of the under sleeve must match the upper, as can be seen in this plan.

the following way—divide line A—B into half and then into quarters, and indicate each with a dot.

Counting from A measure half an inch down from the first dot, and mark this spot, from the next dot measure one inch and from the third two inches. Draw the curve for the head of the sleeve starting from A at the folded edge and passing through each dot, finishing at the top of sleeve seam curve on line B—D.

The distances given to obtain this curve are average but they may vary slightly with different sized sleeves. Adjust them when necessary to keep a good evenly shaped curve.

Keeping the paper folded evenly cut out the curve for the head of the sleeve, the wrist curve and the inside sleeve seam, through both sheets of paper.

Turn the paper over and draw the under part of the sleeve on the second side. The fold of the paper should be on the right of the rectangle for this.

Continue the dotted line for the elbow line right across from the first side.

Divide the top of the sleeve into half and mark this point A, measure two inches vertically from this point and make another dot D.

Draw the underarm curve from the top of the sleeve seam B to the top of fold at C.

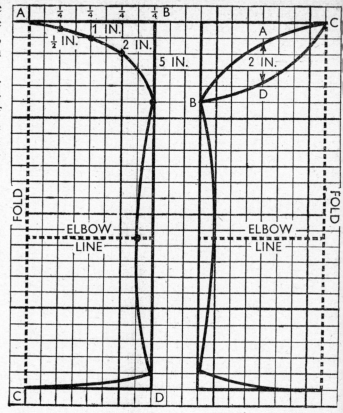

The one-piece sleeve is drawn in two halves but on doubled paper, when the pattern is opened out it will give the complete sleeve. This block can be adapted to make many different patterns.

Open out the paper and cut out this curve, making sure that it continues in a good line with the curve for the head of the sleeve.

Neither of the sleeve block patterns are cut skin tight to the arm, so that it is possible to use these as working patterns without further alteration. It is permissible, however, to adapt these blocks, particularly the one-piece sleeve, to make a variety of different shaped sleeves. This is described under the manipulation of patterns.

The seam to seam sleeve is an adaptation of the one-piece sleeve. A description is given in the next chapter.

General Notes on Pattern Making. —Accuracy in every detail is the keynote to good pattern making. If the measurement is so much as quarter of an inch wrong it will upset the fit and finish of the garment. Remember, quarter of an inch on a half back, or front, will add half an inch to the width of the garment all round.

The block patterns described in this chapter are only for use as a foundation but they must fit the figure perfectly if good working patterns are to be obtained from them. Fit them all very carefully and make any necessary adjustments, then if need be cut them out again, allowing for the alterations.

74

MANIPULATION

Cutting Patterns from the Foundation Block

Having made the most important block patterns you can now cut working patterns from them. They can be adapted to cut any style of garment. With practice you will be able to do this without difficulty and be able to copy the most up-to-date fashions saving yourself the trouble of searching for ready made patterns in that particular style.

These block patterns are not working patterns. They are flat representations of your figure and are used as the basis for the cutting of working patterns which can finally be used for cutting the finished garment. There are a few instances when the block can be used as the working pattern without alteration, but only when the measurements are very small.

Some extra measurements may be needed to obtain the particular style you have chosen. For instance—fashion may dictate that the waist line will be worn higher or lower than the normal position; shoulders may be made square one period and they may be slanting the next; sleeves may be cut high instead of flat, at the top. Such fancies of fashion will require special measurements to obtain the position of the changed line.

Do not cut the basic patterns themselves, they are to be used only as a guide.

When cutting working patterns from the block all turnings should be made in addition to the actual size. It will not then be necessary to allow turnings on the pattern when cutting out the material.

Before cutting the working pattern decide what style of garment you want to make. Have a picture to which you can refer if need be. Failing that, you must have a very clear idea in your own mind how the design will look when finished.

Note carefully all the points which are additional to the block pattern—fulness in the bodice in the form of gathers, tucks or darts; is there to be a yoke; what style the neck will be and the type of collar, if any. Then consider the skirt—whether it will be flared, gathered or pleated. The style of the sleeves must be suited to the garment.

An opening down the front needs especial attention as it will be necessary to allow extra material for the wrap-over.

This chapter deals, in a general way, with the adaptation of block patterns—how to introduce fulness in simple ways; how to join a bodice to the skirt for a very easy frock. Individual blouse and skirt patterns are dealt with in their own chapters, as are the different styles of sleeves, collars, cuffs and other accessories.

The principles of manipulating a basic pattern are always the same however complicated the style may be.

When the figure is slight it is not necessary to alter the block pattern for plain garments. If the bust measurement exceeds thirty-four inches fulness at the shoulder must be introduced, otherwise the bodice will pull across the bust.

With the skirt block this rule is reversed; it can be used as a working pattern for someone with large hips as this will allow enough width round the hem line for striding and walking.

Front.—To make a basic pattern into a working pattern a dart may be introduced at the waist line, on the shoulder or in the underarm side seam. It is practical to insert the dart in any part of the bodice providing the basic shape of the block is retained. For a simple pattern the waist dart gives a good fit but with a full busted figure the shoulder darts and side seam darts are needed.

Any dart that is made in the front of the bodice block should taper off to nothing at the point of the bust.

Waist line: measure from bust point to bust point and divide this measurement by two to get the distance between centre front and dart, A—B on Diagram 1. A—C is the length from bust point to waist line, B marks the point of bust. From B drop a perpendicular to X, C—X equals A—B.

Subtract half front waist measurement (quarter waist size plus half an inch) from waist measurement of half front bodice block, this will give the width of dart, X—Y. The lines B—X and B—Y indicate the opening of the dart.

Shoulder: make a fold in the paper taking up the amount allowed for the waist line dart and pin it, Diagram 2. This will make a bump at the bust point, to flatten it make a cut from this point to the centre of the shoulder line. Smooth the pattern out so that it is quite flat and this will give the width of the dart, Diagram 3.

Side Seam: continue the line A—B to the side seam and cut through from D to B. When the waist line dart is closed this will give the size of the underarm dart, Diagrams 4 and 5.

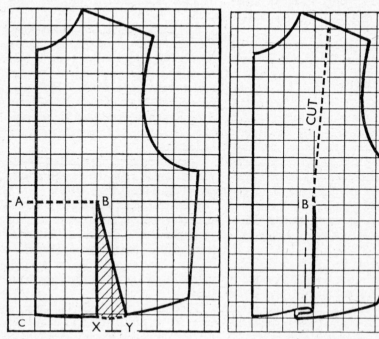

1. *A waist line dart.* X—Y *equals the amount to be taken up in the dart.*

2. *Fold the paper, making a pleat to take up the amount allowed for the waist dart.*

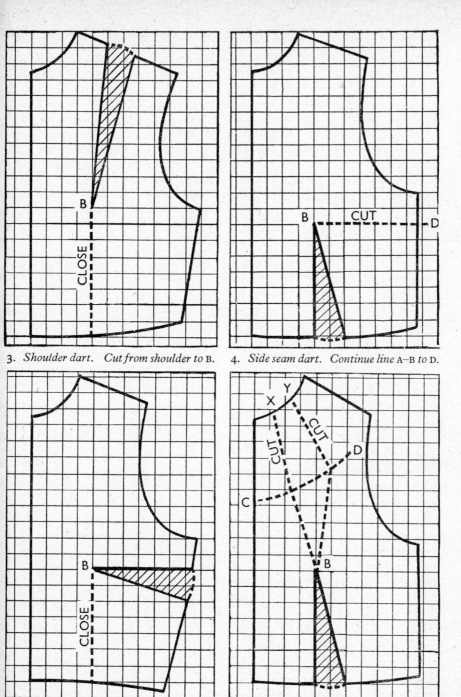

3. *Shoulder dart. Cut from shoulder to* B.

4. *Side seam dart. Continue line* A–B *to* D.

5. *Close waist dart in a pleat and cut from the side seam to* B *at bust point.*

6. *Neck darts. Draw* C–D, *parallel with neck line. Then draw position of darts* X–Y–B.

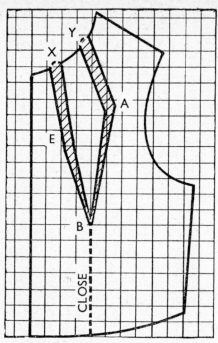

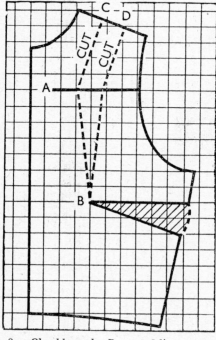

Neck line: draw a curve D—C half way between the bust point B and the neck line, and parallel to the neck. Draw two lines from X and Y at the neck to B, Diagram 6. Close the waist line dart and cut along X—B and Y—B. Open the pattern out to make it flat. Tucks or darts may be made to take up this fulness; if small darts are made they must taper off to nothing at E and A, Diagram 7.

Tucks at the Shoulder: tucks may be used instead of darts to introduce the shaping at the shoulder, to cut the pattern in this case the underarm dart pattern is used. First draw the width of the tucks at the shoulder line C and D and join these points to the bust point B through line A, Diagram 8. Fold the underarm dart and cut through lines C—B and D—B, and flatten the pattern, Diagram 9.

Cut another paper pattern, when the allowance for the darts has been made; marking the position of the dart.

7.   *Close waist dart and cut lines* X-Y-B.

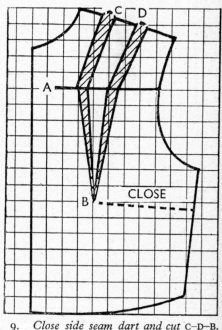

8.   *Shoulder tucks. Draw tuck lines* C-D-B.   9.   *Close side seam dart and cut* C-D-B.

Fulness can be introduced into a garment at the centre of the armhole, giving the appearance of a half yoke. Draw a line on the bodice block at right angles to the armhole edge about two inches long, and about four inches from shoulder seam. Extend this line beyond the armhole edge for the same distance, drop a perpendicular from the end of the line to the underarm curve.

When making the garment, cut along line A, gather the additional material to fit the slit, see Diagram.

Back.—For a plain blouse or bodice the back blocks need no adjustment of any kind.

If the shoulders are rounded three or four tiny pin darts or tucks should be introduced at the neck line as described for the front neck, see Diagram.

It may be more satisfactory if the waist line is darted to allow for the rounded shoulders. As the block pattern is wider than the actual waist it is not necessary to allow extra width.

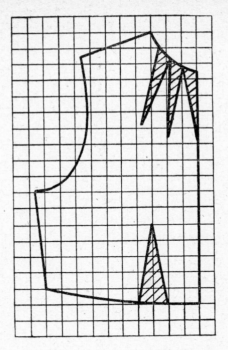

Fulness at the neck is taken up in radiating darts or tiny pin tucks.

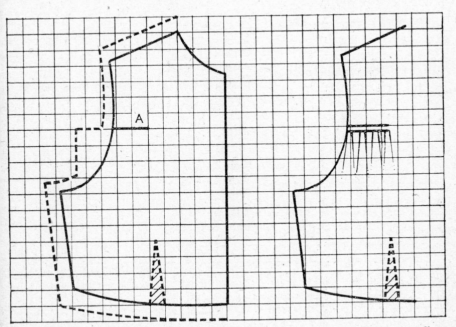

A plain shoulder and gathers at the armhole edge give a pleasing half yoke effect.

79

To make a plain skirt with extra width round the hem use the block pattern as it stands, adding extra width to each side of the hem line at front and back. Draw a straight line from this point to the hip line. Then allow for turnings. If desired an extra half an inch can be allowed on and below the hip line, both back and front, this allows for spring and prevents seating.

The skirt will have a better fit if an extra inch is cut on each side of the back, at the waist. This surplus is taken up into two darts, see Diagram on this page.

The block pattern can be used with

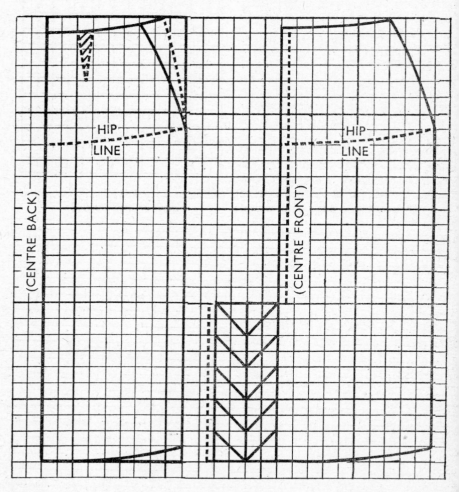

The skirt block can be easily adapted to make a simple straight skirt with one or more pleats. Add twice the width of the finished pleat to the centre front, back or side seams. To make a centre panel with pleats each side, cut a section from the quarter skirt pattern, half the width of the panel. The extra material for the pleat is cut on to one or both sections of the skirt in the same way as above.

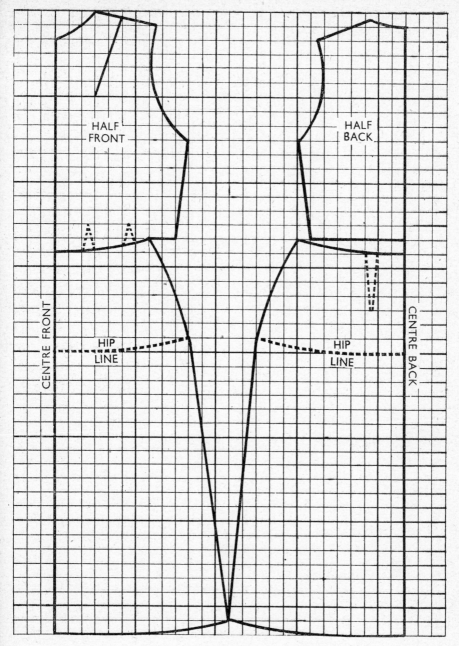

HALF
FRONT

HALF
BACK

CENTRE FRONT

CENTRE BACK

HIP
LINE

HIP
LINE

A simple frock can be made by joining the bodice block to the skirt. Make any necessary fitting features, such as darts, tucks and gathers, to each pattern before joining them together. Here you see the shoulder dart in the bodice, extra width cut on to the front bodice waist, and added width cut on to the back skirt to allow for darts and sitting room. The skirt is shaped at the side seams.

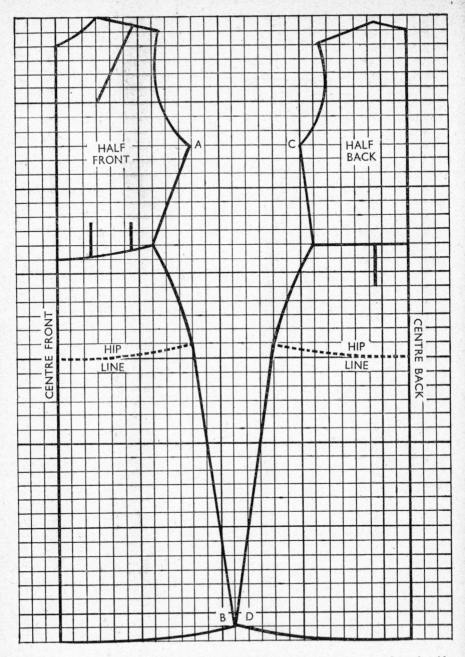

HALF FRONT

HALF BACK

A

C

CENTRE FRONT

CENTRE BACK

HIP LINE

HIP LINE

B D

Having made all the necessary darts and joined the bodice and skirt together, the side seams can then be joined. The garment will have a better line if the side seams are curved slightly at the waist. Care must be taken to match A to C, B to D, the waist line seams and the hip line, without puckering either side of the garment. The frock is then completed with sleeves and some sort of neck finishing and a collar.

little alteration for a straight skirt with short pleats. Decide the width and length the pleats are to be, add a rectangular piece to the hem allowing twice the width of the finished pleat and the required length, plus turnings. This will make a seam above each pleat, as shown by the dotted line in Diagram.

Allow for darts at the back waist.

JOINING BODICE AND SKIRT

A simple frock can be made by using the bodice block pattern and the skirt, with little alteration.

The manipulation previously described can be applied to the patterns, which must be cut in conjunction with each other. Allow for a dart at the shoulder on the front bodice, and for extra fulness at the waist.

Cut the extra width at the back waist of the skirt to allow for darts, see Diagram on page 81.

Pin the darts in the pattern and fit all the pieces together. The waist lines of bodice and skirt should fit exactly. The waist lines and hip lines should meet exactly at the side seam and the side seam should be the same length so that A matches C and B matches D, see Diagram on page 82.

SLEEVES

The sleeve block patterns need little manipulation for them to be usable as working patterns.

The two-piece sleeve, which is tailored in design, can be used as it is drawn without any alteration.

The one-piece sleeve block, without adjustment, gives a straight sleeve, wide at the cuff. If the cuff edge is gathered into a tight fitting band at the wrist it will make a bishop sleeve.

A tight fitting sleeve is made by adjusting the one-piece sleeve block. A dart is made between the elbow line and the wrist on the under side of the sleeve close to the fold. To judge the size of this dart—take the exact wrist measurement and deduct this from the cuff measurement, used when drawing the block, the difference between the two gives you the width of the dart at the cuff edge. Taper the dart to a point at the elbow line. It will be necessary to allow turnings on the inside of this dart when cutting out the garment, see Diagram below.

These three sleeves need careful setting into the armhole and the seam should be placed at a point 2 or 2½

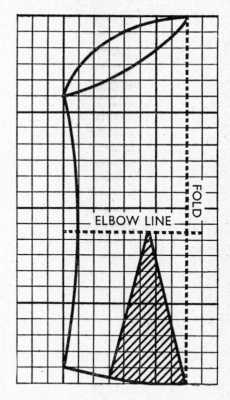

To make a tight fitting sleeve from the one-piece sleeve pattern a dart is made from the wrist to the elbow line.

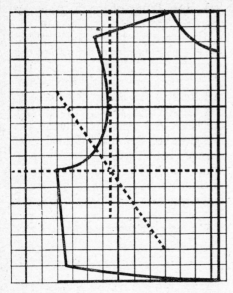

Mark where sleeve seam joins the armhole.

inches in front of the bodice side seam. To find this point on the front pattern drop a vertical line from the shoulder, just touching the edge of the armhole. Draw a horizontal line from the armhole point, divide the angle thus made with a diagonal line, and where this cuts the armhole curve is the setting-in point, see Diagram.

The seam-to-seam sleeve pattern is cut from the one-piece sleeve block. Lay the pattern out flat and re-draw the curve at the head of the sleeve, so that the highest part is in the centre. Draw a new curve for the cuff line, as shown in the Diagram below.

When setting this sleeve into the armhole the sleeve seam is matched to the side seam. The sleeve may be inserted before joining the side seam.

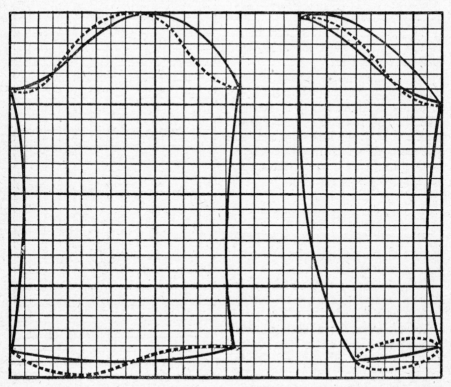

To make a seam-to-seam sleeve re-draw the one-piece sleeve pattern, as the dotted line.

BOUGHT PATTERNS

These patterns are made to fit stock size figures, and they are not, as a rule, obtainable in the in-between sizes. If you are not able to buy a pattern which is the exact size it is better to get a size larger and adjust it to your own measurements.

Each pattern is marked with the bust, waist, hip measurements and length from shoulder to hem. When choosing a design compare the sizes on the pattern with your own measurements and select the one which is nearest to them, and will require the least amount of adjusting.

All alterations to a paper pattern, whether in the length or width, must be made before cutting the material. The original outline of the pattern should be retained as far as possible. Therefore adjustments, unless they are very slight, should not be made on the edge of the garment. When adjusting any pattern care should be taken to avoid upsetting balance marks, darts, and fitting marks.

It will generally be found that detailed instructions on the cutting and making of the garment are given with the pattern. These should be studied in great detail before work commences, especially if the design of the garment is of an intricate nature.

A pattern for a style which has gathers, pleats and other details of fashion may appear rather peculiar in shape at first glance. It is, therefore, advisable to study each piece carefully, comparing it with the cutting chart, before commencing work. Get to know the pattern pieces thoroughly, learn which are balance marks, fitting notches and other guides. Learn how one shape fits in with another so that you have a clear picture in your own mind how the making up will be done.

When you know the pattern in detail then you can test it for size, with your own measurements, and decide what adjustments are necessary and how they can best be made.

The cutting chart given with the pattern will be helpful, when it comes to laying out the pattern on the material. There will be no doubt which edges must be placed to a fold, which part of the pattern can be cut on the bias, and other peculiarities. It is sometimes possible, especially when the pattern has been made smaller, to fit the pieces into less material. Juggle with these into the most economical layout, making sure that the straight of the pattern is on the grain of the material, where necessary. One point to remember: if a pattern has been made larger to any great extent it will require more material. It is always a good plan, therefore, to measure up for the amount of fabric required, as described on page 96.

When large adjustments have to be made to the pattern, you may find it helpful if a second pattern is cut from the altered one, in plain paper. Mark this new pattern with all the necessary fitting and cutting marks, so there will be no slipping up in the making.

Finally, having made all adjustments, and learnt all there is to know about the pattern, pin the pieces together and fit them to your figure as a final check for size.

You should now have a perfect pattern, with the darts in the correct places, the width the right size and the length to your liking. If care is taken in the cutting out, fitting and all making details, the finished garment should be flawless.

Study this chapter closely. Detailed hints on the alteration of patterns are given and will be of great help.

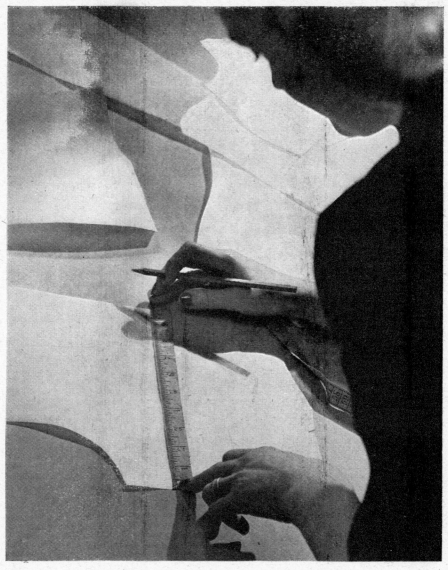

Check the measurements of a ready made pattern carefully with your own before cutting.

Test the bought pattern for size before fitting it to the figure. Lay each piece flat on the table and measure every part carefully.

The best plan is to have your list of measurements by you and take each one in turn. Check this size with your own size and mark the difference on the pattern. Allowance must be made for gathers, darts or pleats in the style of the garment. Having marked the differences of size, alter the pattern.

ALTERING THE PATTERN

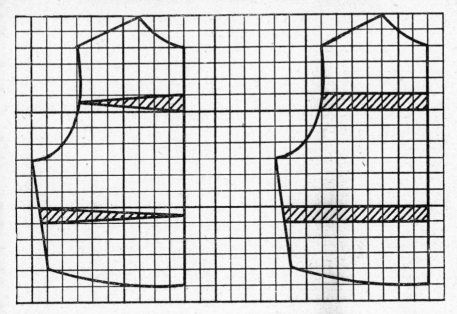

When the length of the bodice pattern has to be altered, whether it be a ready made pattern or one cut to measure, adjustments must be made in the middle of the pattern, halfway between the shoulder and armhole or between armhole and waist line.

The Bodice.—Can be lengthened or shortened by slitting the pattern.

Lengthening: to lengthen the bodice back and front above the armhole, cut right through from the centre line to the armhole edge and insert another piece of paper into the gap to give the extra length required.

Extra length is added below the bust line when the lower part of the bodice is too short.

It is sometimes necessary to add length to one edge only. If this is the case cut from the edge to be lengthened right across the pattern, and spread the two pieces out to form a V-shape, inserting another piece of paper.

Shortening: the bodice is shortened in the same positions where additions are made. Fold the pattern into pleats, taking up the required amount, straight across the pattern.

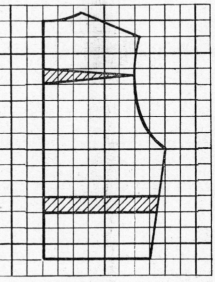

The length of the back bodice is adjusted in the same way as the front, either right across the pattern or at one edge.

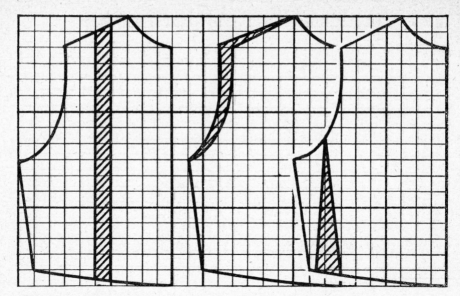

Adjustments to the width of the bodice pattern can be made in three ways—reading from left to right in both diagrams—a cut from the shoulder to waist line; addition at the shoulder and armhole edge; and a dart between armhole and waist. The pattern outlines shown in the diagrams on this page are a basis for showing how alterations are to be made. They are not intended as working patterns.

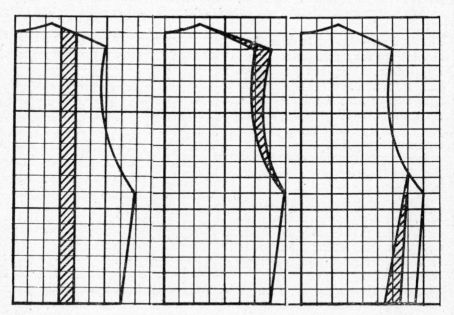

The back bodice is adjusted in the same way as the front. Never add to or take away from a bodice pattern at the centre front or back, as this would upset the neck size. When adjusting the width at the waist line avoid altering the armhole edge.

Making wider: there are three ways in which a bodice can be made wider:—

(1) Cut straight down the pattern from shoulder to waist and insert another piece of paper.

(2) Extra width on the shoulders is cut on to the end of the shoulder seam and the armhole edge.

(3) To make the waist line larger slit the pattern as far as the armhole and open out to a V-shape.

The back bodice is altered in exactly the same way as the front.

Making narrower: fold the pattern from shoulder to waist in a pleat, taking up the amount needed. Take up any surplus in the shoulder and armhole edge with a dart, or make darts at the waist line.

Collars and neckbands: these should be adjusted at the centre back either by adding additional paper to enlarge or making small pleats to decrease.

Sleeve.—Should be lengthened above or below the elbow, but never at the elbow line. Widen down the centre fold, as explained below.

Lengthening: before making any alterations to the length of a sleeve mark the elbow line on the pattern.

Cut straight across the pattern, from seam to seam, above or below the elbow line, wherever the added length is needed, and insert a piece of paper.

Shortening: again, these alterations must be made above or below the elbow line. Fold the pattern into a pleat.

Widening: cut the pattern right down the centre from the top to the cuff. Insert paper into this or spread the slit out into a V-shape, if the top of the sleeve is to be unaltered.

To make narrower: make a pleat in the pattern down the centre line.

When adjusting a two-piece sleeve both pieces must correspond.

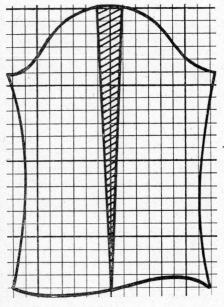

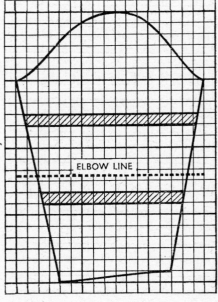

ELBOW LINE

Make adjustments to the width of all sleeve patterns down the centre of each piece, and not along any of the seams.

Alterations to the length of sleeves must be made above or below the elbow line, so there is no change in the separate lengths.

The Skirt.—Is lengthened or shortened below the hip line.

Lengthening: a skirt is always lengthened below the hip line, to prevent interference with the hip size. Cut right across the pattern and insert another piece of paper.

Shortening: a fold is made in the pattern below the hip line, to take up the correct amount required right across the skirt.

To widen: extra width is added to each quarter of the pattern. Make a cut from the waist line to the hem, parallel to the centre line of the skirt, and insert a piece of paper for the necessary addition.

To make narrower: fold the pattern into a pleat down the centre of each quarter of the pattern, from the waist to hem line.

Circular skirts: these patterns can be lengthened and shortened at the bottom edge, unless it is desired to keep the original width of hem, then the skirt must be adjusted in the centre, as previously described, below the hip line. Level up the side seams.

Tight-fitting skirts: with straight side seams can be lengthened and shortened at the hem edge.

Never, under any circumstances, must these alterations be made at the waist line of a skirt pattern.

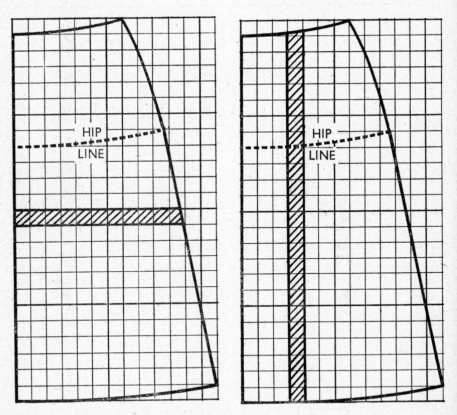

The skirt pattern is adjusted in width below the hip line to avoid interference with the fit over the hips. Alterations to the width are made down the centre of each pattern piece, especially if the side seam is shaped.

90

FITTING
PATTERNS

Having made all the necessary adjustments and alterations to the pattern, fit it to the figure to make sure it is correct. If you have no one who can fit the pattern for you then it can be fitted on the dress form.

Paper is rather difficult to pin in the normal way, as it tears so easily, especially the thin paper used for patterns. Here is a tip how to join the pieces together without spoiling the patterns.

Cut several small squares of paper, about the same weight as the pattern itself, place the seams of the pattern together and pin two or three of the paper squares across the join, pinning securely each side. If there are turnings allowed on the pattern they must be wrapped over so that the seam lines join exactly, otherwise the fit will be thrown out of true.

As only half the garment is supplied in pattern form it is a good idea, when fitting the pattern, to cut duplicate pieces. Use these in conjunction with the original ones and the garment will be completed.

When the pattern pieces have been pinned together and fitted to the dummy in this way, it is then possible to check the balance and fitting marks to ensure that they fall in the correct positions. Pay special attention to the centre back and front, if these do not lie down the middle of the figure the whole hang of the finished garment will be ruined. See, too, that darts, pleats and style lines lie in straight lines.

Make any further adjustments by making darts in the pattern, or by inserting extra strips of paper if necessary. Re-cut the pattern from another sheet of paper, allowing for these alterations.

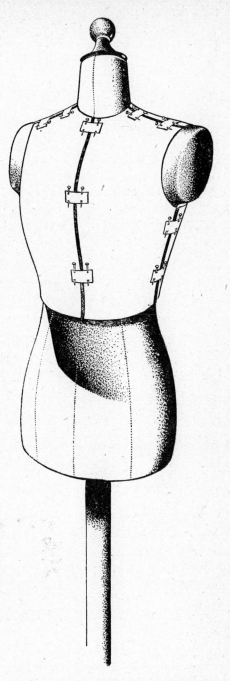

When fitting a paper pattern on to the dress form, join the seams with small strips of paper pinned across the edges.

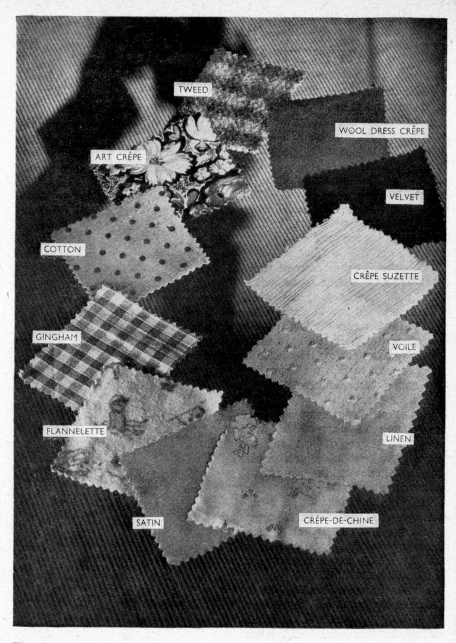

The choice of materials is important in dressmaking. Suitability of texture to suit the style and purpose of a garment needs careful consideration. Here are a few examples of the many fabrics from which a selection may be made. Tweeds and woollens for suits, with the light-weight wools for dresses; velvets, heavy satins and crêpes, for evening and afternoon wear; ginghams, voiles and cotton fabrics for tub frocks and blouses; flannelette for children and the lighter crêpes and satins for lingerie.

MATERIALS

HOW TO CHOOSE THEM

Materials play a very big part in dressmaking and, if the best results are to be obtained, careful thought must be given to the selection and suitability of the fabric for each particular style and purpose. Study the various peculiarities—texture, weight, pattern, and colour—carefully, and in relation to the garment being made. For instance, do not select a heavy tweed for a dress that is draped or has fulness in the skirt; alternatively light-weight silks and cottons are most unsuitable for tailored styles.

Patterns which are bought ready to use are supplied with a list of suitable materials. If, however, you are using your own pattern study similar style models in the shops, this will help you in the choice of fabric.

Material chosen for pleated styles must be firm in texture, if it is springy and wiry the pleats will not stay in their creases; crease-resisting fabrics are not recommended for this purpose. A soft material that falls well into folds is the best choice for gathered or ruched styles, and designs where smocking is being used, or in fact, any other form of fulness.

Give careful thought to the buying of plaid and patterned materials, extra length will be required to allow for the matching of the pattern. Fabrics with a definite right and wrong way of the cloth, whether it be in the pattern or the texture, are more extravagant than plain materials.

Material for tailored styles must be firm and have plenty of weight. Linen must be crease-resisting and fadeproof, and fabrics for washable frocks should be chosen for their unshrinkable and colour fast qualities.

Most cotton materials make up well into summer frocks, blouses and children's wear. The majority of these fabrics can be made into semi-tailored styles with pleats. If not too heavy in texture they will gather quite successfully. In recent years the improvement in design and texture of cotton fabrics has been so great that it is now possible to use them for charming evening frocks. Organdie, which is a transparent "stiffened" material, can be used for the full-skirted crinoline type evening dress, fluffy blouses and children's party frocks. Voile is another light-weight cotton, soft in texture it will drape and gather gracefully; some of these voiles are charmingly embroidered with delicate designs, and make up beautifully into simple styles. The good quality lawns and cambrics are obtainable in lovely pastel shades, as well as white, suitable for lingerie.

Linens are made in varying weights, and nowadays it is possible to get heavy, crease-resisting material in fashionable shades, which is admirable for summer tailored suits and frocks. The linen lawns, which are soft and dainty, can be used for blouses and lingerie.

Pure silk is the basis of all the finest and most luxurious fabrics. There is a certain amount of resilience in this yarn which lends itself to perfect fitting.

The varieties of silk materials are many, ranging from filmy chiffons and georgettes for billowing and draped evening dresses, to the heavier marocains for dress and suit wear.

Taffeta makes up well into the stiff "frou-frou" crinoline and bustle styles for evening. This is most charming in the softer shades, and bright colours should be avoided.

Heavy-weight satins and crêpes range with velvet in the "clinging" variety and give grace to the sylph-like styles. If cut generously they drape and fold most beautifully, but tend to give a fattening effect.

The less luxurious types of silk, such as shantung and shap silk make up well into semi-tailored summer frocks and shirt blouses. The thinner crêpe-de-chines, satins and jap silks are used for lingerie and linings.

Rayons are varied and, in the main, hard wearing. They take the place of linens, wool materials and all types of silk fabrics, and they can be used for similar purposes. It is sometimes difficult to distinguish a good quality synthetic material from the real thing.

For tailored suits, coats and frocks woollen fabric is always the best choice. Wool is made up into fabrics of different weaves and textures, from the heavy tweeds and suitings to the sheer georgettes and crêpes for dress wear. As a general rule tailored styles should be chosen when woollen fabrics are being used, but the lighter dress weights can be draped successfully. Simple, well cut lines, without "fuss" are the best to choose.

Jersey cloth and knitted materials need careful handling as they stretch a great deal. The design of the garment should be simple and well cut to avoid "cling." It is a good plan to hang the fabric over a rod before cutting, the weight of the material will take away some of the stretchiness and promote a better hang when made up. Careful sewing is needed, try to avoid double hems and tight stitching.

Fabrics which have stiff metallic threads, or cords, woven with the warp of the material should be cut with this thread running through the length of the garment, otherwise it will stand out and be quite unmanageable.

Heavy fabrics with a slight cord effect, such as bengaline or heavy marocain, can introduce new interest of line into a design if cut crosswise to the grain.

Avoid using light-weight and heavy materials together for the same garment, this combination would upset the balance. For instance, if a sheer yoke and sleeves are desired on a thicker material frock, choose georgette rather than chiffon.

Before buying material make sure that you have chosen a style of garment that you really like, something that is not too old or too young in design. Have an eye for smartness and fashion, but avoid eccentricities of which you may tire before the garment is finished, and hate before you can wear it. Careful consideration at the beginning saves wasted time and money later. Then select a material which is the most suitable for the style.

Be especially careful in the choice of patterned materials. As a general rule elaborate styles should be made in plain materials. When the design is plain and tailored the pattern in the material can be bold and gay. Remember, large patterns are fattening.

The mixing of two entirely different fabrics in one garment is not recommended. Silks match up with wool better than with cottons and rayon, but the arrangement must be carefully planned beforehand, with a very definite idea as to the finished result in mind.

Wool crêpe for dresses; heavy tweed for suits and coats; and barathea for suits.

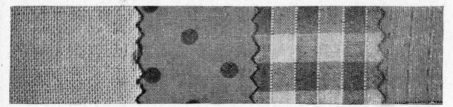

Dress weight linen; printed dress cotton; cotton gingham; and fancy cotton voile.

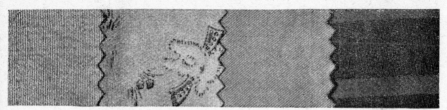

Pure silk shantung; silk crêpe-de-chine; rayon satin; and rayon, satin striped, crêpe.

QUALITY OF FABRICS

To judge the quality of materials well is a highly specialized job which requires experience. It will be found, however, that pure fabrics are stamped with a manufacturer's guarantee which states if they are fully shrunk, crease resisting and colour fast. As a rule these guarantees are to be relied upon, as they signify the material has been scientifically tested.

Pure wool and pure silk fabrics are more expensive than mixtures and synthetic materials, but they do give more satisfactory results. Wool and silk materials into which a certain amount of cotton has been introduced are hard wearing and make up quite well. Rayon fabrics are frequently mixed with cotton

as this gives stability to the fibre.

Here are a few tips on how to judge fabrics:—

Wool: the texture of the material should be soft. Unravel a few of the strands, both warp and weft should have the soft appearance of wool. Burn the ends with a match, they should smoulder slowly into a brown "blob," with a strong smell.

Silk: both strands are soft and pull apart easily. The material is smooth and soft in textures, when burnt it turns filmy and transparent.

Rayon: the fabric feels cold and is heavy. There is often metallic sheen to the surface. Owing to the acetate content it will flare up when burnt.

Cotton: the feel and appearance give the impression of a stiff fabric, this is often due to the dressing. If dampened it does not absorb moisture immediately.

Linen: heavy in weight and frequently uneven in weave, owing to the threads of the fabric being slightly bumpy. It will absorb moisture easily.

ESTIMATING MATERIAL REQUIRED

Comprehensive directions are supplied with most ready made patterns, and you can't go far wrong if guided by the amount of material suggested.

When using a pattern you have made yourself judge the amount of material required in the following way:—

First cut out all the pieces required for the garment then:—

(1) Take a length of paper as wide as the material to be used, or mark this area on a large table or the floor, with tapes or string. Arrange the pattern pieces in this area exactly as they will be when material is used, keeping the "straight" of the pattern parallel with the edges and allowing for turnings. Take into consideration "up and down" of the material and remember the pieces that have to be cut twice.

Measure along the tape from where the pattern starts to where it finishes,

and this will give you the amount of material required.

(2) This method needs a little mathematical calculation but, when space is scarce, it is a satisfactory method.

Make miniature pattern pieces, one-quarter scale of the originals, and on a sheet of paper draw two parallel lines a quarter of the width of material. Arrange the small patterns in this area and measure it up as before. Multiply by four and you will have the amount of material required.

Lining material is estimated in the same way, using only the pattern for the portion to be lined.

Remember — patterned and plaid materials cut extravagantly as the matching of the pattern must be allowed for . Half a yard extra for normal designs will be sufficient, more will be needed if the pattern is very large.

NORMAL MATERIAL WIDTHS

Fabrics are woven in standard widths —single width and double width. It is fairly safe to work on the principle that dress weight materials are thirty-six inches wide and woollens are fifty-four inches wide. There are exceptions, however, so it is always advisable to

make sure of the exact width before buying the fabric chosen. Two or three inches on the width make a big difference to the total quantity of material required.

The following list will give you some idea of the standard widths:—

STANDARD WIDTHS TABLE

	INCHES		INCHES
Cottons, plain or printed	36	Chiffon and georgette .	36
Spotted muslin . . .	30 to 36	Velvet	34 to 36
Organdie . . .	44	Velveteen	27 to 36
Rayons and linens . .	36	Light woollen material	36 to 54
Lining materials . .	28 to 44	Heavy-weight woollens	54
Silk dress materials .	30 to 38	Tweeds, single width .	28
Shantung	28 to 36	Tweeds, double width .	54

Lay the pattern pieces out carefully on a strip of paper or between two tapes, allowing the width of the material to be used. Measure the length taken up by the patterns to estimate the amount of material required. The patterns must be arranged correctly.

Choosing a style from a picture is not so easy as walking into a shop and trying the garment on. The long slim lines of a drawing may lead you astray into believing that the style is slimming, whereas, if you were able to try on that same frock made up you would see immediately, it was not for you. Don't despair, the designs from which you can choose are unlimited, there is sure to be something suitable.

Firstly, consider your personality—are you the tailored type or feminine and frilly?

Secondly, study carefully lines that are slimming against those that add width.

Thirdly, decide for what purpose the garment is to be used.

Fourthly, have a very definite idea of the kind of material to be used.

Fifthly, remember your age, choose something that is neither too old nor too young.

With these points in mind select a good design that is most suitable. It is a difficult task but, if you are critical and firmly discard those that emphasize imperfections, and concentrate on those that will flatter your good points, all should be well.

Widening lines: are those which run round the figure and cut across the length, detracting from the height.

Wide sleeves, square necks and collars, yokes straight across the shoulders or hips, stripes going round, full skirts and loose-fitting coats, are all points which add width to the figure. They should be avoided by the short woman and one who is plump.

Lengthening lines: which are at the same time slimming and should be avoided by the very thin woman are— lines running straight up and down the figure in the form of seams and stripes, long tight fitting sleeves, V-shaped necks and diagonal lines. Straight tight fitting skirts are to be recommended for slim appearance.

Finally a word about patterned materials. Checks and plaids should be avoided by the not so slim. Very large and gay floral patterns give a broadening effect. A regular all-over pattern is kind to most figures, but small niggling sprig patterns can only be worn satisfactorily by the very slim or small person.

The woman with an average figure has few troubles as she can, with care, wear almost any style. Few of us are blessed with such perfect proportions and have to decide which are our best points to be emphasized, and which are those to be hidden. Here are some suggestions.

When the legs are long and the body is short, jacket coats and skirts should be made longer than average, and belts to short coats should be avoided. Alternatively, someone who is long in the waist can wear belted styles and have short jacket coats. Skirts must not be too long if the legs are short.

Built-up shoulders and widening yokes flatter the figure with large hips and narrow shoulders, especially if combined with slim-fitting skirts. Panels, wide on the shoulders and tapering at the waist, also add width to a narrow figure. Swathing round the hips and skirts with yokes lend width to the hip line. To lessen the shoulder width have narrow cut shoulders and V-necks.

The woman who is small in the bust finds the gathered and draped bodice flattering, but the plain styled bodice is the best for the stout person.

Narrow waists are accentuated by tight fitting belts which should be avoided.

For the very broad figure, long loose fitting lines are the rule, always.

99

Pressing plays a very big part in dressmaking. Each seam, dart and every little detail must be pressed in the course of making if a smart neat finish is to be obtained.

PRESSING
SOME SIMPLE METHODS

It is bad dressmaking to leave all the pressing until the garment is completed. Each seam and every detail must be pressed, step by step, if the garment is to have that smart professional finish. With a few exceptions all materials should be pressed on the wrong side.

Wool materials need steam pressing

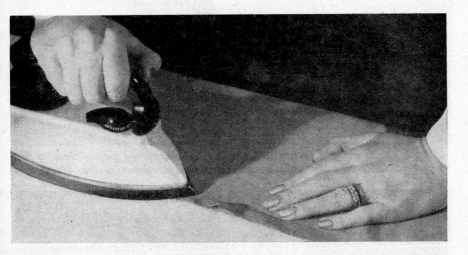

First press a seam with the two edges level, then open them out flat, and press again.

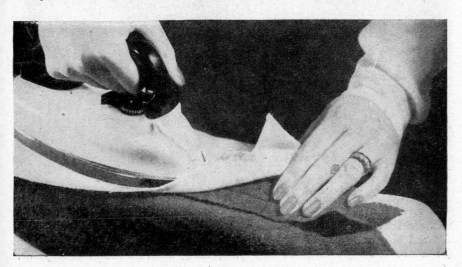

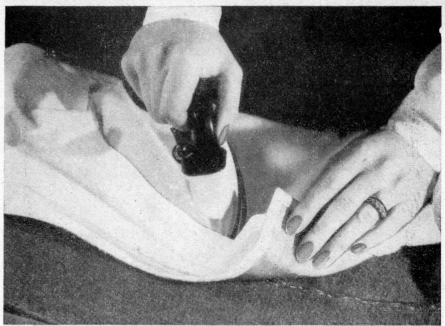

A lapped seam is neater if pressed on the right side. Always use a damp cloth for this to prevent shine, or better still, an anti-shine pad, as shown in this photograph.

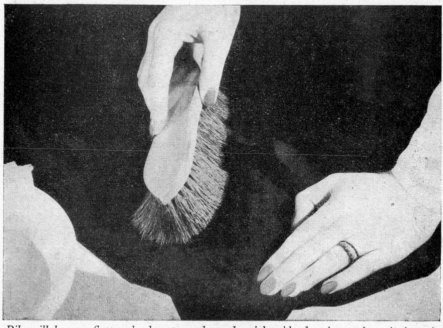

Pile will become flattened when pressed on the right side, but it can be raised again if brushed with a stiff brush immediately after pressing, whilst the steam is in the fabric.

with a hot iron and a damp cloth (or old piece of linen) which has been wrung out very well. Dry the cloth slightly with the iron before use.

When pressing, hold the iron over one spot for a few seconds and then lift it right off. Repeat this until the fabric is dry. Pat in the steam with the hand, a dry cloth or a flat piece of wood.

Seams.—Will have a neater finish if pressed to one side first. Lay the garment flat on the board with the seam to one side, and press in this position. Whilst the material is still damp pull the stitching gently to ease any contraction, and dry off with the iron. Open the seam out and press in the usual way.

When pressing open seams, slip a roller underneath so the join is pressed more than the edges. This method prevents marks on the right side of the garment. The centres of the seams in woollen materials can be dampened with a sponge, then covered with a dry cloth and pressed. Seams that are pressed to one side should lie in the same direction for the complete length.

Pressing seams, pockets and buttonholes on the right side needs care. Do not leave the iron on one spot too long. Always use a damp cloth or a piece of garment material under the iron and pat in the steam to prevent shine. Dry out the garment on the wrong side

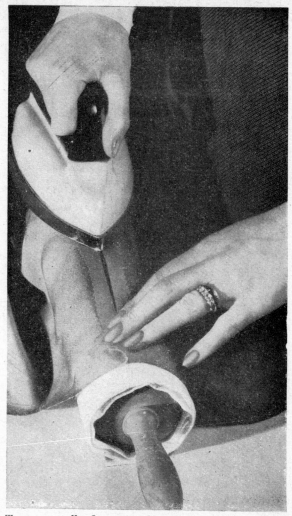

To get a really flat seam place the join on a rounded surface when pressing the edges open.

after pressing with the warm iron.

The pad described on page 43 will prevent shine and improve the pressing.

When material has become shiny through pressing, place a thoroughly damp cloth over the spot, press with a very hot iron and pat in the steam.

Materials with nap, other than velvet, should be ironed the way of the pile. To prevent it from becoming flattened brush up the pile with a stiff brush.

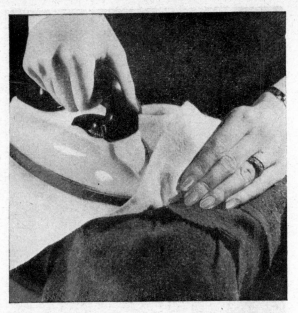

Sleeve Seams.—The sleeve board can be slipped inside the sleeve so that when the seam is pressed the remainder does not become crushed.

This miniature board can also be used for pressing the seam at the top of a sleeve, or it may be substituted by the tailor's cushion described on page 43. This seam may be pressed, either with both the edges flat over the top of the sleeve, or with the edges divided as an ordinary opened seam.

The tailor's cushion is ideal for pressing darts at the top of sleeves, it can be made to fit the shape exactly and so prevent the sleeve being pressed into

The armhole seam can be pressed with the edges opened out as in an ordinary flat seam. Use the tailor's cushion as a foundation for this to get a clean sharp join that is absolutely flat. It may be necessary to snick the seam edges.

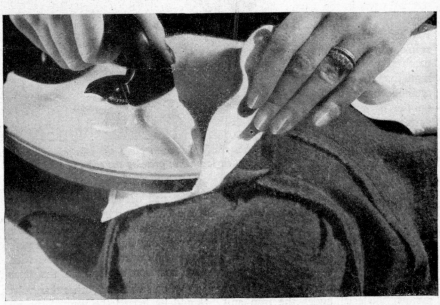

Another way of pressing an armhole seam is to let both the edges lie to one side, level with each other, preferably over the sleeve itself. Press these edges in this position, still using the tailor's cushion. If the latter piece of equipment is not available use the sleeve board.

an ugly shape. These small darts can be pressed uncut or slit along the centre and opened out.

Pleats.—Careful pressing is needed for pleats or they will hang badly and not fold properly. It is most important that they should first be tacked very well indeed so that they will not slip. Press both the wrong side and the right. Do not pull the edge of the pleats while pressing as this will stretch them and cause them to hang badly. Make the hem at the lower edge before finally pressing pleats, otherwise they will be creased the wrong way and not fall into the natural folds.

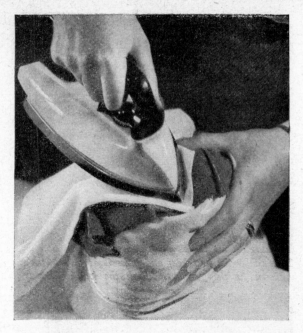

The small darts at the top of a sleeve are pressed on a rounded surface. The tailor's cushion is ideal for this.

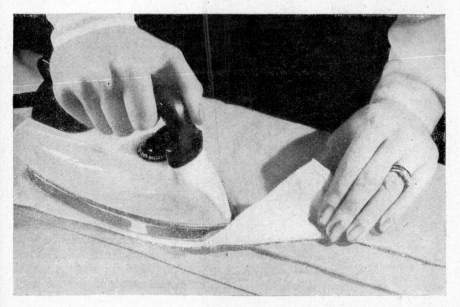

Pleats need very careful pressing both on the right side as well as the wrong. Use a damp cloth for woollen materials and a dry one for silks and light-weight fabrics. The hem of a garment that is pleated should be pressed flat before the pleats are set into folds.

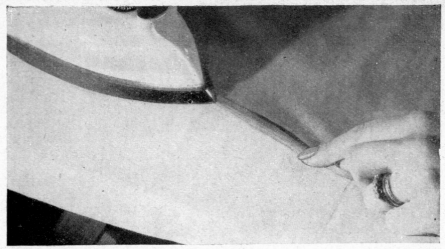

Turn under the first hem and press it down. Make the second hem, sew the darts to make it fit the garment. Tack the hem well and press under a cloth, see below.

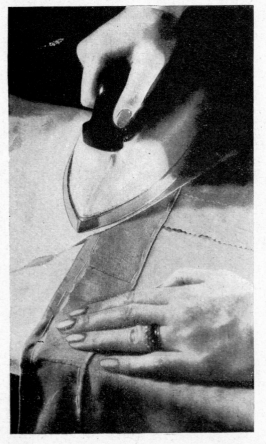

Hems.—First fold the single hem, then press it. If the material is heavy it may be found easier if the hem is first tacked. Turn under the main hem, tack it, and press again. Make the final stitching, remove the tacks and press the hem very well. If the garment is made in thick material give the hem a final pressing on the right side, taking the anti-shine precautions.

Circular hems must be absolutely flat on the board when being pressed, avoid pulling of any kind or the hem will become misshapen.

Velvet.—There are several ways of pressing velvet. The most usual is the steaming method—heat the iron until it is the right temperature, and stand it on end. Hold the material with a cloth between it and the iron, pile side outside, pulling it fairly tightly so there are no creases. Move the velvet backwards and forwards, gently, in this position until it has been well steamed and the creases are removed. Do not handle the fabric whilst it is still warm or the pile will flatten and become finger marked.

The needle board described on page 43 is of great assistance in pressing velvet. Lay the fabric flat, pile side down on the board, place a cloth over the wrong side and iron very gently with a warm iron.

Panne velvet, which has a long flat pile, can be pressed in the normal way

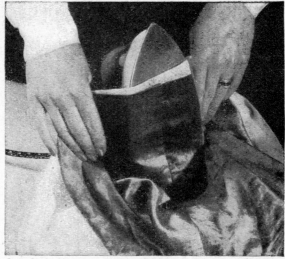

Stand the iron on end and pass the velvet across it pulling gently so the steam will take out the creases.

under a cloth. Press on the right side and always iron with the way of the pile. If stroked the wrong way it will mark badly and permanently.

There is yet another good way of pressing seams in velvet. Pin one end of the seam firmly to the ironing board cover, hold the other end with the left hand and pull it taut. Iron up and down this tight seam with a warm iron.

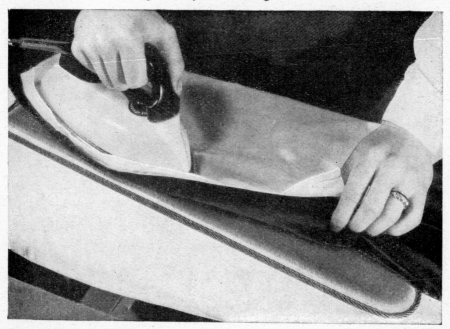

If a needle board is used the velvet can be placed flat, pile side down, and pressed.

Silk.—Delicate silk fabrics require careful pressing. They are apt to water mark if a damp cloth is used and if the iron is too hot it will scorch or leave an impression of the iron on the fabric.

Fine materials such as chiffon and other expensive silks should be pressed underneath, or even between, two pieces of tissue paper. Test the iron for heat on a scrap of the same material, or on a corner that won't show. Never dampen materials in which there are metallic threads.

Rayons vary in texture so much that the heat of the iron must be regulated for each particular type. Always test the iron on a spare piece of material before pressing the main garment, and press quite dry.

Cotton can be pressed dry or very slightly dampened all over. It is not a difficult fabric to press.

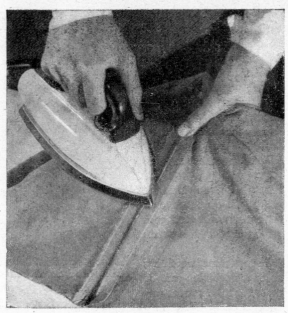

When pressing seams in velvet pin one end to the ironing board, hold it taut and press with the point of the iron.

Linen scorches easily so do not use a too hot iron, and be sparing with the damping.

It is always advisable to remove tacking threads before the final pressing as they will leave marks, especially in lightweight materials.

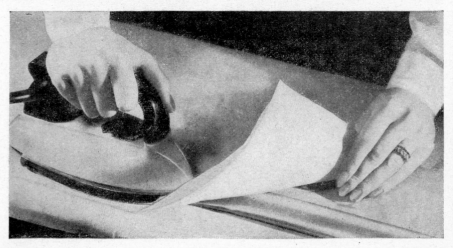

To prevent silk from marking, place a piece of tissue paper between the iron and the fabric.

SHRINKING

This chapter covers shrinking before making, and the removal of fulness.

Before Making.—There is a school of thought which believes that all materials, cotton and woollen, should be shrunk before making up. This is an old-fashioned theory which belongs to the time when manufacturers gave all fabrics a good stretch before they left the factory. In these days of fully shrunk fabrics further shrinkage at home is not necessary.

If, however, you feel happier if the material is shrunk at home, this is how it is done. First make sure that the material will not spot or crinkle when it comes into contact with moisture. Take a piece of old linen fabric a little wider than the material itself, or half the width if it is folded, and a little longer than the yardage. Wring this out well in water and squeeze until most of the moisture has been disposed of. Place the damp material flat on a large table, or the floor, with the material to be shrunk on the top of it. Roll the two together tightly, damp cloth outside, stroking away all creases and folds. Wrap the bundle in a dry cloth and leave overnight. Shake the material out well and press with a warm iron in the normal way. Leave to hang, quite straight, until dry.

Do not attempt to shrink fancy and delicate fabrics.

Tailor's canvas must always be shrunk, otherwise when it gets wet it will shrink again and ruin the sit of the collar and lapel. Be quite ruthless about this, dip it in water and leave it until it is thoroughly wet, wring it out and leave to dry. Press when slightly damp.

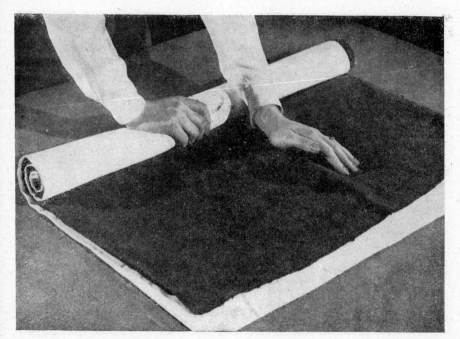

To shrink woollen material before making up, roll it in a damp cloth, removing all creases.

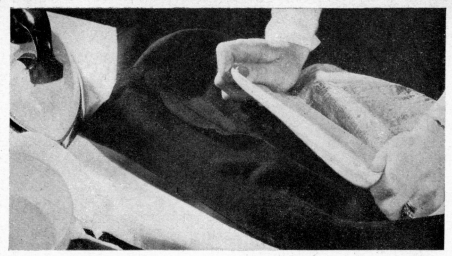

Place a damp cloth over the bump at the point of a dart, and press well with a hot iron.

After Making—Darts.—It is sometimes necessary to shrink a portion of a garment after making up. The bubble that occurs at the points of darts, after they have been stitched, is something that must be removed by shrinking to make a flat, smooth fit. First press the dart on the wrong side. Place a rather damp cloth over the fulness and then place a fairly hot iron on to it and

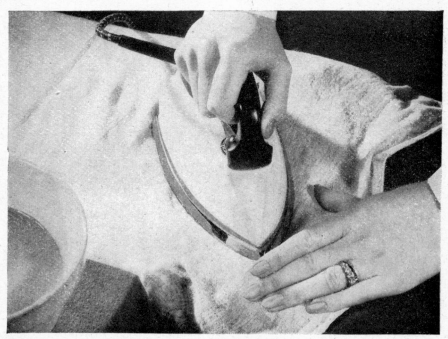

When shrinking with a damp cloth, keep the iron firmly in one place until almost dry.

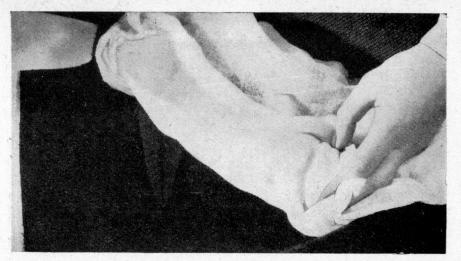

Remove the cloth and dry the dart with the iron, or press with the hand to keep in the steam.

leave until the cloth is almost dry. This takes away the bulk of the surplus.

Now turn the garment over, right side uppermost, and repeat the procedure on the right side, using a drier cloth and not such a hot iron. Do this carefully to avoid scorching. Whilst the material is still full of steam pat it with a dry cloth to prevent shine and help the shrinking.

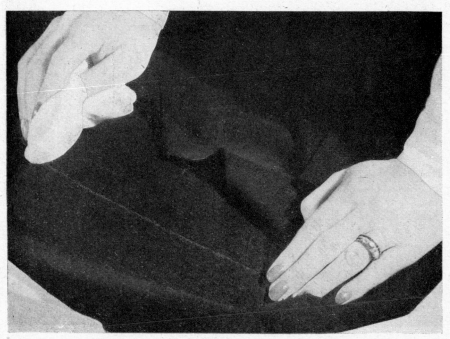

To prevent shine when pressing the right side, pat the steam into the fabric with a dry cloth.

Gather the edge to be shrunk, and steam press with a hot iron and damp cloth.

round the area are pressed flat. Dry the fabric of the garment with the iron.

When the sleeve is too big for the armhole the consequent fulness can be shrunk away after the sleeve has been fitted into the armhole. Tack the sleeve in place with the fulness at the top. Using a wet cloth and a hot iron shrink the sleeve as previously described.

When the armhole is too large, the sleeve is fitted into place and the fulness of the armhole is stroked to the back and evenly distributed between the side seam and the shoulder seam. Shrink with a hot iron and a damp cloth.

Fulness at the waists of tight-fitting jackets, elbows and, after wear, the seats and knees of skirts, can be disposed of by shrinking in a similar way. Lay the portion to be shrunk flat on the board and stroke all the fulness to the centre of the area concerned. Cover with a wet cloth and using a hot iron smooth all round the part to be shrunk, working towards the centre.

Armholes and Necks.—Slackness at the armholes and neck make for ugly fitting and the dreaded home-made look. The method of shrinking in these instances is always the same, it can also be used for shrinking away fulness at the top of skirts when they are to be eased into a waist band.

Run a gathering thread into the portion that is to be shrunk and pull this up until the garment is the correct size. Place this section over the sleeve board, cover with a very damp cloth, and hold a hot iron on to the place, until the cloth is dry. Repeat this until all the gathers have been shrunk away, and make sure that all the bubbles

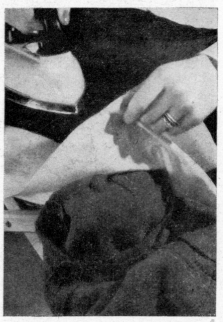

Shrink armholes on the sleeve board.

Shrinking Hem Fulness.—The inside edge of a circular hem is always too full to fit the garment, consequently this fulness has to be disposed of. Run a gathering thread along the raw edge of the hem, all round. Turn up a single hem to the required width and draw up the running threads until it lies quite flat and the gathers are evenly distributed. All this should be done with the skirt spread out quite flat on the table. Tack the hem down firmly, then shrink the fulness away as previously described, using a wet cloth and hot iron.

Stretching a Hem Edge. — The stitched edge of a hem that has been faced with a second piece of material sometimes becomes rucked and tight. This can easily be remedied as follows:— lay the edge of the hem flat on the board and place a wet cloth over it, press quickly with a hot iron and, whilst the hem is still damp, stretch the edge until it is the right size.

This method is sometimes used when a line of machining is too tight.

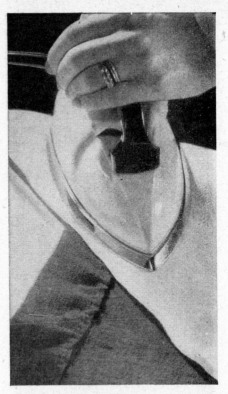

Gather the edge of hem and draw it up.

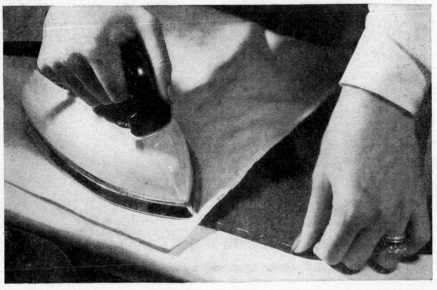

Press with a hot iron over a damp cloth, and pull the edge to be stretched at the same time.

It is important, when cutting out a garment, to have the material laid out for the full length, so that all the pattern pieces can be arranged in position at one time. If there is no table large enough then the floor is a good substitute. Pin the pattern carefully.

CUTTING OUT

MATERIAL CHARACTERISTICS

All material is made up of warp and weft threads. The warp threads are those which run through the length of the fabric, with the grain; and the weft is woven in and out of them, across the grain. When these fibres are being woven the edge of the material is given a firm finish to prevent fraying; this is known as the selvedge.

The bias of the material runs diagonally across the warp and weft and, as there are no threads running directly across this way, the fabric is stretchy.

To find the true bias—fold the material across one corner diagonally, so that the weft edge is level with the selvedge. This cut edge must be absolutely straight along the thread of the material.

Before attempting to cut out a pattern examine the material carefully, making quite sure in your own mind which is

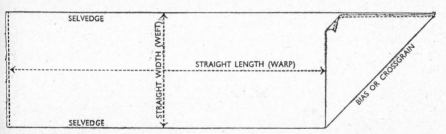

Get to know all the peculiarities of the warp, weft and bias of a fabric, before cutting.

The weft threads of these materials are silky in texture and are woven into damask patterns.

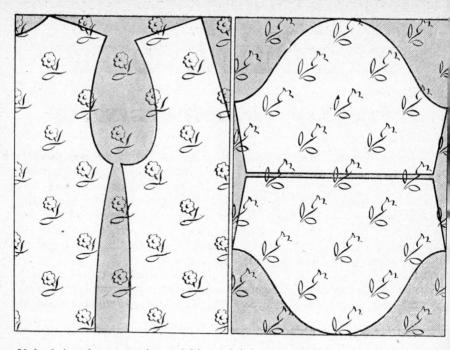

If the design of a patterned material has a definite up and down, the pattern pieces must be arranged facing all one way, as on the left; and not up and down as on the right.

the grain of the material, across the grain and the bias. This knowledge is necessary so that the patterns may be placed on the material correctly. The slightest twist, which will take the straight of the pattern off the grain of the fabric, will cause the garment to hang incorrectly when finished.

Examine the material carefully for any flaws, and mark them with chalk, or tacking thread. These spots can then be avoided when arranging the pattern for cutting.

It is sometimes difficult to distinguish between the right and wrong side of the material. Usually the right side is folded inside when the fabric is bought or, if supplied in single width, the right side is rolled inside against the roller. Printed materials are sometimes folded with the right side outside, but the two sides are easy to distinguish as the

wrong side is not so bright in colour. Patterned fabrics which have the design woven in a damask weave have two very definite sides which cannot be mistaken. Fabrics with simple woven designs, such as ginghams and tweeds, are frequently the same both sides and can be used either way.

It is sometimes possible to determine the right side by the feel of the fabric, especially when the material has a nap. If there is any doubt at all examine the selvedge, this should be smoother on the right side than on the wrong.

Having decided which is the right side of the material mark it with a large cross in chalk or tacking cotton to avoid mistakes.

If a material has a definite right and wrong side it is important to watch that the two sides of the garment are cut as definite right and left, in other words

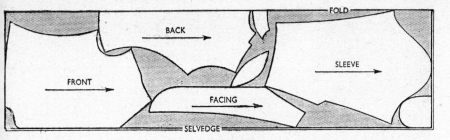

The straight of all pattern pieces should be marked with a line, and this line must be placed on the grain of the material. Here the patterns of a blouse are correctly set.

avoid having two left sleeves, two right bodices and so on.

You have now sufficient knowledge to judge when the pattern is correctly placed: (1) straight with the grain of the cloth; (2) all the same way of the design, and (3) on the bias when necessary.

Press out any creases in the material before cutting and iron the pattern with a cool iron so it will lie flat on the material.

The texture of the material plays a big part in the fit and finish of a garment. Cloth that is softly woven and slightly stretchy will give to the figure, it is in consequence much easier to fit and handle. On the other hand, material that is hard in texture will not mould itself to the contours of the figure as it has no stretch. It is generally advisable to cut generous turnings when dressmaking with fabrics of this kind.

Bias cut garments will cling to the figure as they are very stretchy. A skirt that is cut on the cross way of the fabric should be allowed to hang for several days before the hem is made. The weight of the fabric falls with the hanging and makes the hem line uneven. If the hem has not been made the edge can be re-cut and evened up. On the other hand if the hem is made, stitched and pressed straight away the skirt will drop whilst being worn, giving an ugly hang and hem line to the garment which can only be rectified by unpicking the hem and re-cutting the edge.

Some fabrics, such as stripes, are most attractive if cut with the cross grain in the length but the design of the garment, in this instance, must be chosen with great care. One point to remember—the weft way of the material does not hang so softly as the warp length and will not gather well.

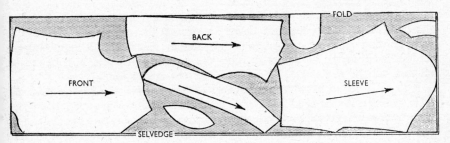

If the straight of the pattern is allowed to cross, or even slightly cross, the grain of the fabric, as shown here, the finished garment will pull and hang in ugly lines.

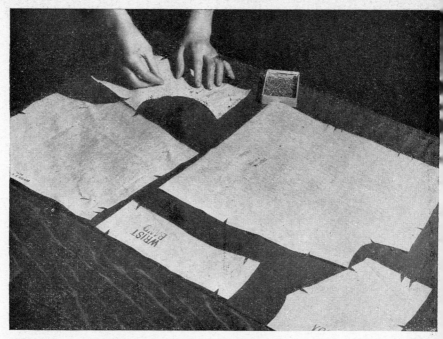

When the material being used is plain, and without nap, the pattern can be arranged facing up or down; this is more economical on yardage. The straight of the pattern must be on the grain of the material. Avoid placing the length of the pattern on the weft.

ARRANGING THE PATTERN

A table, large enough to take the whole length and full width of the material, is ideal for cutting out; failing this the floor is a good substitute. All the pattern pieces can be laid out at one time and arranged more economically, so that they fit in with each other. Cover the floor with an old sheet, or white paper, fastened down with drawing pins; newspaper is not recommended as the ink is apt to rub off and soil the material.

If there is not room to keep a large table permanently, a good plan is to have a board made of plywood; this can be placed on an ordinary dining or kitchen table, or between two chairs for cutting out, and stored in some small

corner when not in use. In a household where there is a large amount of dressmaking to be done, but not a great deal of space, this is an excellent plan. There is one advantage in this table top; as it is unpolished the material will not slip about.

If a small table has to be used, place a chair at the end to hold the surplus material. This method is not advantageous as only part of the pattern can be laid out at one time.

When using a pattern you have cut yourself, you will know all the peculiarities and be able to make allowances accordingly. Make sure that all the necessary identification and fitting marks have been made, before cutting

Patterned material is the most difficult to cut. Not only must the pattern pieces be arranged all the same way, but the design must be matched on each section in length and width.

Striped and check materials must be carefully matched, at the seams and centre front and back. When cutting out on double material make sure that the stripes of both sides match.

the material. It is a good plan to draw a straight line on the pattern to indicate which way the grain of the material should lie.

Most ready-made patterns have all the fitting notches, darts, pleats, straight of the material and cutting details marked on them. Study these with care before cutting. Ensure that the balance and fitting marks have not been thrown out of place with any alterations that have been made.

The next step is to arrange the pattern on the material, which has been laid flat with all creases smoothed out.

Even if there is ample yardage to cut into, it is fun to juggle with the patterns and arrange them as economically as possible. You may be able to save enough material to make some other garment or small accessory.

Plain fabric, without nap or pile, is the most economical to cut as the pattern can be turned either way, but the "straight" of the pattern must be kept on the grain of the cloth. Be timid about placing the pattern against the grain as this may have a different texture, which will show when the garment is worn. It is advisable to cut facings the same way of the fabric as the garment. The latter rule can be broken to introduce a trimming note. Straight pieces for belts should be placed along the selvedge, or else they can be cut against the grain to save material, and on the bias for trim-ming. In the latter case the finished belt must be strengthened with a straight grained strip to prevent stretch-ing.

When the material is self-coloured but has a definite "up or down," such as velvet or face cloth, then all the pattern pieces must be placed facing in the same direction. The pile should stroke upwards towards the shoulder, in the opposite way to a cat's fur. If velvet is cut the reverse way there will not be the richness of colour and the skirt will creep up and wrap round when worn. An easy way to find the right and wrong way of velvet is to hold it towards the light, level with the eyes, and look along the grain, first one way and then the other. In this posi-tion velvet looks darker against the pile than with it. Panne velvet can be smoothed with the hand, it has a flat pile with a very definite up and down.

Patterned materials are the most extravagant and difficult to cut. Not only must the patterns be kept all the same way, but the two fronts, the back, the sleeves and the skirt pieces must match. Pick out some prominent feature of the design to use as a guide

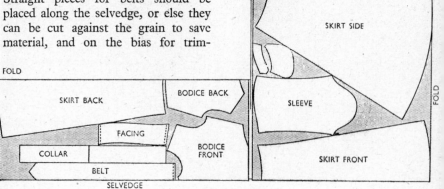

It is often more economical to refold part of the fabric, or to cut some patterns singly.

in placing the pattern, making sure that it appears in a similar spot on each piece. Match pocket pieces and facings as well.

Stripes and checks must be meticulously matched. Nothing looks worse than a seam where the stripes differ by a fraction of an inch, or a bodice or skirt with the stripes slightly to one side of the centre line. When cutting on doubled material match the stripes of one layer with the other. Here is a tip which might help you in the cutting. Place the front pattern on the fabric and mark the position of each stripe, then mark the back pattern to correspond so that it can be cut with the stripes in the same place. Both sleeves and cuffs must match, and the centre of the collar should correspond with the centre back.

When all the pattern pieces are small it is possible to arrange them on the material as it is folded, when bought. This simplifies the arranging of the patterns considerably as the two sides can be cut at the same time, ensuring they are both alike. The edges where a seam is to be avoided can be placed to the fold in the material. Take the precaution first to have the fold through the centre of the design, the selvedges level with each other, and the two sides matching exactly.

It is sometimes more economical to cut the patterns on single material. In this case pieces which have to be cut double with a fold down the centre, need special treatment. Either—cut a second piece of the pattern in paper. Place the pattern on a sheet of paper and draw all round it with pencil or the tracing wheel, cut round the tracing. Arrange this shape side by side with the original pattern, on the material. Or— place the pattern on the material leaving an equal amount of material at the outer edge of the fold, hold the pattern in

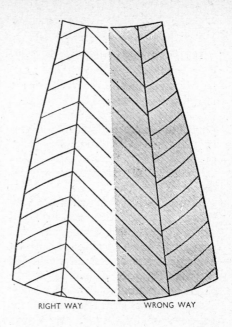

RIGHT WAY   WRONG WAY

Take great care with the cutting and fitting of stripes cut on the bias. If they do not match perfectly at the seams, as shown on the left, the result is ugly, as can be seen by the right of the skirt.

place with weights and draw all round it with tailor's chalk. Turn the pattern over so that the fold edge is along the same chalk line, pin the pattern in this position and cut round the outer chalk line and paper.

Some of the pattern pieces may be wider than the material when it is folded in half, but not the full width of the fabric. In this case the cloth can be refolded so that half the length is cut single and the remainder is cut double. This method gives a fold to which the centre front and back of the garment can be placed.

Alternatively, it is sometimes found more economical to cut out the pattern with part of the material folded along the length and with the remainder folded across the width, so that all the pieces are cut in double material.

When all the pattern pieces have been arranged on the material satisfactorily, pin them down well, making sure that the paper and fabric are quite flat. Flimsy silk material may be pinned to a piece of thin paper to prevent slipping. Cut through this paper as well. Handle the material as little as possible to prevent unnecessary creasing.

If turnings have been allowed for on the paper pattern, the pieces should be placed close together without any extra allowance. If no turnings are allowed a margin must be left all round the pattern. Be quite definite as to the width of the turning allowance, which should be the same throughout the garment, or the fit will be wrong. Turning widths are determined by the

material concerned, they can be from half an inch for firm cloth, to one inch for fabric which frays easily. Large turnings make clumsy seams but sufficient should be allowed for fitting adjustments, especially in materials that have no stretch. Mark the turnings with chalk or tacking threads before cutting.

Balance Marks.—The notches, which are made in a pattern as a guide to making up, darts, tucks, the centre back and front, and all other balance marks, must be transferred to the material before the pattern is removed. If this is done before cutting, not only will it help to keep the pattern from slipping, but, if it does move there will be an indication of the correct position. Balance marks may be made in one of three ways—1. With tailor's chalk, which

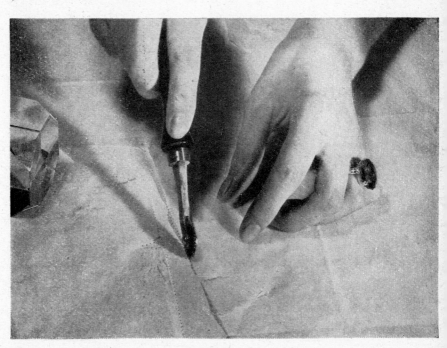

When a second pattern is needed for cutting on single material, or a design is being adapted, use the tracing wheel for marking round the outside edges.

Mark all the fitting notches and edges of the pattern before cutting out. It is not advisable to cut the notches as they might fray. On plain materials tailor's chalk can be used, as it shows up clearly and rubs off afterwards. Pin the pattern in position first to avoid slipping. Arrange the patterns carefully to fit in one with the other, for economical use of material.

Patterned and striped materials need clearer markings than tailor's chalk. Make thread marks round the pattern with a contrasting shade. Make a loose back stitch in each notch.

123

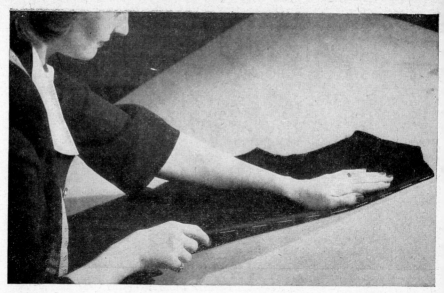

Mark the centre front and back of a garment before cutting out; use plain tacking or tailor's tacks for this. After cutting and when the pattern has been removed, fold each section, matching the edges, as shown, to test that the tacks are absolutely central and correct.

can be rubbed off after making up. This method is not to be recommended for use in light coloured and flimsy materials.

2. Tailor's tacks, which can be made over the paper pattern; the long stitches are snicked so that the pattern can be removed easily, see page 151. To mark notches and single points with this method—make one large loose back-stitch at each point. After cutting out the two layers can be pulled apart and the stitches snicked in between them. There will be a few threads left on each piece of the garment. This is the most satisfactory way of marking sheer fabrics as it is more permanent. Use a contrasting coloured cotton.

3. The tracing wheel, a quick method which can be used on stiff materials or when making a second paper pattern.

The centre back and front of a garment should be marked with long tacking threads; make them along the edge of the pattern before it is taken off the

material. Check the position of this carefully after the garment has been cut.

The shears used for cutting should be large, well set and very sharp. If small scissors are used the blade is so short that the cut edge will be hacked and uneven.

It is inadvisable to cut darts before making up; if they have to be adjusted in the fitting the material allowed may not be sufficient. Also, the raw edges of materials fray, therefore, the less cutting made into the garment the better. Because of this avoid cutting the small V's for notches, especially in loosely woven materials.

When cutting out do not lift the material away from the table. Slip the larger blade of the shears under the fabric at one edge and hold the pattern, which is being cut round, firmly with the left hand. Make long cutting strokes, opening the scissors as wide as possible and cutting for the full length, thus making an even, straight edge.

If the material is lifted off the table whilst cutting out is in progress the pattern is liable to slip, and the material will be pulled out of place, thus upsetting the size and shape.

Cutting on the Cross.—Needs special care. It is important that the centre back and front should be kept on the true bias, otherwise the hang will be unbalanced. Mark the pattern with a line which is to be placed on the cross grain and make sure that it is very carefully placed. It will help if the bias of the material is marked with a tacking line. Find the cross grain as explained on page 115 and make long tacking threads along the fold. The line marked on the pattern can then be placed on these tackings or parallel with them.

A skirt pattern that is cut on the cross is usually wide and full and it is often found that the sides extend beyond the selvedge of the material. When this is the case small pieces can be joined on at each side to get the full width. The grain of these additional pieces must be matched with that of the main fabric. If the edge is selvedge then it is a good plan to choose a small piece with a selvedge and join the two. If patterned or striped material is being used, then this must be matched as well.

Careful Cutting.—When there is a shortage of material, as sometimes happens if a remnant or very expensive material is being used, extra consideration has to be given to the cutting out. The arrangement of the patterns on the fabric must be meticulously planned, and only the right amount of turnings must be left on the seams. It is a good plan in this instance, especially if the pattern is complicated, to cut the garment out in mull, fit it accurately to the figure, making any adjustments necessary, and then cut the garment material from this foundation.

Cutting Linings.—These are cut from the garment pattern, omitting facings and any extra length on the skirt and sleeves allowed for hems. Linings should be made slightly larger than the garment itself, especially across the back, to prevent pulling. Make a small pleat at the centre of the back neck. Leave the extra width for all the length.

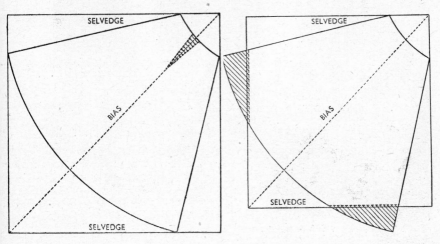

A skirt that is cut on the bias has the centre line placed on the cross grain. If the material is not wide enough to cut the full extent of the skirt, join pieces each side as required. Cut turnings to allow for the join and match the grain of the fabric on the two edges.

Accurate fitting, both of the paper pattern and of the garment throughout the making, plays a big part in the appearance of the finished garment. Every minute spent on fitting is well spent and will help to eliminate that home-made look that is so despised.

FITTING
DURING MAKING

The putting together of the various parts of a garment needs care and should be tackled with great precision and method, otherwise the whole effect and style of the garment will be lost.

When fitting a garment keep all the pins, chalk, scissors, tape-measure and necessary equipment by you.

It is a good plan to make a small pin cushion that will pin on to your frock, or sew one on to a band of elastic that will slip on to the wrist. This will keep pins handy and easy to pick up.

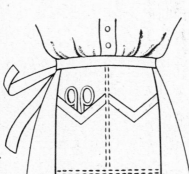

A small apron with two big pockets for tools.

Another aid to keeping equipment handy is a small apron with two large pockets in which scissors, chalk and other necessaries can be kept.

Make this from a square of material attached to a waist-band as shown in the Diagram on this page.

As a general rule, pin all the seams of the garment on the marked fitting line. Keep the seams flat on the table whilst this is being done to avoid any stretching or pulling out of shape. Insert all the pins

Pin seams carefully matching the fitting marks, and making gathers and darts beforehand. The two edges should be flat on the table so there is no fear of one edge being puckered.

facing one way. Replace the pins with short tacking stitches for security.

Be methodical about pinning a garment together. First find the centre lines of bodice and skirt back and front. Match the centre lines of the bodice to those of the skirt. Pin all darts at shoulders and waist line. Then pin the shoulder and side seams. Pin all seams from the top to hem line.

A simple garment made in thin material can be pinned up on the dummy. First tack the shoulder seams, then drape the fabric over the dummy and pin the seams and darts to get a perfect fit.

Pin and tack the sleeve seams, making all darts and easing the fulness in at the elbows. Fit this on the padded arm, making necessary adjustments.

The first fitting is made on the wrong side of the garment so that the seams can be adjusted easily. Then turn the garment right side out and fit again, preferably on the person herself.

Many people have one side of the figure slightly different from the other. When this is the case the garment must always be fitted on the right side, otherwise it will never fit. To do this make the fitting adjustments with pins and chalk marks in the normal way. Remove the garment from the figure and mark each alteration with thread marks and tacks, then these adjustments can be made on the wrong side.

When the garment has been fitted and sewn correctly then the sleeves, with the seams already sewn, can be inserted. Make sure that the armhole is a good fit before trying to put the sleeve into it. If the shoulders are to be padded, the padding must be placed in position when the shoulder and sleeves are fitted. Having made quite sure that the sleeve is set correctly and that the hang is right, then mark where the seam appears on the garment, and the fold of the sleeve turnings, with tailor's chalk. Remove the garment and the sleeve from the figure, turn to the wrong side and pin and tack the seam, matching the chalk marks on sleeve to those on the garment.

The particular style of the garment should be borne in mind during fitting, otherwise, with careless fitting the design might be completely altered.

Keep the seam flat on the table whilst inserting the tacking stitches which should be made along the pin line. All seams should be tacked carefully before the garment is fitted.

Line of tacking marking centre front and back of a garment.

FITTING A DRESS

Balance marks play a big part in the fitting of a garment and the first thing to watch for is that they are all correctly placed. The centre line of the front and back must lie along the centre front and the spine of the figure. The grain of the material in a straight cut garment lies straight round the bust line and across the hips. A bias cut garment must have the true bias corresponding with the centre.

Having ensured that the balance marks are set correctly continue with the fitting one step at a time.

Adjusting shoulder seam for neck fitting.

BODICE

Take careful note of the seam lines and make sure that they lie correctly. Have a picture of the style in front of you, then there will be no fear of making a loosely fitting bodice too tight, or a tight bodice too loose.

When fitting the shoulder seams and the armhole insert the padding, which is the correct size and thickness, into the shoulder. If the padding is omitted the armhole will appear to be too big and there will be a tendency to make it smaller. Then the sleeve will not fit and the shoulder padding will have to be omitted altogether. Adjust this seam to get a neatly fitting armhole and a snug neck. Never be too hasty about trimming off the turnings on armhole and neck edges. Remember that it is always easier to cut away than to fill in the gaps.

It may be necessary to adjust one side of the seam more than the other, for instance, the line may be too far to the front, in which case the turnings will have to be made narrower on that side.

The seams in a panelled bodice, which meet at the shoulder, must be matched exactly so that they run in a continuous line from back to front.

There is nothing more unsightly than a badly fitting neck. Make sure that it fits quite snugly. Tiny darts at centre back may be needed to improve the fit.

Darts.—These should always be tapered off to nothing at the points. Shoulder darts reach almost to the bust line and waist darts extend a few inches, to just below the bust. If the figure is full busted it is advisable to make small darts in the side seam at the bust line, this gives the extra spring required. In a loosely fitting bodice these darts will

Darts in shoulder and waist of bodice.

not be necessary. The style must be borne in mind whilst fitting so that darts are not made unnecessarily; avoid breaking into the line of design.

When there is a seam running from the shoulder to waist it must be fitted in the same way as darts. The seam is tapered off at the bust line and run in at the waist to fit snugly. In this style of garment it will be necessary to cut extra length on to the shoulder seam to allow for the amount taken up in the seam.

When fitting the bodice, first make quite sure that both the front and the back are the correct length, and make any adjustments at the shoulder seam. Keeping the line of the shoulder seam

Lengthening front at shoulder seam.

correct, let out or take up the side which requires adjustment. The right line for the shoulder is from the base of the neck just behind the ear to the edge of the shoulder, just behind the centre point. It is bad fitting to have the seam so near the front that it is visible.

The back neck should be kept small or it will bulge in an ugly way. Watch this point when adjusting the shoulder seam.

When the front bodice is too short it will hang badly with an uneven hem line, which pooks out from under the bust line. Adjust this fault by dropping the front edge of the shoulder seam to give extra length, as shown above, keep the shoulder line in the correct position, and ensure that the side seam is right.

Bodice which is too short at the front.

Lifting front to overcome sagging bodice.

Sagging Armholes.—If the distance between the shoulder seam and the armhole level is too great the armhole will sag. To rectify this lift the shoulder seam, front or back as required, thus shortening the length of the armhole edge. Keep the shoulder seam in the correct position.

Downward Drag at Armhole.—This is caused by the front bodice not fitting correctly through insufficient spring. To adjust this error make a small dart in the armhole edge, at the shoulder or in the side seam, whichever seems best.

When introducing darts into the side seam care must be taken to keep the seam in the correct position and to ensure that back and front match at the armhole and waist line.

At all times during fitting retain the correct hang of the garment.

Sagging Bodice.—This is usually caused by the balance of the bodice being incorrect. Pin the bodice to the dress form or the underclothes, with the balance correct, and then stroke the fulness upwards and outwards. Take up the extra material in the shoulder and side seams, or in darts, to get a perfect fit. Do not fit the bodice too tightly or there will be puckerings.

Dragging Across the Bust.—This is caused by the bodice being too tight, usually the front. To rectify this fault let out the side seams. This adjustment may cause the armhole to be too large. Do not, however, take up the shoulder seam in this case but make a small dart in the side seam or the armhole edge to get the play needed over the bust, see sagging armholes.

Bodice too tight causing dragging at front.

Downward drag from too large armhole.   *Shoulder and armhole darts to adjust drag.*

Sagging overcome by side seam darts.

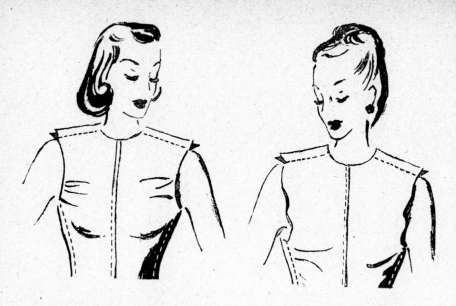

Armhole too tight causing pulling.   *An armhole that is too large sags.*

An armhole that is too tight will cause creases across the chest and also across the back. This fault may be rectified by letting out the side seams, unless the armhole is too large and the garment is too loose across chest and round the bust. If necessary release the shoulder seam as well. At all costs avoid making the armhole too large; there is nothing more ugly and the sleeve will never fit.

An armhole that is too large is a difficult problem unless there is plenty of room on the bust line, then the side seams can be taken in. If there is no alternative insert extra material into the space, taking great care to match the grain and pattern of this piece with that of the garment. To insert a piece of material in this way place the extra piece in the gap, turn under the edge of the garment and tack through the

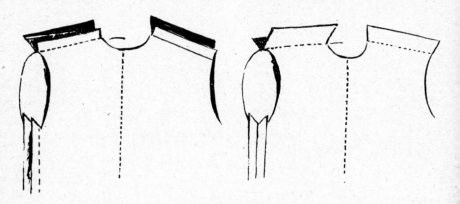

An incorrect armhole is adjusted at the side or shoulder seam, back or front.

Tightness pulling the bust line.   _Fulness round the bust line._

fold. Neatly hem the folded edge to the patch and neaten off the raw edges on the wrong side, with catch stitches, see page 155.

The best way to overcome this fault is to lift the garment at the shoulder seams and re-cut the armhole. To do this it will be necessary to have plenty of room and extra length at the waist line and to refit the bodice at the side and shoulder seams.

The Bust.—If the bodice is too tight it will pull into ugly folds across the bust, the revers will pook in an ugly way and the bodice will hang badly below the bust.

The remedy is to let out the side seams, more at the front than the back if necessary, keeping the seam in the correct line.

A bodice that is too loose will sag across the bust in ugly folds, and if the

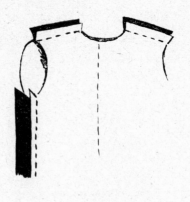 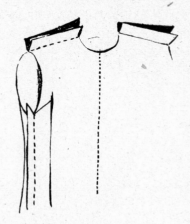

An adjustment to the bust line is made in the side seam as necessary.

The Back.—If the back measurement of the bust line is too large, the bodice will sag in folds right across. This fault is adjusted in the same way as the front by taking in the side seams. It may be that the bodice is too long from the shoulder to the waist in which case lift the back at the shoulder seam, keeping it in the correct position.

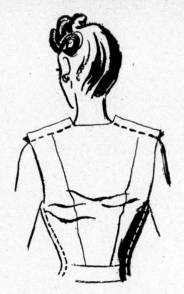

Too large back bodice causing sagging.

waist is tight fitting it will fall over in a blouse-like way. Take the extra width up into the side seams, still keeping them in the correct position.

Adjust the back like the front.

A too large neck line sagging badly.

Uneven shoulder seams are puckered.

Puckering at the Seams.—This is caused by one side being shorter than the other or the seam being wrongly sewn. Unpick the stitches and adjust, re-cutting where necessary.

The Neck Line.—This must fit neatly and snugly. If it is too large it will sag, if too tight the shoulder seams will pull to the back and the garment will crease across the back.

If there is too much fulness in the front of the neck line, smooth it away to the side and take it up in the shoulder seam, this may mean that the shoulder dart will have to be increased slightly.

Tiny darts can be made radiating from the neck line in the centre back. These will dispose of any extra fulness and improve the fit. They are especially helpful when the bone at the nape is rather large, or when the shoulders are slightly rounded. These pin darts need very careful fitting as it is such a minute adjustment.

Having fitted the bodice perfectly and made all the adjustments, sewn the seams and pressed them, trimmed off surplus turnings, and you feel really happy about the whole thing; then the sleeves can be fitted and inserted into the armholes.

Slip the bodice on, right side out. Make sure that the shoulder seam lies in the correct position and that it is not too long. See that the armhole fits snugly but is not too tight. Then run a tacking thread all round the armhole to indicate the correct position for the sleeve seam and the amount of turnings that are to be taken up.

Tacking round armhole for sleeve fitting.

SLEEVE

First make sure that the sleeve itself fits correctly. If it is too wide take more material into the seams. If too tight let out the seams accordingly. Take care to get the elbow fulness in the correct position when making a one-piece sleeve.

Now fix the sleeve into the armhole. Find the top point of the sleeve and mark it with a pin or thread mark. Turn under the turnings and match this point to the top point of the shoulder, with the fold of the turnings placed to the tacking line round the armhole. Continue pinning the sleeve to the garment all round the armhole, keeping the fold to the line of tacking stitches.

The seams of the sleeves must be matched to the garment. Seam to seam sleeves are arranged with the

Small radiating darts in large neck line.

Arranging elbow fulness in sleeve seam.

sleeve seam placed to the underarm seam. The two-piece sleeve has the front seam placed to a point on the bodice front, as shown on page 84. If these points do not quite match, adjust the seams. Do not move the centre point or the hang of the sleeve will be wrong. If, however, the sleeve does hang badly, either too far forward or too far back, then this point must be adjusted to rectify the error.

Having fitted the sleeve into the

1. *Sleeve set too far back in armhole.* **2.** *Sleeve set too far forward in armhole causing bad hang and wrinkles.* **3.** *Sleeve set correctly with a straight hang from shoulder.*

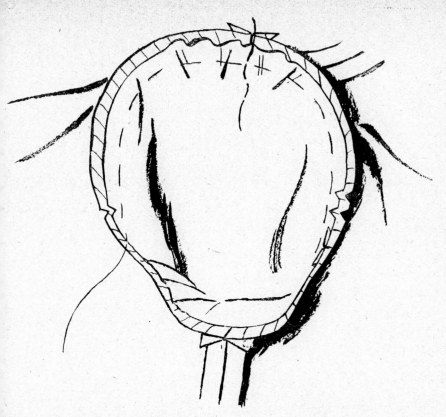

Setting sleeve into armhole matching notches and arranging fulness at the top.

armhole correctly on the right side, mark the edge of the sleeve turnings with tacking stitches or chalk, and make any fitting marks, the position where seams occur, and similar marks. Remove the sleeve from the garment, turn the armhole on to the wrong side and refit the sleeve with a normal plain seam, tack and then sew.

A seam-to-seam sleeve may be fixed into the armhole before the side seam is sewn up. It is advisable to fit it in the normal way as before. The sleeve

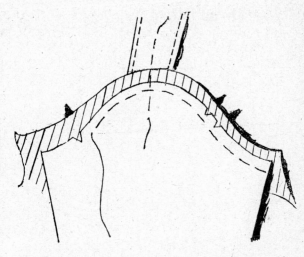

Arranging seam-to-seam sleeve in armhole before sewing the side seams. Note how the notches are matched.

seam and side seam can then be sewn.

When the sleeve is too big at the top the fulness can be shrunk away, see Diagram, if woollen material is being used. Silk and rayon fabrics will have to be darted or re-cut.

A too big elbow can be shrunk in this way as well, if the fabric is wool.

Finally fit the sleeve for length, and turn up the bottom hem.

A sleeve too full at the shoulder line.

Shrinking fulness away at head of sleeve.

Sleeve too wide and bulging at the elbow.

Bulge in the elbow being shrunk away with a wet cloth and hot iron, on sleeve board.

SKIRT

If the skirt is to be attached to a petersham waistband, make the belt first. Cut a length to fit the waist, adding turnings. Make a small hem at both ends and then sew on the hooks and eyes. Use the loop eyes which are sewn so that the bump of the loop is level with the edge of the hem, to correspond with the underlap. The bend of the loop is placed level with the edge of the overlap.

Fasten the petersham belt round the waist and then pin the skirt on to it for fitting. Match the centre front and back, and ensure that the side seams are placed correctly. A skirt always hangs from the waist and the seams must be absolutely straight.

Arrange the fulness evenly round the belt. If it is very great take it up into darts at each side of the front and in the back. When there is only a little fulness to dispose of it can be taken up in the side seams and darts, or, in woollen fabric, it can be shrunk away with a hot iron and damp cloth.

Do not have the skirt too tight over the hips or it will drag and seat badly, especially if it is a straight skirt. There must be room to allow for sitting down without stretching.

If the skirt drops at the hem, either

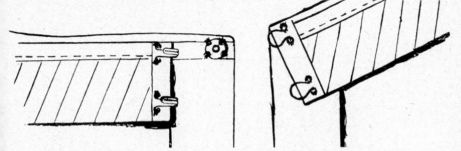

Sewing hooks and round eyes on the ends of petersham belting for skirt.

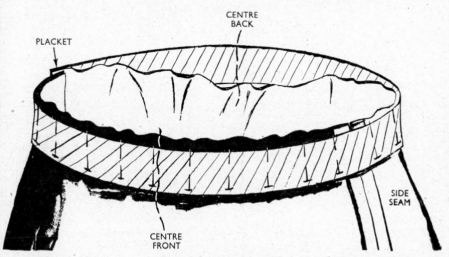

Fixing skirt on to petersham belt, arranging fulness evenly between pins.

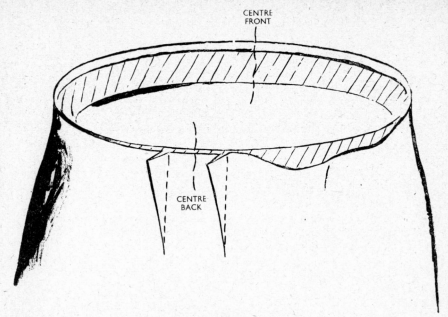

Making darts in centre back of skirt, taking up fulness to fit the petersham belt.

back or front, then lift it up at the waist and take the surplus into the side seams, but keep the seams in the correct position. If it is shorter, drop it at the waist and adjust the side seams accordingly.

Padding for hollow waist at skirt back.

The hem line of a straight cut skirt should not require much adjusting, especially if the waist and hips are fitted correctly and the straight grain of the skirt runs straight round the hips. If the hem does appear to be very uneven check over the fitting to ensure that there is no major fault causing the trouble.

Make all the adjustments necessary, sew and press seams and darts, before turning up the hem.

A waist that is very hollow is not easily fitted with a skirt. It is not usually a good thing to try and make the waist fit with too many darts. Leave it slightly loose and pad the hollow with a light padding made in the following way.

Take a small square of lining material, the right size to fit the hollow, and hem the edges. On to this sew two or three slightly gathered frills, with the edges hemmed, of the same material. Then stitch this square on to the waistband.

Turning the Hem.—This is something which needs careful attention, a badly turned hem or one that is uneven can ruin the appearance of the most beautifully cut and well-fitting garment.

If you have a tailor's dummy or someone who can fit the garment on to your own figure the whole thing is fairly simple. If, on the other hand, there are no amenities of this kind then another method will have to be devised. There are one or two ways of getting over this. One is to stand against a table and make a chalk mark round the hip, level with the table top. If there is no suitable table available then a yard stick can be used in the same way. Place one end of the stick on the floor and mark the top level with chalk. The yard stick must be kept absolutely straight all the time or the measurement will not be correct.

Then lay the skirt flat on the table. Decide the length the skirt is to be, it is a good plan to measure an old skirt to get this length, then calculate what the distance should be from the line just made at the hips, to the hem of the skirt. Using the yard stick measure from the line at the hips all the way round and make a chalk mark at the correct distance to indicate the edge of the hem.

If there is a tailor's dummy available or if the garment can be fitted on to the person for whom it is being made,

then the measuring can be done with the hem guide, page 36, or the yard stick. Decide the required distance between the floor and the skirt hem, then mark this height with chalk all the way round the hem. A tape measure

Measuring hem length with yard stick.　　*Marking hip line by the table edge.*

143

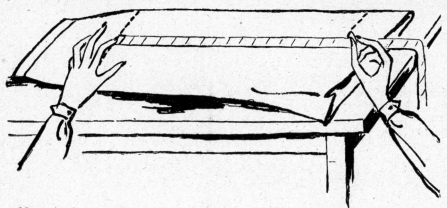

Measuring length of hem from the chalk line at hip, already indicated against table edge.

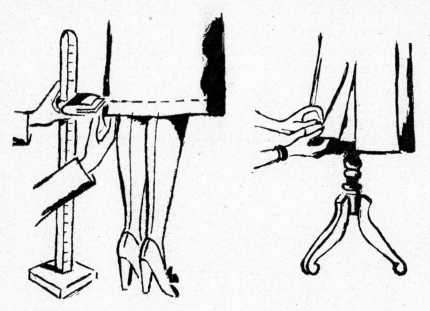

Measuring hem length using hem guide. Turning up hem with garment on dummy.

can be used for this purpose but it is not satisfactory as it is inclined to sag and the measurement will not be correct.

Turn the hem up whilst the garment is on the figure. Fold along the chalk line and pin loosely at frequent intervals. In this way it is possible to tell if the bottom edge is correct.

Then tack the hem in the normal way and try the garment on again to ensure that it is correct and straight round the bottom.

Hips.—If too tight the skirt will crease across the front and hang badly. Release the side seams, back or front or both, to rectify this fault.

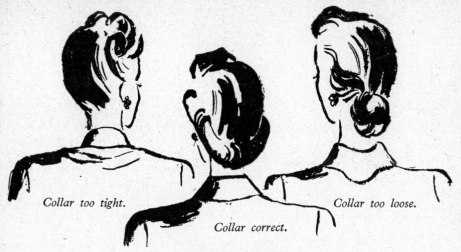

Collar too tight.

Collar correct.

Collar too loose.

COLLARS

Collars must be carefully fitted. It is a good plan to cut out a collar in a spare piece of material of the same weight and texture as the garment fabric. Fit this on the garment and cut and re-cut until it fits exactly. The collar must be set closely to the neck at the back. If it is too high the garment will wrinkle. If too low the collar will sag and stand away from the neck. Make sure that the stitching is made along the correct fitting line.

Dragging across the hips is caused by the skirt being too tight.

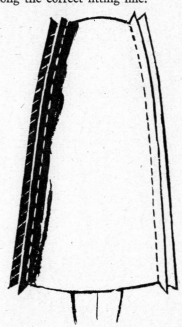

The side seams of the skirt are released to rectify dragging at hips.

JOINING SKIRT TO BODICE

A frock that is joined at the waist can be either tight or semi-fitting to suit the style being made. Fit the bodice and skirt separately as previously described, leaving the waist line of both loosely fitting, so that the dress will not pull into ugly wrinkles. The waist measurement of the skirt must be the same as that of the bodice.

Join the skirt to the bodice, matching all darts and seams together carefully. The hang of the skirt must be watched, the seams must be absolutely straight from the waist to hem. Do not turn up the hem of the skirt until it has been joined to the bodice so that there is no fear of the balance being wrong and the hem will be quite level.

When a frock is tight fitting it will be necessary to make a placket in the side seam, in order to get the garment over the shoulders. Consider this when fitting the dress and make a note of the position and the length it needs to be when finished.

Having joined the bodice and skirt together try on the garment, wrong side out, once more, and check all the fitting points. See that the shoulder seams are in the correct position, that the side seams are straight and hang correctly, that the darts taper off to nothing and do not finish in an ugly bulge. Mark the placket for the fastenings and make sure that both sides are exactly the same length.

Press the seams very carefully and then turn the garment on to the right side and try it on once more.

Then make sure that the fit is perfect in every detail, that the pockets are in the correct place, the cuffs and collar are the right shape and width and that the belt is suitable, then give a thought to other trimmings. A loose white collar perhaps, with cuffs to match. Braid is smart and gives a chic finish, buttons of the correct size and colour with belt or buckle to match. When all these points have been settled, then neaten the seams and give the garment a final pressing.

Bodice joined to skirt for simple dress.

A ONE-PIECE DRESS

A dress made in one piece does not as a rule fit closely to the figure. This fact should be remembered when the fitting is being done.

The fitting is done in the same way as for bodice and/or skirt, but in one complete operation. The garment should have a good straight hang from the shoulders. If the sleeves are magyar they will tend to wrinkle at the armholes.

With this style of garment there is sometimes a drooping of the side seams which causes the front to pook out. When this happens make a small seam at the waist line to rectify the error.

The waist line is shaped with darts, two or three at the back and two at the front, which taper off to nothing at the bust line and below the waist.

Darts in waist for one-piece dress.

Simple one-piece dress finished.

COAT

The general directions for fitting apply to a coat but it must be remembered that this garment is to be worn over other clothes and allowance must be made for this.

The Back.—If the back is too long or too short a faulty balance is indicated. In the former case there will be sagging across the shoulders and it will be necessary to lift the back and take the extra material up into the shoulder seams. A too short back causes it to pook in an ugly way, and it will be necessary to unpick the side seams and re-adjust the fit so that the balance is correct across the shoulders and the hips. This adjustment may throw the armhole out of line, in which case the shoulder seam must be adjusted and the armhole re-cut.

The bottom edge will need attention, too, as this will most likely be too short. It is always better, when making this adjustment, to lift the back rather than lower it, to avoid making the armhole too big.

When the shortness is not very great then it may be possible to make the adjustment by letting out the shoulder seams. Care must be taken, however, to avoid making the armhole too big.

Back too small, causing dragging at shoulders.

FINAL FITTING

When the lining has been inserted into the coat and is stitched in place, then make a final fitting. Slip the garment on to the figure, right side out, wrap over the front correctly and pin, then check up all the fitting points—collar, sleeves, shoulders, side seams, width and hem. Having ensured that no further alterations are necessary, mark the edge of the wrap over and the position of the buttonholes, and, if applicable, the place for the belt loops.

Fitting lining into coat on wrong side.

FITTING LINING

The lining of a coat should be made slightly larger than the coat itself. Join the seams of the lining, slip the coat on to the figure, wrong side out, and fit the lining, right side out, over it.

The lining should just cover the raw edge of the facing. The hem, when turned up, should be about half an inch shorter than the coat and the sleeve should just cover the cuff raw edge.

Make a pleat in the lining at the centre of the back neck, and ensure that lining and garment seams correspond.

Final fitting, marking the wrap-over edge.

STITCHES

CONSTRUCTIVE

Constructive stitches are those used for the sewing together and making of a garment. Small neat stitches are the keynote of good sewing and security. Commence and finish off with two or three small stitches made over each other. This method is firm and neat. When commencing a hem the end of the thread can be tucked underneath and sewn in with the stitching. On a stitched seam edge the thread end is tucked between. Never use a knot, unless stitches are of a temporary nature, as this makes an ugly bump on the sewing line and right side.

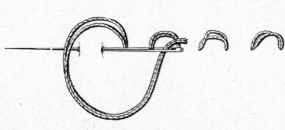

Tailor's tacks. Made into two thicknesses of material. Long loops should be left on the right sides to give play.

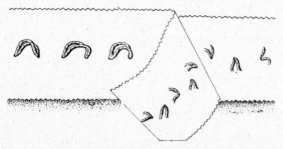

Cutting tailor's tacks. The fabric is pulled apart and the stitches between are cut, leaving short ends on both sides to indicate the position of the fitting line.

Except for tacking, which is removed when the garment has been completed, use a good quality matching thread.

Tailor's Tacks.—This stitch is used for making fitting marks through two thicknesses of material, so that the marks are identical on both sides. Use double cotton in a contrasting shade.

Work from right to left starting with a knot, take the needle in and out of the two layers of fabric making fairly large stitches, and leaving loops of double cotton on the working side. Fasten off loosely. When all the tacks have been made pull the two thicknesses apart carefully, snick the stitches between the two layers which can then be parted, leaving threads in both sides.

When making the fitting marks of a paper pattern, the tailor's tacks are made through the paper and two layers of material as well. Snick through each loop on the right side and remove the pattern. When pulling the material apart take care not to pull out the stitches.

To make single marks, such as fitting Vs on side seams, make one single back stitch leaving the ends of cotton and a loop on the right side, snick the loop as before, then pull the layers apart and snick the stitches in between.

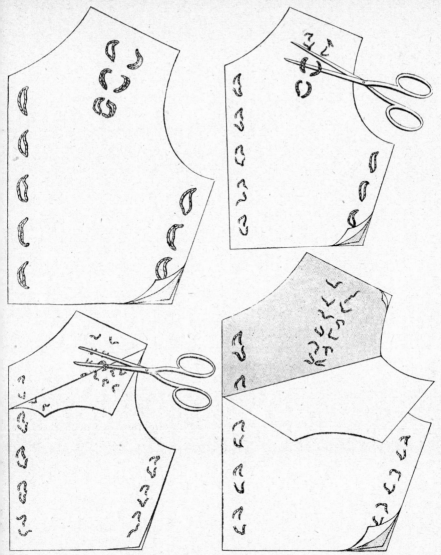

Pull the two thicknesses of fabric apart and cut the threads between, as on the left. When all the loops have been cut the pattern can then be removed as bottom right.

If the garment is to be handled a great deal in the making, and there is fear of the tacks being pulled out, then it is a good plan to mark the tacking line with tailor's chalk after the stitches have been snicked.

For more permanent markings make a line of simple tacking stitches.

Thread Marking.—Fitting marks made with thread. Tailor's tacks are used on two or more thicknesses and simple tacking on single material.

It is a good plan to make brightly coloured balance marks when cutting out, and white fitting marks in the making so they can be distinguished.

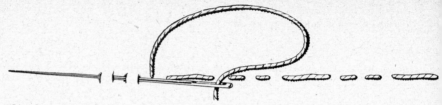

Simple tacking. Is more secure if one or two short stitches are made in between the long ones. This method should be used on the seams of a garment before the fitting.

Simple Tacking.—This is worked with single thread. The stitches can be made all one length or one long and two short for extra security. Use for holding the seams or hem during making. Tacking stitches are more easily made and the correct fit is retained if the garment is allowed to lie flat on the table.

Chevron Tacking.—The needle is inserted horizontally, as in ordinary tacking, first in one line, then in the other. Snick the stitches before removing. **Diagonal Tacking.**—A form of tacking used when large surfaces have to be held firmly. The stitches are made between two parallel lines—the needle is inserted vertically from the top.

Chevron tacking. Covering a wide area it is worked between two imaginary parallel lines. Do not pull the stitches too tightly or the material will pucker in between the lines.

Diagonal tacking. Is worked between two imaginary parallel lines. The long stitch between the two lines on the wrong side makes it very firm, so it will stand a lot of handling.

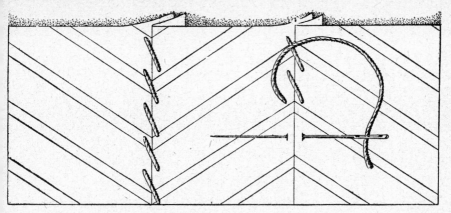

Slip basting. Useful for tacking a lapped seam, especially when there is a pattern or stripes to be matched. The stitches are made across the seam, diagonally, on the right side.

Slip Basting.—A method of tacking used when joining seams in material with a pattern that must be accurately matched. Work on the right side of the garment. One edge of the seam is turned under and lapped over the other. The needle is inserted from right to left at right angles to the seams and at equal distances. The thread between these stitches passes over the seam diagonally. A line of simple tacking is made along the seam on the wrong side after slip basting.

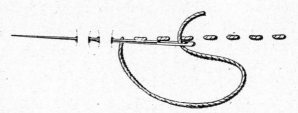

Running stitch. A simple joining stitch where the needle is taken in and out of the fabric in small even stitches.

Running.—A simple stitch similar to tacking but with smaller stitches. The needle passes over the same number of threads of the material as are picked up.

Use this stitch for lingerie seams, tucks, darts and bindings in light-weight materials, where there is not much wear and tear.

An occasional back stitch will strengthen the line of stitching.

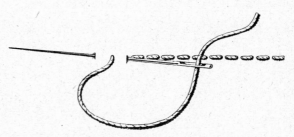

Back stitch. The needle is inserted into the ends of the previous stitch making one continuous line, like machining.

Back Stitch.—A stronger stitch used for sewing seams in heavier material. Start as for running but make the subsequent stitches by passing the needle back into the end of the previous stitch and bring it out beyond the stitch just made. The finished effect is the same as a line of machine stitching.

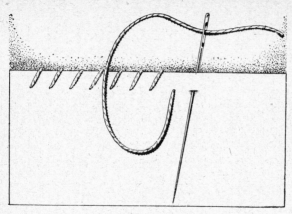

Overcasting. Worked from left to right, it is generally used for neatening raw edges.

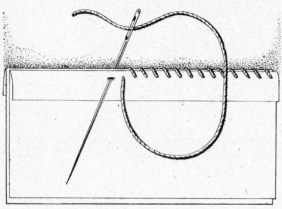

Oversewing. Similar to overcasting but worked the reverse way, it is used for joining edges.

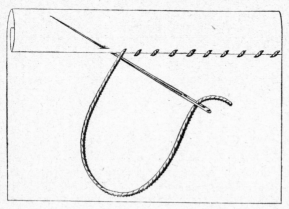

Hemming. The stitches are made very tiny on the hem edge so as to be almost invisible.

Overcasting.—This is a stitch used for neatening seam edges, especially on firm materials, to prevent fraying. Trim the edge evenly and then, working from left to right, pass the needle through the material from the back. Repeat this at equal distances making even slanting stitches over the edge. Do not pull the stitches tightly.

If the fabric frays easily the stitches can be made closer together, but they must be kept quite flat.

Oversewing.—A stitch used for joining two edges together. It is strong and hard wearing. The movement of the stitch is similar to overcasting, but it is worked from right to left. Pass the needle behind both edges and bring it through at the front, a little below the edge. Repeat this at equal distances making small neat stitches fairly close together. Press the seam flat, after sewing, between the thumb and finger.

Hemming.—This is the strongest stitch used for sewing hems. Start at the right hand side and pick up a fraction of the garment material, then take the edge of the hem on the needle which should slant diagonally.

The stitches should be made small and even on the very edge of the hem fold and into the garment fabric just under the hem.

Uneven Hemming.— This is used for sewing down bindings where light stitching is needed. Leave a long thread between the stitches, which is tucked along the fold. A small hemming stitch is made into the garment material or the first line of sewing in a binding.

Herringbone.—Used to fasten down hems with raw edges. Work from left to right. Insert the needle into the hem from right to left, taking up a few threads of the material, pass over the edge of the hem and insert the needle into the garment, from right to left, taking the same number of threads. Repeat this procedure all the way along. The finished stitch consists of a double line of crosses.

Catch stitch. — This is used to fasten down a hem on a garment which is to be lined and where only light stitching is needed. The stitches should not be visible on the right side. Working from right to left take up a few threads of the hem on the needle, pull the thread through and pass it diagonally over the hem, take up a few threads, or the top surface, of the garment material and repeat this all the way along.

The threads between the stitches should not be pulled tightly but allowed to lie easily across the hem.

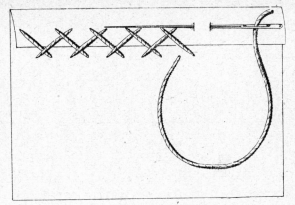

Herringbone stitch. Worked from left to right over the raw edge of a single thickness hem.

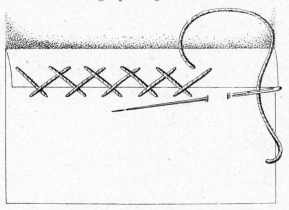

Make each alternate stitch into the hem and the in-between stitches into the garment.

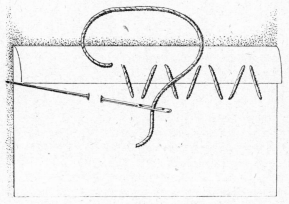

Catch stitch. A stitch worked lightly over the hem edge when strong sewing is not needed.

155

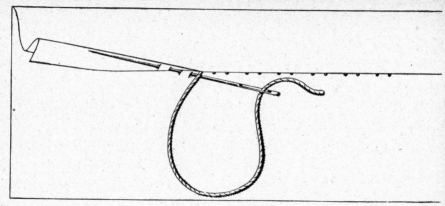

Slip stitch. This stitch is worked just under the fold of the hem with one stitch into the second turning and one into the garment material. It should be quite invisible.

Fishbone stitch. Used to draw two edges together, work into each side alternately.

Fishbone stitch.—A stitch used to join two edges together without overlapping, such as a tear before darning.

Attach the thread to one end of the join and pass the needle point between the two edges, bringing it out just inside one edge. Repeat this on the other side and alternately all the way along.

Slip stitch.—This stitch is used for fastening down hem edges invisibly, and also for sewing folds and facings. It will not stand up to hard wear and pulling.

Work from right to left, making a tiny stitch in the garment at the edge of the hem or fold. Take as little of the material as possible so the stitches will be invisible on the right side. Before pulling the thread through fold the hem back a little with the left thumb and take up a few threads underneath the hem. Pull the thread through and repeat this all the way along.

Slip stitch can also be used to join two folded edges together. Fold the two edges under towards each other and tack them. Join the thread to one edge at the right hand side, take up a few threads of the opposite fold on to the needle and then make a stitch in the fold nearest to you. Repeat this from side to side all the way along.

Do not pull the thread too tightly or it will pucker.

Blind Hemming.—This is used on thick materials. It is worked in the same way as ordinary hemming. The top surface only of the garment is picked up, so there are no stitches visible on the right side.

Blanket stitch.—Is used for neatening the raw edges of material which does not fray easily, or fastening down a hem with a raw edge.

Join the thread to the material edge at the left-hand side, insert the needle into the material vertically, bringing the point out just below the edge. Pass the single thread under the point of the needle and pull the thread through. Repeat this at equal distances all the way along. The distance between the stitches should be equal to the depth of the stitch.

To make a decorative edge with this stitch work several rows as a border. The first row is worked about one inch from the edge and parallel with it. The second row is arranged so the tips of the stitches hook into the loops of the previous row. The third row hooks into the second and covers the edge of the material.

Other variations of this stitch are worked by making the stitches different lengths—each alternate stitch short; two short ones and two long and so on.

The length of the stitches can be varied but the pattern must be kept uniform.

Fly Running.—This stitch is used for gathering threads in soft material.

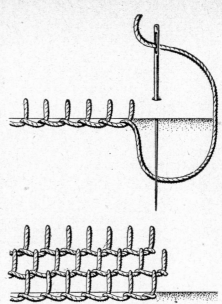

Blanket stitch. A stitch which can be worked over a raw edge to prevent fraying.

It is a quick method of working running. Several stitches are made on the needle at a time. Starting at the right insert the point of the needle into the fabric, with the left hand move the material up and down on to the point, at the same time pushing the needle with the right hand. Pull the thread through and draw up the fabric.

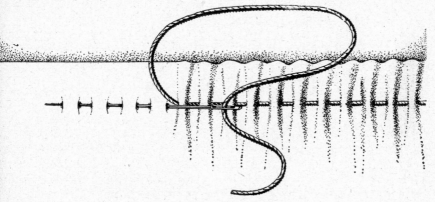

Fly running. A form of running stitch used when a gathering thread is to be inserted. The needle is held in the right hand and the material worked with the left on to the needle.

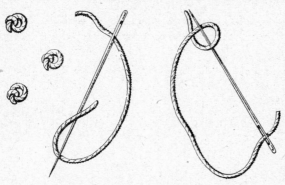

French knots. The thread is twisted round the needle point which is then inserted into the material.

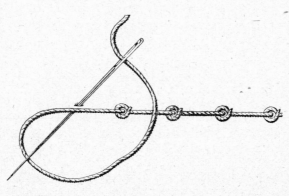

Snail's trail. The knots are made equal distances apart. The thread is held taut with the left hand.

Run and darn. Two parallel lines of running stitch are made first, the darning is worked into them.

French Knots.—A stitch used for the centres of flowers, borders and, in fine embroidery, the filling of petals.

Bring the thread through to the right side, make one twist of the thread on the needle and insert it back almost into the same hole. Before pulling the thread through push the loop down the needle close to the material. When the thread is pulled through there is a small stitch tying the loop down.

Snail's Trail.—Work from right to left. Lay the thread along the line of stitching flat on the material, and hold the thread with the thumb of the left hand. Pick up a few threads of the material with the needle slanting diagonally from right to left under the straight thread. Pull the thread through and continue making knots in this way at equal distances.

Run and Darn.—A composite stitch simple to do. First make two lines of running stitches, making the stitches of one line opposite the spaces of the other. With a contrasting shade, darn up and down through these stitches.

The darning stitches must not be pulled or the running stitches and material will pucker.

Feather Stitch.—There are several variations of this stitch which is used mainly for trimming lingerie and children's clothes.

The most simple form is single feather stitch which is worked as follows:—join the thread to the centre of the line of stitching and work towards yourself. A line can be made on the material as a guide to straight stitching, but this should not be of a permanent nature. A line of coloured tacking thread is a good method, as this can be removed later.

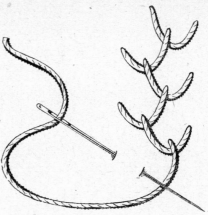

Insert the needle a little to the right of this line; the point should be pointing downwards and slanting slightly towards the centre line; let the single cotton pass under the needle and pull the thread through. Work a similar stitch on the left of the centre line and repeat this procedure to the end. Try to avoid pulling the cotton too tightly when working this stitch and do not take too much of the material on to the needle at a time, or the finished result will be clumsy. Likewise, if there is too great a space between the stitches the final appearance will be untidy.

Feather stitch—single. Work first to the right and then to the left alternately.

Double Feather Stitch.—This is more decorative than single feather stitch, and gives a wider band when finished. Commence on the centre line, work one stitch to the right as previously described, then two stitches to the left, then two to the right. Continue in this way making two stitches each side of the centre line.

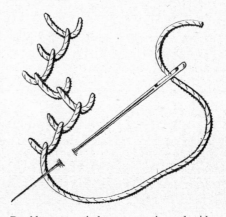

Double—two stitches are made each side.

One stitch of each movement will be made on the centre line and the outer stitches will be made to left and right of this.

Triple Feather Stitch.—A stitch similar in movement to double feather stitch. Make three stitches to the right and then three to the left. Still keep one stitch of each movement on the centre line with two loops each side.

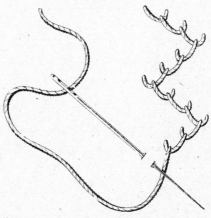

Triple—make three stitches each side.

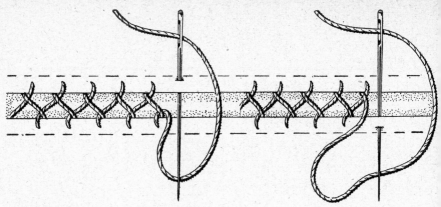

Faggot stitch—twisted. Tack the two edges parallel on paper and work into each alternately.

Faggot Stitch. — A joining stitch which can be used in a decorative way for seams, false hems and rouleaux.

First turn under and press the edges to be joined making double hems, after sewing the first turnings. Tack them on to stiff brown paper, making sure they are the correct distance apart and parallel. Working from left to right, join the thread to the bottom edge. Insert the needle vertically into the top edge with the point towards the join. Pass the thread under the point of the needle and pull through. Now make a stitch into the bottom edge, inserting the needle point under the hem, pass the thread under the point and pull the needle through, pulling the thread towards the space. Repeat this movement all the way along, keeping the stitches evenly spaced.

Bar Faggotting. — Tack the edges on to the paper as previously described. Join the thread to the bottom edge on the left side of the work. Insert the needle vertically, towards the join, into the top edge. Pull the thread through, making a straight stitch across the join, and twist this bar three times round the needle. Draw the needle through and pass it along inside the hem to the position of the next stitch.

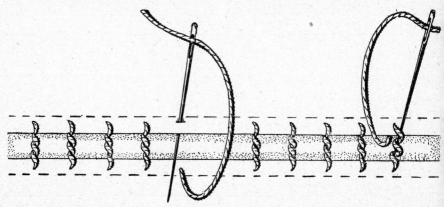

Bar faggot. The bar across the gap is twisted round the needle to give a cord effect. Slip the needle along the hem between the stitches which are equidistant and straight.

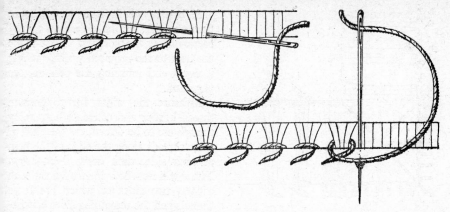

Hemstitch. When the cross threads have been drawn tie the remainder into neat bundles.

Hemstitching.—A stitch which can be used to fasten down a hem, or for the working of decorative borders. In order to work this stitch it is necessary to draw out the threads of the fabric first.

To draw the threads of the fabric— first decide the position of the border and the length it is to be. Mark this and the width with tacking stitches. Cut both ends of the threads to be drawn, pick up each one with a pin and draw it out. Buttonhole stitch along the raw edges at each end.

If a hem is being fastened down, first make the hem and tack it down and then draw away threads, to the width desired, level with the edge of the inside fold. Work with the outer fold of the hem towards you. Join the cotton to the left-hand end of the hem. Pass the needle from right to left under about four of the undrawn threads, then make a vertical stitch into the hem, to the right of this group. Repeat this procedure, tying the loose threads into groups of four, for the full length of the hem.

If hemstitching is being worked on the opposite side of the drawn thread border then the stitches must be made

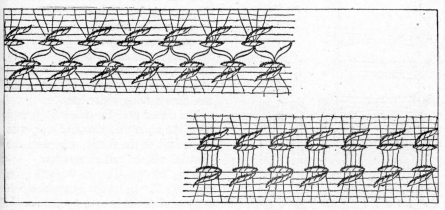

Twisted hemstitch. The groups of threads are divided when working the second line.
Double hemstitch. Work the same way as single hemstitch sewing both sides of the gap.

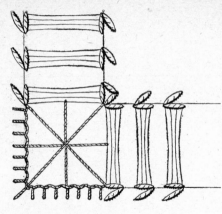

The basic threads for a hemstitch corner.

through all thicknesses of the hem. If, however, it is preferred that the stitches should not show on the reverse side, then the folded edge only is taken in the needle for each stitch.

Double Hemstitch.—This is worked both sides of the drawn threads. The working of the hemstitch on the opposite side of the border is exactly the same as for the hem. The same four threads may be tied into groups making a series of straight bars, or each group may be split into two to give a chevron effect.

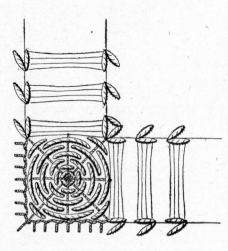

Hemstitch corner finished with weaving.

A border which runs round more than one side will have to have special treatment at the corners. First make the hem to the required width, tacking it down and mitreing the corners, see page 208.

Measure the width for the drawn thread border and calculate how many threads are to be drawn, cut the ends of these threads along the edge of the hem at each side, then draw them away. There will now be a square hole at each corner, two sides of which are loose threads and the remaining sides consisting of a raw edge and a hem fold. Make small buttonhole stitches over these sides to prevent the raw edge from fraying. Work the hemstitching normally.

Corner Motifs.—Work as follows:—join the thread to one corner of the square and pass a strand over to the opposite corner. Slip the needle along the threads on the wrong side to the centre of one side, pass a strand to the opposite side, then repeat this at the remaining corners and sides.

Now take the thread back to the centre of the square, where these threads join, and weave under and over them in a spiral direction, rather like a spider's web. The simplest way to finish the corner is to fill the whole space with the weaving, but with experience other designs may be devised. For instance—the centre may be woven and the threads into the corners and sides oversewn into bars, or, with a small circle in the centre weave under and over two of the threads at a time making wider bars.

The thread used for this work should be of the same thickness and weight as the thread of the fabric, otherwise the material will be pulled and tear.

Chain Stitch.—This is worked from right to left. Bring the cotton through at the end of the line, insert the needle again into the same spot and take up a small stitch along the outline, pass the

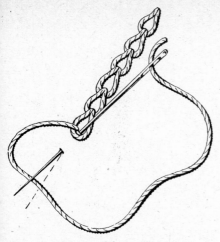

Chain stitch. Work vertically from the top.　　*Lazy daisy stitch. Single loop petals.*

thread under the point and pull the needle through. Repeat this movement into each stitch.

Stem Stitch.—Commence by joining the thread to the left-hand end of the line. Make a small stitch by inserting the needle, from right to left, along the outline. Continue in this way.

Lazy Daisy Stitch.—This is a single chain stitch. Bring the thread through at the centre of the flower, insert the needle in the same spot and bring the

point out at the other end of the petal. Pass the thread under the point of the needle and pull it through. Make a tying stitch over the loop.

Satin Stitch.—This is worked from left to right. Insert the needle into the top edge of the shape and bring it out at the bottom. The stitches are made so that they lie flat side by side. Lines of running or stem stitch may be worked inside the outline first, to give a raised effect.

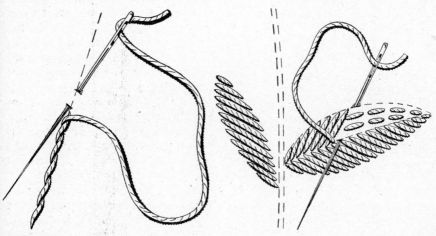

Stem stitch. Work from left to right.　　*Satin stitch. Make the stitches so that*
Insert the needle at an angle across the line.　　*they lie flat on the fabric side by side.*

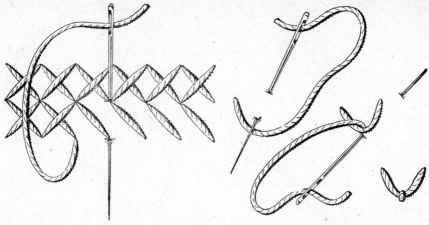

Cross stitch. Is worked singly or in rows. All the stitches must cross in same way.

Fly stitch. Is similar to an open lazy daisy. The tying down stitch can vary in length.

Cross Stitch.—This can be used as a decorative outline stitch, in the same way as feather stitch, or it can be worked solidly to completely fill flower shapes, or in geometric designs. The finished result of cross stitch is more satisfactory if worked on coarse thread material which can be counted, working over an even number of threads for each stitch.

When making borders or solid masses of cross stitch work the first slanting stitch for the full length, then work back completing the crosses. Single stitches are completed in one operation. The stitches on the wrong side of the work should be vertical or horizontal, never diagonal.

Fly Stitch.—In movement this stitch is similar to lazy daisy stitch, but there is a space left at the top, forming the threads into a V or Y shape.

Bring the thread through at the top left of the stitch and insert the needle level with this spot and to the right, bring the needle out again in between these two points leaving the loop of thread under the point. Pull the thread through and make a tying down stitch over the loop.

Arrowheads.—Used for reinforcing and strengthening as well as being decorative. They are worked at the tops of pleats, the corners of pockets and places where there is strain.

First mark the position and size of the arrowhead with a triangle of cotton. Small tacking stitches can be used, or one long stitch, at each side of the triangle, the base across the pleat.

Join the thread securely to the bottom left-hand corner. Insert the needle from right to left into the topmost corner leaving a long stitch between the two corners. Now insert the needle into the right-hand bottom corner and bring it out at the left, immediately to the right of the previous stitch.

Repeat this procedure making the stitches close together until the shape is completely filled. The stitches at the top point become larger working towards the base, while the stitches at the base meet in the centre.

Bar Tack.—Another method of strengthening the ends of pockets and plackets. Make three or four stitches over the end of the opening, right through all thickness of material. Work solid satin stitch over these bars.

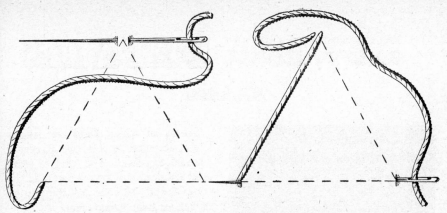

Arrowhead. Mark the triangle with a line of tacking stitches. Pick up a small stitch at the apex of the triangle and make a large stitch across the base of the triangle.

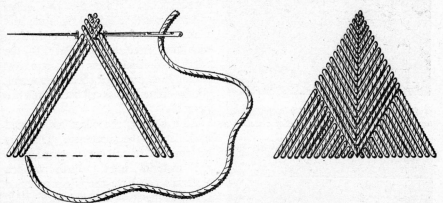

The finished arrowhead. This is filled solidly with threads. Continue to work the stitches under each other at the top and inside each other at the base until the triangle is filled.

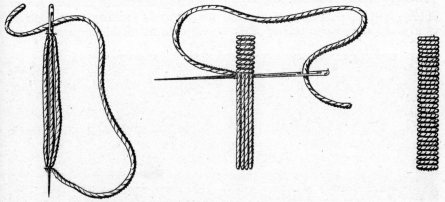

Bar tacks. Make three or four long back stitches where the bar is to be made. Then work satin stitch over these stitches and through a few threads of the garment material.

SEWING DETAILS

SEAMS

A plain seam is simply two edges joined together with one central line of stitching.

A line of machine stitching along the fold of a plain seam gives a tailored finish.

Seams, of which there are various kinds, are used to join two pieces of material together. The kind of seam used is determined by the nature of the material and the style and the portion of the garment being sewn.

Plain Seam.—This is a straight seam used for the sides of garments and other simple joins. Place the two edges together, with the right sides inside, and make a line of stitching about half an inch away from, and parallel with, the edge. Machining is the strongest sewing line, but back stitch or running stitch with an occasional back stitch can be used.

After sewing, the edges are pressed open flat and then neatened. This may be done in several ways according to the material used. Firm woollen materials can have the edges trimmed with pinking scissors to prevent fraying. Thinner fabrics can have the edges turned under and sewn, either with machining or running stitches. A very usual way of finishing seam edges is with overcast stitch, see page 154.

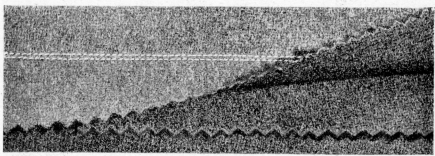

When the seam is flat sewn on the right side the turnings are pressed together on one side of the sewing line. The second machine stitching will hold them in this position.

166

Binding is used for neatening the edges of seams on loosely fitting coats that are not being lined, or on loosely woven fabrics that will have hard wear and fray easily.

Fold the binding into two lengthwise and press it. If bias binding with a raw edge is used turn under the edges as well. Place one edge of the braid on the underside of the seam turning so that the raw edge is along the centre crease. Stitch this edge with machining, backstitch or hemming. Fold the binding over the raw edge and sew the second edge.

A line of machine stitching each side of the join in a plain seam keeps the turnings flat and gives a neat tailored finish.

Additional interest may be given to plain seams by the addition of machine stitching. After pressing the seam open and neatening the edges press both to one side again and tack them down. Now on the right side, make a line of machine stitching close to the seam line. Or, the seam can be left open flat and neatened, then on the right side two lines of machine stitching are made one each side of the seam line.

A plain seam that is stitched flat must first have the turnings pressed open. Neaten the edges with pinking or oversewing.

The secret of success in both these methods of finishing is to keep the machine stitch absolutely straight with the seam join.

The seam edges of fine materials can be neatened by turning under the edges.

Seam edges are finished with binding on fabrics that fray, and on unlined garments.

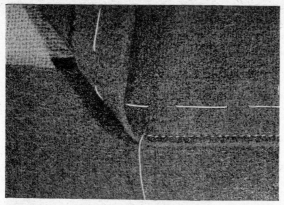

The turnings of the top portion of a lapped seam are folded under, pressed and the edge machine stitched.

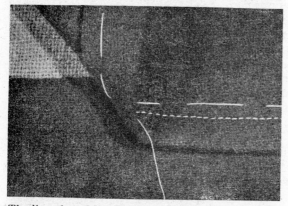

The line of machine stitching on a tucked seam is made down the centre of the turnings parallel with the edge.

A welt seam is flat and neat and has the same appearance on both sides. Make a line of machine stitching along the seam line on the right side for a tailored finish.

Lapped Seam.—Is similar in appearance to a plain seam stitched to one side. The method of use is different as it is found round the edges of yokes and as a trimming.

First decide which part of the garment is to be lapped over. Turn under the edge of this for the amount of turnings allowed, on to the wrong side. Leave the underside flat and place the top fold over it so that the raw edges meet. Sew with a line of machine stitching on the right side close to the folded edge. Neaten the raw edges with overcasting or binding.

Tucked Seam.—Is made in exactly the same way as a lapped seam except that the line of machine stitching is made halfway between the fold and edges.

Welt Seam.—Is used on tailored garments made in heavy materials and without lining. Make a plain seam on the wrong side. Press this quite flat to one side. Trim away the underneath turning close to the seam, leaving enough for the stitches to hold. Turn under the other raw edge and press the fold. Tack this part of the seam flat to the garment, taking care to avoid twisting. Machine stitch along the tacking on the right side. A second line of stitching may be made close to the welt. Give a final press.

Run and Fell Seam.—A strong seam especially suitable for shirts and underwear, tub frocks and children's clothes, where there is hard wear and washing.

Make a simple plain seam on the wrong side, press the turnings to one side and cut away the surplus from the underneath layer. Turn under the edge of the wider turning and tack it down flat. Sew this close to the edge with machining or hem by hand, if preferred.

This seam may be made on the right side, it is a matter of personal choice.

Mantua Maker's Seam.—Should only be used on very light-weight materials as it is a double seam and tends to be clumsy. Use it for lingerie, chiffon blouses and similar garments.

First tack the seam line on the wrong side, but do not stitch permanently. Trim away one edge of the turnings. Turn under the raw edge of the second side and fold it over until the hem fold is level with the tacking. Stitch firmly through all thicknesses of the seam. Press the turnings to one side.

To make a run and fell seam really flat cut the under section away as close to the seam line as possible, after the turnings have been pressed to one side. This seam may be made on the wrong side or the right. The double stitching gives a tailored finish.

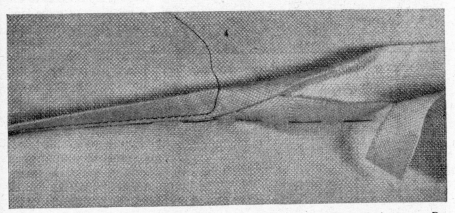

A seam that is made and neatened in one operation is the mantua maker's seam. Do not use this method on thick materials or the result will be bulky. This seam lends itself to garments made in transparent material as it can be made narrow and strong.

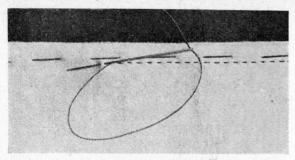

The first step of a french seam is made on the right side.

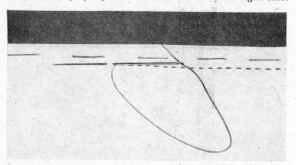

Complete the seam on the wrong side encasing the raw edges.

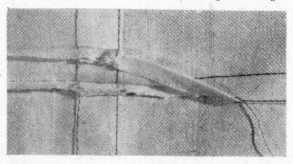

The crossing seam must make one continuous line.

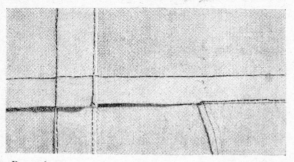

Press the seams to be joined very carefully and well first.

French Seam.—Is a seam used mainly for lingerie, blouses and other washable garments. It is not recommended for use with intricate fitting.

First make a plain seam on the right side, allowing very small turnings, about one-eighth of an inch. Trim off the raw edges and press the seam with the two edges together. Turn the garment on to the wrong side, folding the seam so that the raw edges are encased. Press the sewing line on both sides and tack along the inside of the raw edges. Sew the seam firmly on the wrong side and press again. When making this final line of stitching feel for the raw edges and make sure that they are within the seam.

Crossed Seams.—It is often necessary to join two seams in the centre of a third. When this is to be done it is advisable to use a flat seam of some kind rather than box type, such as a french seam. If, however, this type must be joined fold one seam one way and the second the other. First press the two seams to be joined very well to avoid any bulkiness. The lines of stitching must be matched perfectly when making the third seam. Having made the line of stitching for the third seam trim away surplus turnings of the joined seams to prevent thickness.

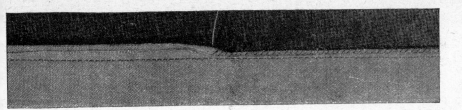

A rolled seam is used on transparent fabrics as it can be made almost invisible. Trim one turning close to the first sewing line and roll the other side over it. Stitch with oversewing.

Rolled Seam.—This seam is used for garments made in fine transparent materials where an ordinary seam would be clumsy and unsightly as it would show through to the right side.

Start by making a plain seam, sewing with running stitch and an occasional back stitch. Trim the front edge of the seam to about one-eighth of an inch in width leaving the other side a quarter of an inch in width. Join the thread to the right-hand side of the seam and, with the thumb and first finger of the left hand, roll the wider turning over the narrow one almost to the sewing line. Make neat even oversewing stitches over this roll to hold it in place. It is sometimes easier to work this oversewing if the right-hand end of the seam is pinned to a board, or the knee. It can then be pulled taut, helping the roll to turn over more easily and simplifying the sewing.

Press the seam well, making a neat flat roll which will be almost invisible on the right side.

Herringbone Seam. — Sometimes known as flannel seam. This is used on flannel and similar materials which do not fray easily. It is most frequently found on children's underclothes and babies' garments.

First make a plain seam in the usual way. Press both the edges on one side and trim the under one to half the width of the other. Tack both thicknesses flat to the garment and then work herringbone stitch along the cut edge, fastening this to the main material.

If a flatter seam is needed press the edges open flat and sew each one to the garment with herringbone stitch.

Strap Seam.—Is a decorative method of finishing a seam. It is particularly useful for unlined garments.

Make a simple plain seam on the right side of the garment, open out the turnings and press them flat. Cut the strip, used for the applied piece, the width required plus half an inch for turnings on both sides. This strap can be made in self colour to match the gar-

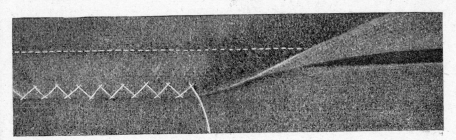

The herringbone seam, or flannel seam, is used on materials that do not fray easily. Sew the turnings to one side with neat herringbone stitches, as for a run and fell seam.

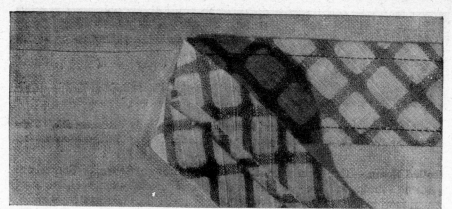

A strap seam is a plain seam with a decorative finish. Make the join so that the turnings are on the right side of the garment, trim away surplus edges and press open quite flat.

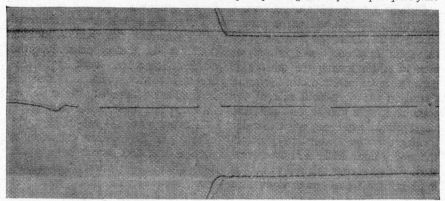

The strap, which can be of a contrasting fabric or a matching piece, is laid over the seam turnings and stitched each side neatly with machine stitching close to the edges.

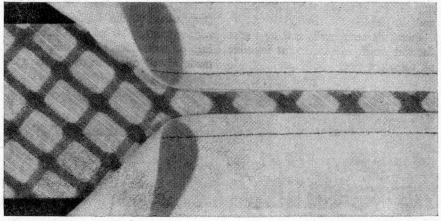

The slot seam is the reverse to the strap seam. The contrasting strip is laid underneath the two edges, which are turned under and sewn. The stitching should be straight.

ment or a contrast either in material or colour. Further decoration may be added by cutting the strap on the bias. Fold the strap into two, make a crease down the centre, and press under the turnings at each side. Place this crease on the seam line and tack the strap in place. Machine stitch down each side keeping level with the folded edge.

It is permissible to apply the strap to the inside of the garment as a means of neatening, but remember that lines of stitching will show on the right side, and must be very straight.

Slot Seam.—Is another decorative seam, made the reverse way to the strap seam. This is also a means of adding extra width to a garment. The turning allowance can be omitted from the seams.

Turn under the edges of both sides to be joined and press them and tack them down. Cut the strip for the slot allowing enough width to take the opening plus the width of the turnings on both sides. Place the folded edges of the garment one each side of the strip, placing the raw edge of the fold with those of the strap. Tack both sides in place and then make a line of machining parallel with the folded edge both sides. Neaten the raw edges by working overcasting over them together or binding with bias cut strips.

Curved Seam.—Is made in the same way as a plain seam but the edges are notched so the seam will press flat.

Bias Seam.—Must be sewn with a loose tension to prevent puckering. Never pull edges that are cut on the bias when sewing them together or they will stretch permanently. If the material is at all flimsy make the stitching over thin paper when machining. If a straight edge is being sewn to a bias edge have the bias on the underside.

Special Notes.—The width of turning allowed for each seam is governed by the material being used. Leave sufficient to prevent fraying but not so much that the hang of the garment is spoilt or the finish bulky. Keep the width uniform throughout.

All seams must be pressed at each stage in the making. Remove all pins and tacking threads first.

Trim the turnings straight before neatening the edges. Cut away odd corners. Where turnings appear under folds or double thicknesses, such as hems, trim them down to the minimum.

All seams should be neatened to prolong the life of the garment, as well as improve the appearance.

Do not make the stitching too tight or the seam will pucker. If too loosely sewn it will pull apart and look ugly. Use matching thread for the sewing.

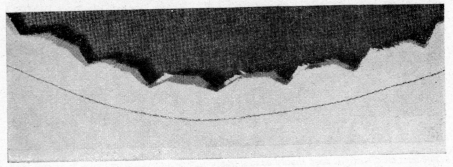

As a general rule the seam used on a curved edge is a plain seam. In order that the turnings can be pressed quite flat the edges should be snicked at regular intervals.

HEMS

Hems are used to neaten the edges of single thicknesses of material such as the bottom edges of skirts, sleeves and the edges of frills. The secret of a good-looking hem is to have the width uniform for the full length. Measure very carefully with the transparent ruler, or with a cardboard guide made to the correct width.

To make this guide cut a strip of firm cardboard one and a half inches by six inches. Measuring from one end draw a line to indicate the width the hem is to be. Cut along this line for one inch, and then make a second cut at an angle to form the slot. The distance between the end of the card and the straight side of the slot is the width of the hem.

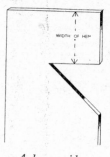
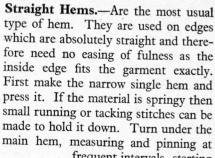

A hem guide.

All hems must be very carefully measured and the width indicated either with tacking threads or pins, all the way along. Measure again after the hem has been turned up, and before pressing. Check the width occasionally.

Straight Hems.—Are the most usual type of hem. They are used on edges which are absolutely straight and therefore need no easing of fulness as the inside edge fits the garment exactly. First make the narrow single hem and press it. If the material is springy then small running or tacking stitches can be made to hold it down. Turn under the main hem, measuring and pinning at frequent intervals, starting with the two ends to keep them level. The pins are inserted at right angles to the edge of the hem. Tack the hem in place and then press. The method of stitching varies according to the purpose. The hem of a garment should be slip stitched with invisible stitches on the right side. Machine stitching can be used for cotton garments.

Skirt Hems.—The edge of a skirt is seldom straight and even a slight curve will affect the making of a hem. Make a narrow hem, tack and press it. Have the skirt flat on table, match the seams,

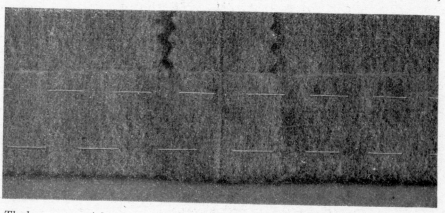

The hem on a straight edge should be absolutely flat without gathers or tucks of any kind. Match the seam line of the hem to that of the garment and tack carefully close to the fold of the hem as well as at the edge. Press well before making the final stitching.

174

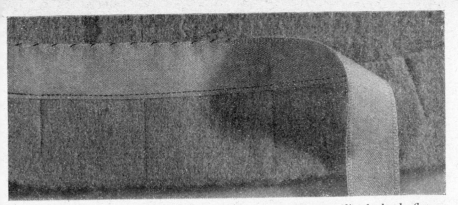

The hem of a circular edge needs careful handling. The hem must lie absolutely flat on the garment with the fulness arranged evenly all the way round the hem. Stitch the darts to keep them quite flat and finish the edge with tape or braid, which is lightly sewn.

then divide hem into six-inch sections with pins and have the fulness evenly distributed between. Pin and tack the hem, pressing before sewing.

Braided Hems.—Are used on thick materials or where the edge is very curved. First make and pin the hem in the way described for a skirt hem, and tack close to the folded edge. Run a gathering thread along the raw edge and pull it up until the hem lies flat on the garment, or arrange this fulness into tiny darts, hemming down the folds. Arrange the braid over the inner edge of the hem for about quarter of an inch. Tack the braid and then sew the edge firmly. Slip stitch the braid to the garment.

This method of disposing of fulness may be employed on a plain skirt hem if necessary. In this case the hem must be made first and the running thread inserted, or the darts made before making the single hem. If wool material is being used shrink the gathers and flatten them as much as possible to avoid bulk. Thin materials need only be dry pressed.

Gathers can be used, instead of darts, to dispose of the fulness in the edge of a circular hem. In woollen fabrics these gathers can be shrunk away so that the hem lies quite flat on the garment. The braid is sewn to the hem after shrinking, and neatens the raw edges.

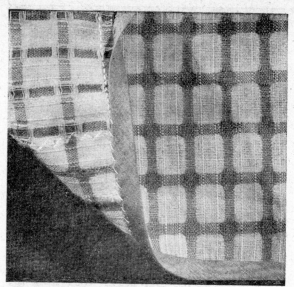

A bound hem is a useful way of finishing an edge that has no spare material for turnings. The binding is bias cut.

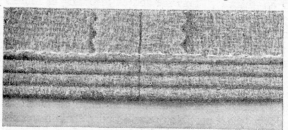

Several lines of machine stitching made on a single hem.

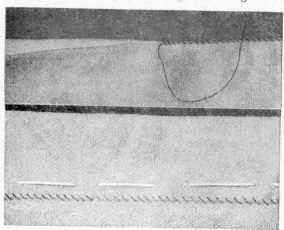

An oversewn hem should have a similar appearance on both the right and wrong sides. Press the hem flat.

Bound Hem.—Useful for finishing the edge of a circular or gored skirt in light-weight material. Cut and join strips of bias-cut material for the full width of the skirt, see page 207. Place one edge of this to the hem edge, right sides together, and stitch loosely. Press the edge and then turn the binding over the stitching and raw edge, and press again. Turn under the edge of the binding and hem the fold to the first line of stitching.

The edge of a plain hem in very thick material can be bound in this way, before it is sewn down. In this case it will not be necessary to turn under the binding the second time.

Single Hem.—Used on firm materials when neatening is not necessary or on lined garments. In the former case make parallel rows of machine stitching for the full width, and trim the edge close to the last line. In the latter case sew with catch stitch, page 155.

Oversewn Hem.—A strong hem which can be used on straight edges which need laundering.

Make a simple plain hem, tack it and press. Fold the garment back level with the fold and oversew through the two, taking the stitches right through to the other side and keeping them very even. Flatten and press.

Faced Hems.—Are used for lengthening or decorative purposes. This is also a neat way of finishing a flared skirt hem.

To obtain the shape for the facing piece of a circular skirt, lay the edge of the skirt flat on a sheet of paper and draw round the curve. Draw a second line inside this curve half an inch wider than the finished hem is to be and parallel with the first. Cut a strip of material to the shape. Place the larger curve to the edge of the skirt, right sides together, and stitch a quarter of an inch from the edge, fairly loosely. Press the stitching and turn the facing over the sewing and press again. Crease along the stitched edge, turning the facing on to the wrong ' side, tack the edge and press again. Make a small hem along the inside curve and stitch in the normal way.

To apply a decorative hem, sew the right side of the facing to the wrong side of the garment and turn it on to the right side. Finish with slip stitch.

A straight faced hem is applied similarly to a straight edge.

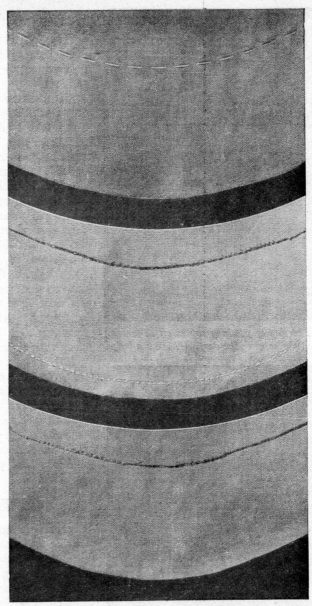

A facing is the most satisfactory way of finishing a hem that is very curved. This is not difficult if tackled step by step. The width of the hem is marked on the garment with tacking stitches. The facing piece is cut to the exact size and shape of the tacked section. The facing is sewn to the garment edge, right sides together, then turned to the wrong side, sewn and pressed. Faced hems can be used for straight edges, in which case the facing strip is cut on the straight.

DARTS

Darts play a big part in dressmaking. Their use is to dispose of surplus material and to give a good fit to the garment.

First measure the position of the dart very carefully, placing a pin where the centre fold should be. Place two more pins, one each side of the first and equidistant, to mark the width of the dart. The distance between the last two pins should be equal to the amount of material to be taken up. From the centre pin measure the length of the dart, and place a fourth pin. Fold the material between the first and fourth pins in a straight line and at right angles to the material edge. Pin the two thicknesses together, matching the second and third pin and tapering off to nothing at the point, where the fourth pin is placed. Stitch neatly along the pin line.

The line of stitching tapers off to nothing at the point of the dart, to prevent a bulge.

If the darts are small and the material thin, the darts may be pressed to one side. With bulky fabric it is advisable to slit the dart down the centre fold, open the edges out and press them flat.

If there is a bulge at the point of the dart this can be disposed of by shrinking and pressing, see notes on page 110.

OPENINGS

There are many different ways of making and finishing openings in the side seams, neck and shoulders of dresses, sleeves and skirt plackets. Choose a method to suit the type of garment and the material being used. Openings should be as inconspicuous as possible and heavy finishings should be avoided on light materials.

Seam Opening.—Used in the side seam of a frock.

Cut a facing strip for the back part of the opening, which is the underlap.

The fold of the dart is slit, the edges are opened out and pressed flat like a seam.

This strip should be about one and a half inches wide and the length of the placket plus one and a half inches.

Sew one edge of the facing to the garment underlap, right sides facing, press the seam flat and fold along the line of stitching. If the fabric is fine a small hem can be made on the edge and the strip then sewn to the turnings with stitches that are invisible on the right side. If bulky material is being used finish the facing edges with braid and sew to the garment as for a hem finished with braid, page 175.

Take a length of braid, the same size as the facing, and sew one edge to the front overlap. Press it flat along the seam and sew the raw edges. The ends of this facing are sewn to the underlap in the wrapped over position.

The seam turnings above and below the opening should be cut almost to the stitches, and pressed out flat.

If the seam of the front facing meets the seam of the underlap facing, the opening will be neat and flat and like a skirt placket in appearance.

Faced Openings.—For finishing the openings at necklines.

Cut a piece of material on the straight, about one inch longer than the opening and about five inches wide.

Mark the position of the slit with a line of tacking stitches. Fold the facing piece into two, lengthwise, and mark the centre line. Place this line on the opening tacks, arranging it so that the edge meets the neckline at the highest point. Pin and tack it in place. Make a line of stitching one-eighth of an inch inside the neckline and each side of the placket line, also across the bottom. Cut along the centre line and snick into the corners. Make notches in the neck curve. Press the facing back over the seam edges and turn it back on to the wrong side, with the sewing line at the edge. Make sure that the corners are

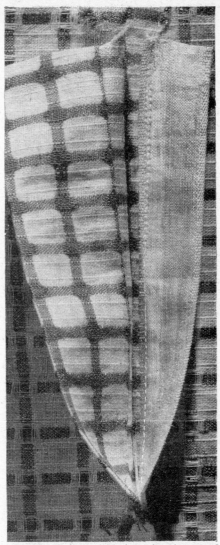

The front edge of the opening is turned under and neatened with braid. The underlap is finished with a straight facing.

well pulled out, tack the facing quite flat and press. Neaten the edges with a tiny hem or overcasting, page 154.

This type of finish is also suitable for a neck opening with revers. In this case cut the facing wider at the top so that it will extend one inch or so along the shoulder line. The width at the

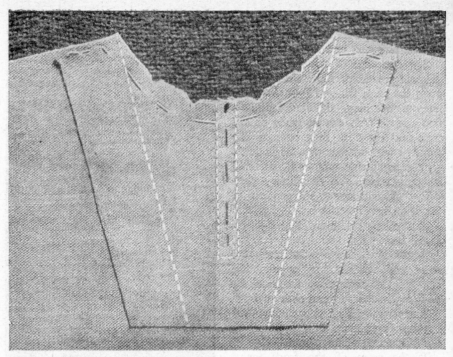

The facing piece of a faced opening is cut to the shape of the neck and extended well below the slit. If revers are to be made then the facing piece is taken along the shoulder seams.

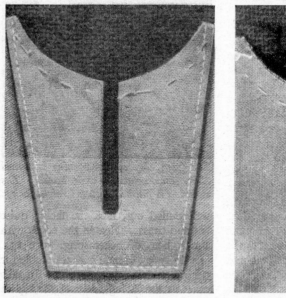

The facing is turned on to the wrong side and folded along the seam line, the edges being neatened with a single hem. Keep the right side flat without creases, and tack the neck edge.

bottom of the facing is about five inches.

The photograph on page 180 shows how this facing should be cut. The larger section is the size to cut facings for rever openings. For a plain-faced opening cut along dotted lines.

The dark tacking stitches indicate the cutting line for the slit.

Note how this facing is carefully tacked in place round the neck edge, and along the shoulder lines.

Bound Opening.—Can be used to finish a front or back opening.

Mark the slit with tacking. Take a piece of material on the straight about two and a half inches wide and one inch longer than the opening. Find the centre by folding it lengthwise.

Place this centre on the tacked line of the opening and pin and tack in place. Right sides should be facing.

Make a line of stitching down each

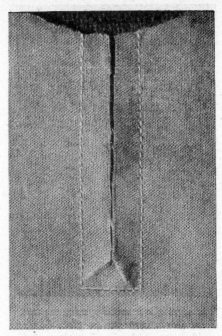

Stitch all round the slit of a bound opening and snick into the corners at the base.

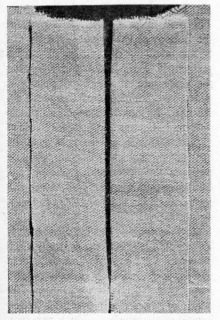
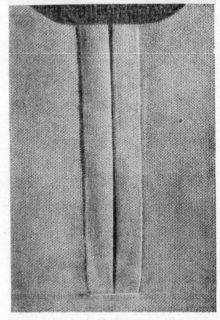

The facing is turned on to the wrong side and pressed with the folds level; a small pleat is formed at the bottom of the slit. Keep the binding, on the right side, of an equal width.

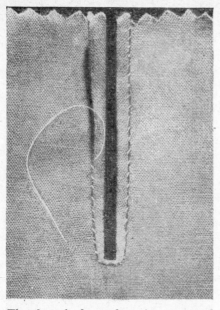

The edges of a hemmed opening are turned down into a very narrow plain hem and neatly sewn with tiny hemming stitches.

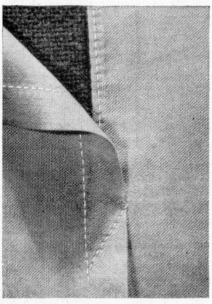

To make a neat lapped opening it is necessary to arrange the material into a knife pleat. This extends from the bottom of the slit to the edge of the garment.

side of the centre line, about one-quarter of an inch from the tacks, also across the bottom of the slit. Cut down the centre line, snicking into the corners. Press the binding over the seam and turn it on to the wrong side, making it quite flat and even so that the edges meet and pull the bottom ends into a pleat to ensure neatness.

Neaten the raw edges, and slip stitch them down invisibly.

Hemmed Openings.—A simple slit used at the neck and sleeves of blouses and children's clothes. It is not suitable for use on heavy fabrics.

First cut a slit the length required, make a narrow hem each side of the slit and sew with hemming stitches. Strengthen the end with a bar tack, page 165.

Lapped Opening.—Suitable for sleeve openings and the back neck of children's dresses in light-weight materials.

Cut the opening the required length. Fold the right side over the left for a girl, and the left over right for a boy. This will make a small knife pleat at the bottom of the opening, which can be extended for the full length of the garment if liked. Make a tiny hem on the underside of the opening and a wider one, the width of the pleat, on the top. Strengthen the bottom of the opening with a line of stitching. Have a piece of tape or strip of material underneath the underside to take the strain of the fastenings.

Continuous Opening.—Used for sleeve, neck and skirt openings in light-weight fabrics.

Cut the opening the length required. Take a length of bias cut material twice the width the placket strip is to be plus half an inch and long enough to pass round both sides of the opening. The width of this strip is governed by the length of the placket. For a two-inch opening make the binding three-quarters of an inch wide when finished, for a longer opening allow more width but avoid a clumsy finish.

Place one edge of the bias strip to the edge of the opening, right sides together. Stitch all round, not too tightly, one-quarter of an inch away from the edge. Press the seam and press the binding over the raw edge. Fold the strip into two, turn under the raw edge and stitch the fold to the sewing line.

The binding is then tucked inside the garment with one side lapping over the other and the seams meeting. Press quite flat so that the finished placket is almost invisible.

A continuous opening has a binding which extends round the whole length of the slit. The binding, which is cut on the bias, is first sewn to the right side of the garment.

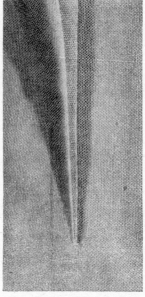

The binding is then turned on to the wrong side of the slit and folded down the centre. A small hem is made at the raw edge and this fold is sewn with neat hemming stitches to the first line of stitching. After pressing fold the overlap over the underlap, so that the stitched edges meet exactly. A few invisible stitches are made at the bottom.

can be added. Cut two straight pieces of material about one and a half inches wide and one inch longer than the opening. Stitch one edge of one strip to the back skirt piece, right sides together, and the other to the front in the same way. Press the seams open and neaten the edges of the back and under piece as before described. Fold the front piece back along the seam and finish as before.

Strengthen the bottom of the placket with invisible stitching made through all thicknesses of material.

The underlap of a skirt opening is strengthened with braid for fasteners.

Skirt Plackets.—When thick material is being used. Cut extra turnings on the left of both front and back to allow for wrap over of the placket. Strengthen both sides with tape or a strip of material where the fastenings are to be stitched. Neaten the edge of the under piece with pinking or binding. Fold the top portion back for the correct width and tack it down. Neaten the edge with braid hemmed first to the hem and slip stitched to the garment.

If this method is too extravagant on material then separate placket pieces

The edge of the opening should continue in a straight line with the seam of the skirt, to be almost invisible, flat and neat.

Shoulder Opening.—

This is made in the seam of the shoulder. It is used on high necked blouses and frocks, and also on children's garments.

Leave a portion of the seam unstitched, long enough to allow for the opening. Fasten off and strengthen the stitching at the placket end. Snick through the turnings just below the end of the opening, open them flat and press the seam.

The front part of the seam laps over the back. Make a hem, the width of the seam turnings, on this

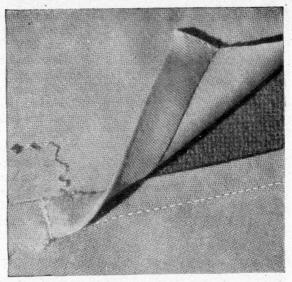

The underlap is bound with a bias binding. Cut the turnings up to the seam so they will fold under the overlap.

Neaten the front edge with a small hem. The single hem can be machined, the sewing to the garment is invisible.

edge and stitch very neatly, making sure the sewing does not show on the right side. If there is to be much strain on the opening, or the garment material is of a loose weave, this hem should be strengthened with tape or material to take the fastenings.

The underneath part of the placket is bound with bias binding in thin fabric. Cut a strip twice the width of the top hem, plus half an inch for

turnings. Sew one edge of this to the edge of the opening, having right sides together. Press the binding over the sewing and the raw edges and turn it on to the wrong side. Make a small hem at the edge and sew the fold neatly to the first line of stitching.

Fold the top layer over the bottom so that the fold of the hem is level with the join of the binding. Press very flat and strengthen the end of the placket with invisible stitching made through all thicknesses of material.

Buttons and buttonholes can be used for fastening this type of opening, in which case hand-made buttonholes are made into the hem and the buttons are sewn on to the binding.

If press fasteners or hooks and eyes are used and neatly sewn this opening is almost invisible when fastened.

side of the garment after pressing the seam. The sewing edge should be at the fold. Tack the facing in place. Turn under the edge opposite to the join. Make a point at the top of the strip, turn under the edges and tack. Machine stitch round the three sides of the facing, leaving the cuff end unfinished. Press again.

This opening should be so arranged that the edge of the wrap over is level with the seam of the binding, which, if made in a seam, should be the continuation of the sewing line. It is usual to finish the sleeve with a cuff when this opening is used.

The underlap of a tailored opening is bound with a straight binding which extends beyond the edge of the slit.

Sleeve Opening—Tailored.—Is

generally found on tailored shirt blouse sleeves or men's shirt sleeves. The underside of sleeve wraps over the top.

Cut the slit the length required or leave a portion of the seam unstitched. Bind the underside of the opening with a narrow bias binding, page 207. For the wrap-over edge cut a strip of material one inch longer and half an inch wider than the facing is to be. Join one edge of this strip to one side of the opening, having the right side of the facing to the wrong side of the sleeve. Stitch about one-eighth of an inch from the edge. Turn the facing on to the right

The top facing extends well below the slit into a point. Make it wide enough to cover the binding of the underlap completely.

One-Piece Sleeve Opening.—This is an opening generally made in the seam of a sleeve. Stitch the sleeve seam leaving the length of the opening unstitched for the length required. Fold the underside of the sleeve over the top, snicking the seam turnings of the under part so the seam can be opened flat and pressed. The edge of the overlap is turned under to have the fold as a continuation of the sleeve seam. Press it down and tack it with a single hem only. Make a tiny single hem on the underlap and turn up the bottom of the sleeve. Tack braid over the raw edges, mitreing the corners, hem one edge of this to the hem and the other stitch loosely to the sleeve making invisible stitches on the right side. The braid should be taken up along the sleeve seam for about one inch for strengthening and to neaten the opening.

If extra finish is desired a line of machine stitching can be made on the right side close to the sleeve and placket edge.

Sew the fastenings to the braid on the inside but avoid letting the stitches penetrate through to the right side, as this will be ugly. Press fasteners are the best. If preferred, however, a single hook and eye can be sewn at the bottom.

The opening of a tight-fitting sleeve is made as a continuation of the sleeve seam. The edges of the slit are turned under once and matching braid is sewn over them.

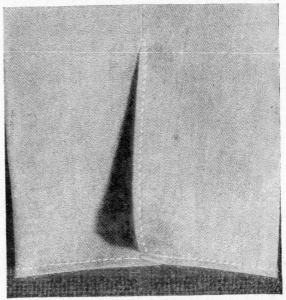

The loose edge of the braid is slip stitched to the sleeve with stitches that are invisible on the right side of the garment. A line of machining gives finish to the opening.

The facing of a V neck is first sewn to the right side of the garment, the facing strip being kept absolutely flat. Make a dart at the point of the neck to get a perfect fit.

NECK FINISHES

There are several ways of neatening necklines; apart from collars the neatest and most used are facings and bindings. Neck edges are, as a rule, cut slightly on the bias. Care must be taken, therefore, to avoid stretching the edge when applying the finishing piece of material. Nor must this be too tight.

V Neck.—Is best finished with a facing, but a bias binding may be used.

Facing.—Cut a crossway strip of material one and a half inches wide and about two inches longer than the length all round the neck. Sew one edge of this to the neck, right sides together, starting in the centre back. Ease the facing to the neck so that the outer edge lies flat on the garment, especially at the corner where the strip must be mitred, see page 208. Press the join and stitching, then press the facing over the raw edges.

Turn the strip on to the wrong side, crease along the stitched line, tack and press flat. Make a small hem on the facing edge sewing with running stitches and then catch it with slip stitches to the garment making the sewing invisible on the right side.

An added finish can be given to the neckline if a row of machine stitching is worked round the inner edge.

Binding.—Is applied in the same way as for facing and turned over the edges on to the wrong side. Fold the raw edge under and sew the fold to the first line of stitching. Mitre the point of the V as for a facing.

The facing is folded along the sewing line and turned on to the wrong side. Neaten the edge with a narrow hem sewn with machine or running stitches, before the final press.

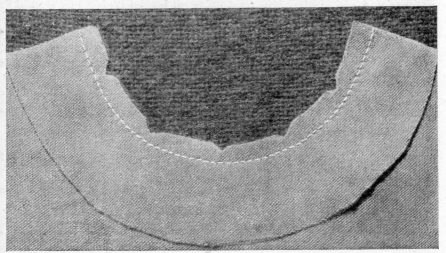

A round neck is faced with a piece of material cut to the shape of the neck line. After making the line of sewing snick the turnings to ensure a flat seam and facing. Press well.

Round Neck.—Can be faced or bound in the same way as a V neck. The bias strip should be eased into the neck edge to keep the outer edge flat.

Make notches into the seam turnings at frequent intervals before turning the binding or facing on to the wrong side, as in a curved seam, page 173. A U-shaped neck is made in the same way.

Never stretch a bias facing or binding when attaching it to a neck edge, but ease it gently so that the seam will not be puckered or pulled tight. Do not apply the binding too loosely.

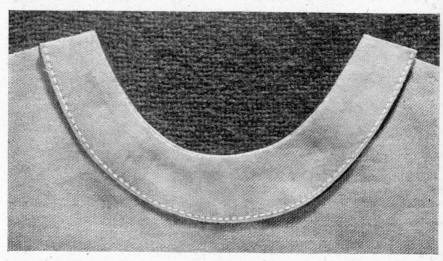

A round neck facing is turned to the wrong side and finished as a V neck.

Square necks are faced with a shaped piece. The corners are snicked up to the stitching.

When the facing is turned on to the wrong side the corners are carefully folded so that they are absolutely square and neat. Finish the edges with a tiny hem as for a V neck.

Square Neck.—Is faced with a piece cut to the shape of the neck. Cut this out before making up the garment from the front and back neck shape. Place each piece of the garment flat on a sheet of paper and draw round the neck edge, then draw a second line outside this shape about one and a half inches away; follow the line of the shoulder. Cut out these paper patterns.

When cutting the material allow the same amount of turnings on the neck and shoulder edges as on the garment. The straight edge of the neck should be placed on the grain of the fabric, try and keep it to a thread. Leave a small allowance of turnings on the outer edge of the facing.

Make up the garment before finishing off the neck, and join the shoulder seams of the facing. Place the two neck edges together, right sides inside, and make sure that the facing piece is quite neat and flat. Tack well. Stitch round the neck edge. Press the sewing line and turnings and make snicks into the corners of the square. Turn the facings on to the wrong side, folding along the seam line. Push out the corners with the points of the scissors. Make sure that the facing is absolutely flat, adjusting the shoulder seams if necessary. Tack round the neck edge. Make a small hem round the outer edge and sew with running stitches. Finally, slip stitch the edge to the garment, page 156, making stitches that are invisible.

The secret of a perfect square neck is to have it cut absolutely on the straight of the material, so that it does not pull out of true, and to keep the seam edge of the facing absolutely flat.

A square neck may be bound with bias binding in the same way as a V or round neck; this needs very special care to avoid pulling and stretching. Mitre the corners neatly, see page 208.

Armhole Edges.—Can be faced or bound with a bias binding in the same way as a round neck.

FASTENINGS

Fastenings of all kinds should be made as invisible as possible unless they serve a decorative purpose as well. The spacing must be regular and the one side of the fastener must be matched perfectly with the other. Make sure that the material is strong enough to take the strain.

Choose a fastening that is most suitable for the type of opening on which it is being used.

The knob side of a press fastener is sewn to the overlap first. Mark the position of the centre of the flat side on the underlap with two crossed pins, top right.

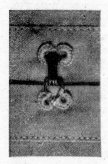 

Round eyes are sewn on the edge of the underlap so the edges meet. A flat eye is placed level with the edge of the overlap to match the position of the hook.

Press Fasteners.—Consist of two round disks, one with a knob and one with a hole to take the knob. Sew the knob side on first to the overlap. To get the position of the other half, rub a little french or tailor's chalk on the knob and press this on to the underlap. This gives the position for the centre of the flat side. Mark this spot with two pins crossed. Some makes of press fastener have a hole through the centre of the knob. This enables the position of the flat side to be found by passing a pin through the hole to the underlap; the spot can then be marked.

To sew the underside of press fasteners in place make three or four oversewing stitches, or buttonhole stitches into each hole. Pass the cotton under the fastener or across the back between each hole. Fasten the cotton off neatly and firmly on the wrong side. The top part of the fastener needs more careful stitching as the stitches must not be allowed to show on the right side. If there is a facing or double layer of fabric, then sew through one layer only and fasten off just underneath the disk. When sewing these disks to single fabric it is a good plan to stitch them first to a separate piece of tape or material which can then be sewn to the garment, invisibly. On thick material the fastener can be sewn to the top layer without penetrating the fabric.

Hooks and Eyes.—Are firmer than press fasteners, but they do not make quite such a neat finish.

Always use the flat type of eye on a wrap over placket and on light-weight fabrics make a hand-worked eye. These are neat but not very hard wearing. Make three large back stitches in the position of the eye, and work buttonhole stitches over these threads. Use round eyes on edges that meet exactly.

Hooks are sewn with the head of the hook just inside the folds of the overlap. Make three or four oversewing stitches or buttonhole stitches into each of the loops at the base of the hook and make two or three backstitches over the back of the hook under the loop, this keeps the hook flat.

To find the position of an eye, fold the overlap into position and place a pin where the curve of the hook rests. This is the spot on which to sew a flat eye and the place for the circle of a round eye.

Hooks and round eyes can be neatened with binding sewn over the loops, leaving the hook part and loop of the eye exposed.

Press fasteners and hooks and eyes, attached to a tape, can be bought by the yard. These are excellent for use on skirt plackets and dress openings as the tape can be sewn on to the garment as a neatening to the raw edge. Neat, firm hemming stitches are made down each side of the tape, but care should be taken to prevent them from showing on the right side.

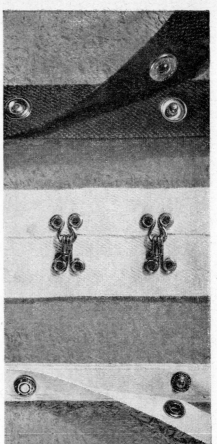

Hooks and eyes, and press studs on tape.

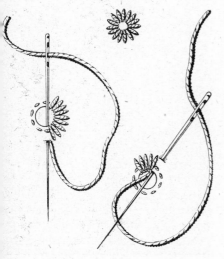

Eyelet holes. Worked with overcast stitch on the left, and buttonhole on the right.

Eyelet Holes.—Are used for headings, in which tape or elastic is threaded.

Mark the position and size of the hole with a pencil and make a row of small running stitches round this circle. Pierce the centre with the stiletto and make two or three more rows of running stitches for padding. Work buttonhole stitches over the running with the knot to the hole, or finish with neat oversewing. Fasten off on the wrong side.

Push the stiletto into the hole to flatten the stitches into a circle.

If wide elastic or tape is being used, then small buttonholes can be made instead of an eyelet hole, see page 200.

ZIP FASTENERS

Whether the zip be made of metal or plastic the method of inserting it into the garment will always be the same.

Zip Fastener in Seam.—Keep the zip closed when inserting it into an opening. The seam should be a plain seam and the turnings should be opened out and pressed flat. Leave the seam unstitched for the length of the zip and machine stitch along the edge of each fold. This stitching can be continued for the full length of the seam if desired. The centre of the fastener is placed behind the folds of the opening which must meet exactly. Tack it in this position and hem along the edges of the tape.

Zip Fastener in Opening.—Cut the opening, keeping it straight with the grain of the material and making it the same length as the metal part of the zip.

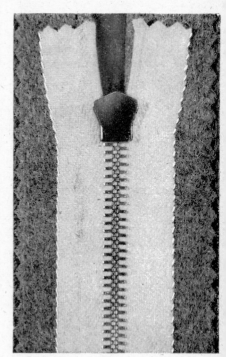

Zip fastener inserted into a seam. The edges of the seam are folded back and machine stitched, and the zip is sewn to the turnings. It is concealed in the seam.

The wrong side of a zip sewn into a seam. Note the hemming stitches on the tape edge.

Make a V-shaped snick at the bottom of the opening and turn under and tack the raw edges, making the width between sufficient to let the slide run up and down. Insert the zip, hemming the folds to the tape on the right side.

Arrange the cord on paper, over the design.

The frog is then stitched on the garment.

FROGS

Frog fastenings are made of cord or braid twisted into interesting designs. They are used for dressing gowns or coats.

First arrange the cord into the design of the frog. The outline of this is drawn on paper, the cord arranged over the pencil line and pinned. Stitch the cord securely where the loops cross and then remove the paper. It should be remembered that a frog must be so designed that it has one loop to take the button. With double frogs this loop is omitted from the button side.

Sew in place on the garment with invisible stitches through the cord.

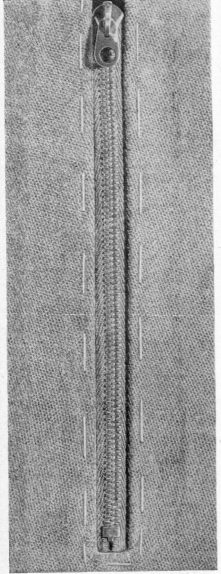

Zip fastener inserted into a cut opening. The slit edges are hemmed to the tape.

LOOP FASTENERS

Loop fasteners with buttons are used on edge-to-edge openings such as the back of a neck, the front of a blouse or a tight-fitting sleeve. These loops can be made with cord, rouleau, or hand-worked in buttonhole stitch.

Cord Loops.—Are easy to make. First make a single hem where the loops are to appear. Sew this lightly with herringbone or catch stitch, and press it. Mark the position of each button and the width of the loops. Calculate also the depth needed for the loop to slip over the button.

Arrange the cord in loops, folding it in between each loop and sewing this fold to the hem of the garment. All the stitches must be made in the single thickness only, so they are not visible on the right side. It is not necessary to cut the cord between the loops.

Single Loops.—Mark the position as previously described. Cut a length of cord long enough to make the loop the size required and to allow for the stitching. Sew this, each end, to the hem. This method also applies to single loops made in rouleau. If the rouleau has been made by hand, each length must be fastened off.

When all the loops are sewn in position neaten the wrong side with a facing. Ribbon or straight binding can be used for this or a strip of the garment material, about one and a half inches wide. In the latter case turn under the raw edges at each side and press them.

Place this strip over the sewn parts of the cord and the raw edges of the hem. Catch stitch the edge of the facing to the garment and hem the other edge neatly on to the inside of the hem.

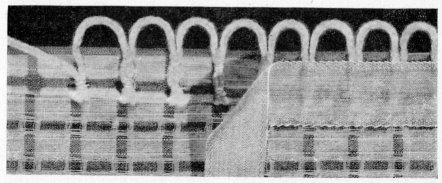

Cord loops are arranged along the opening edge and used with small buttons for fastening. One long length of cord can be used. The fold between each loop is sewn with neat stitches made into the single hem. The stitches should not be visible on the right side.

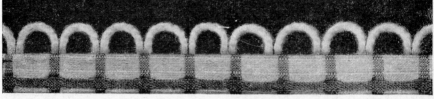

Neaten the stitched part of the cord with a straight facing. When the loops are small this can be ribbon or braid. The facing is arranged over the raw edges of the hem. It is then hemmed to the hem and slip stitched to the garment.

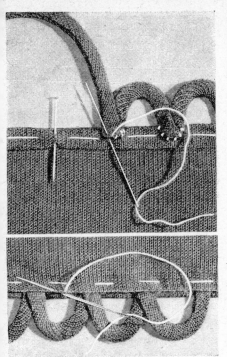
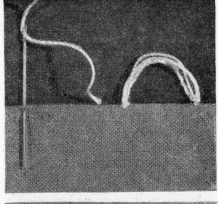
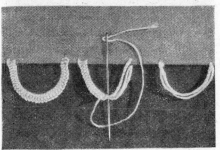

Rouleau loops are made from bias-cut strips of garment material joined into a tubular length with a seam at one side. As shown top left. The stitching of the loops and the hem are neatened with a facing as for cord. Bottom of picture.

Hand-made loops in buttonhole stitch. The foundation threads should be firmly sewn into the fabric each side of the loop, with two or three back stitches. Top right. The buttonhole stitches are made close together on the foundation threads.

Rouleau Loops.—Are made from crossway strips of material. Cut a strip long enough to make all the loops and one inch wide. Fold this strip into two lengthwise and then make a line of stitching just inside the raw edges. Turn the rouleau inside out with a safety pin or bodkin, and press it flat with the seam at one edge.

Make a single hem on the edge of the garment and mark the position of the buttons and the width each loop is to be, as for cord loops. Form the rouleau into loops to take the button, making a flat fold between each. Neatly sew round this fold into the hem only. Neaten the wrong side with facing.

Buttonhole Loops.—Are worked by hand with stout thread. Make a single hem on the garment as before, and mark the position of the button and size of the loop. Join the sewing thread one side of where the loop is to be made, and secure firmly with backstitch. There is quite a lot of strain on both the material and the buttonhole at this point. Pass to the other side of the loop, leaving a length of thread long enough to pass over the button, secure with a back stitch. Repeat this procedure from side to side twice more, then work simple buttonhole stitches over these threads, keeping the stitches flat, close together and firm.

BUTTONS

Buttons being used solely for decorative purposes are sewn flat to the garment with stitches made over and over through the holes.

Buttons that are to be used for fastening need to be sewn a little more carefully. First mark the position of the button with crossed pins or a chalk mark. To find this position wrap the top side of the garment over the other and mark through the buttonhole.

A small button may be sewn behind the large one, to the wrong side, for strength.

The stitches sewing a button are made over a pin or match to get threads for a shank.

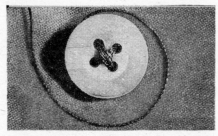

Bind the shank firmly with thread so the button stands away from the garment.

Fasten the thread to the spot where the button is to be sewn, make one stitch through the button to hold it in place. Now slip a pin under the loop just made and continue to sew the button in the usual way, making the loops over the pin as well as the button. If a longer shank is required then slip an orange stick or match stick under the loop in place of the pin. The length of the shank should be regulated to suit the thickness of material used for the garment.

After all the sewing stitches have been made bring the thread through to the right side again, just under the button. Now bind the sewing threads firm by winding the cotton round them. Fasten off securely.

Strengthening.—For buttons on coats and heavy materials which have hard wear. Place a very small button on the wrong side of the garment and secure with one loop, then place the fastening button in position on the right side and stitch as previously described, sewing through the holes of the small button as

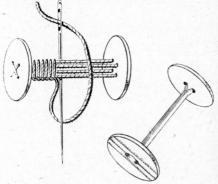

Two buttons joined to form a link, with ribbon, braid or threads buttonholed.

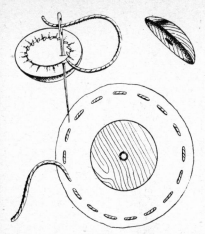

Wooden button moulds are covered with garment material for a perfect match.

Also cut a circle of thick flannel the same size as the mould and place this and the mould in the centre of the larger circle of material, make running stitches round the edge of the large circle and draw it up so that the button is covered completely and tightly. Neaten the back of the button with the small circle of fabric, turning under the edges and hemming round the fold.

Braid and Metal Shanks.—For leather or bone buttons.

Make an eyelet hole in the position where the button is to be, see page 193. For leather buttons take a strip of braid or double material twice the length of the shank, plus one inch.

well as the main one. The strengthening button can be substituted by a small circle of firm material if preferred.

Link Buttons.—Are used for shirt sleeves and edge-to-edge garments. Join two buttons together with threads of sewing cotton covered with buttonhole stitches or with a strip of material, as shown in the Diagram.

Covered Buttons.—Can be made to match the garment, using wooden or metal button moulds.

Cut two circles of fabric, one the same diameter as the button mould and the second twice this diameter.

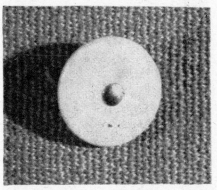

Bone buttons with a metal shank are easily removed when the garment is to be washed.

Leather buttons need a shank of braid. The ends are threaded through an eyelet.

On the left, a braid shank wrong side. On the right, a split pin and metal shank.

Pass this strip through the hole of the button, then slip the ends through the eyelet hole, open them out and stitch neatly on the wrong side.

A metal shank is passed through the eyelet hole and secured with a split pin.

BUTTONHOLES

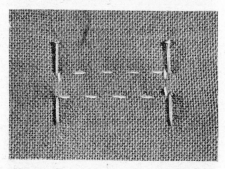

The length of the buttonhole is regulated by the size of the button. The position is marked with a pin each side of the button.

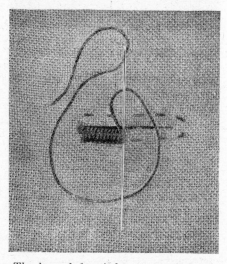

The cut of the buttonhole is marked with a line of tacking stitches which should be made on the straight grain of the fabric.

Worked.—Hand-worked buttonholes are the neatest that can be made and they give a tailored finish to a garment.

Having found the position of the buttonhole mark it for size, using the button. Place the button in position and insert a pin at each side, thus getting the length of the buttonhole.

Next mark the line of the slit with tacking stitches made between the two pins.

The edge of the buttonhole must be strengthened with small running stitches, and, as these buttonholes should be made in double material, the stitches will hold the two thicknesses together. Make these running stitches before cutting the slot. Buttonholes that are made on thick woollen material are more tailored if padded with strands of stout thread or buttonhole gimp. Lay three or four threads along the edge of the buttonhole and work the stitches over them.

Silk buttonhole twist should be used for working the stitch, and wherever possible avoid having a join half-way round. Try to calculate the length of thread required for the size of buttonhole; 1 yard of silk will work a 1-in. buttonhole.

Cut the slit with sharp scissors, buttonhole scissors if possible, and work buttonhole stitch all round, starting and ending at the end farthest from

The buttonhole stitches are worked over the cut edges of the slit with the knot on the raw edge. Keep the stitches flat.

Strengthen the square end of the buttonhole with a bar tack, back stitches with buttonhole worked over them, for extra strength.

the garment edge. Finish this end with three back stitches worked across the slit and work simple buttonhole over them. The other end of the slit should be rounded. If a square buttonhole is desired then the backstitches and buttonhole finish is made at both ends.

The stitch used for buttonholes has a knotted edge. See Diagrams.

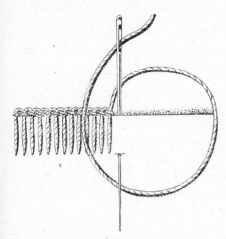

Buttonhole stitch. Take up a small part of the edge of the slit on to the needle. Pass the eye end of the thread under the point.

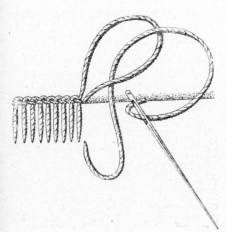

Pull the needle through carefully bringing the knot on to the edge of the cut. The knot should not be pulled too tightly.

Bias Bound.—This is an attractive way of making buttonholes for tub frocks and children's garments. Bias binding as bought by the yard is the best and easiest to use, as the edges are already turned under.

Calculate the amount of material between each slit and cut pieces of material this length and as wide as the facing, or twice the width if it is to be double. Bind the buttonhole edge of these pieces and join them all into one length with binding, at each edge. The facing is then sewn to the garment. When double material is used the folded edge may be left unbound.

A binding of a contrasting colour gives added interest.

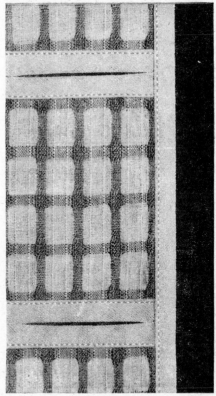

Bias-bound buttonholes are simple to make. The edges of the material are bound and then placed together to form the buttonhole.

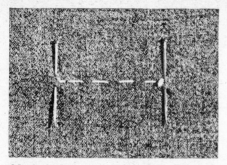

Mark the line of the buttonhole with tacking stitches on the grain of the material.

Bound with Facing.

—This type of buttonhole is used on garment openings where a facing is to be used. If well made they are neat and tailored.

Mark the size of the buttonhole, using the button as described for worked buttonholes, and mark the position of the slit with a line of tacking.

Facing: Cut a square of material on the straight grain, one inch longer than the buttonhole slit and two inches wide. Make a line of tacking across the centre of this to correspond with the tacks on the garment. Place this square on the garment, right sides facing, and the tacking lines matching. Pin it in place and then tack for security.

Sewing: Make a line of backstitching or machine stitching each side of the tacked line, and across each end, allowing one-eighth of an inch each side.

Cutting: With a sharp pair of scissors cut along the tacked line, through both thicknesses, leaving a quarter uncut at each end. Make a triangular cut from each end of this slit into the corners.

Pulling Facing through: After the stitching has been pressed push the facings through to the wrong side. Pull them

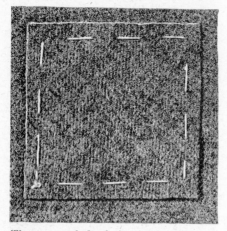

The centre of the facing is placed on the line of tacking, and then well tacked.

Stitching is made each side of the buttonhole slit and across each end. Back stitch or machine stitching should be used.

Cut a slit in the centre of the stitching through all thicknesses and make a triangular cut at each end right into the corners.

at each end of the slit so that a tiny inverted pleat is formed. The binding should be absolutely flat, with the folds meeting in the centre of the buttonhole, and the ends formed into a square.

Tack the facing down and press the buttonhole. Then strengthen each end of the slit with back stitches.

Herringboning: The edges of the facing should be lightly sewn to the garment with herringbone stitch, page 155. These stitches must not show on the right side.

Prick Stitch: Make prick stitches along the seam edge of the binding to hold the garment fabric to the facing. These stitches are made by inserting the needle straight through the seam, leaving a tiny invisible stitch on the right side. Then make a small stitch on the wrong side bringing the needle out a little farther along the seam.

Neatening: After the garment facing has been fixed correctly to the wrapover, make tacking stitches through this and the garment round the buttonhole. Cut a slit in the facing to correspond with the buttonhole, turn under the edge of the slit and neatly hem the fold.

Pull the facing to the wrong side and flatten the binding so it meets in the centre.

The facing is caught to the garment, lightly with neat herringbone stitches.

The wrong side is neatened with the garment facing, as shown at the top. At the bottom a finished bound buttonhole.

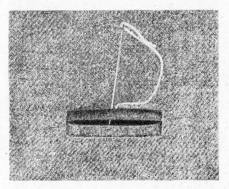

Prick stitches are made through the seam of the binding to prevent the facing from slipping and to keep the buttonhole neat.

FINISHING

Pockets, belts, collars, tucks and gathers are all ways of giving finish to a garment. These finishings must be designed into the style of the garment before it is cut. If the planning of the decorative touches is left to the last there will be a tendency for them to be the wrong shape or size and quite foreign to the design.

PIPING

A crisp finish can be given to hems, seams and edges by the use of piping.

A piping on a straight edge may be cut on the straight of the fabric, but for cord piping and where corners have to be manipulated use bias strips.

Plain Piping.—A strip of material which is inserted into the seam, without padding of any kind. The piping should be cut twice the width it is to be when finished, plus one inch for turnings. Fold the strip in half lengthwise, right side outside, and press the fold. Place the raw edges to one edge of the seam to be joined, or to the edge of the hem on the right side. Make tacking stitches through all three thicknesses.

Cord Piping.—Gives a slight stiffness to the seam; it is, therefore, unsuitable for use on skirts or soft folds.

The width of the bias strip should be the circumference of the cord, plus one inch for turnings.

Piping cord is made in varying sizes. Choose one that is most suitable for the specific purpose. As this cord will shrink when washed it is always advisable to soak it in water before use. Straighten the cord without too much stretching and hang it up to dry.

Fold the bias strip round the cord, right side out, hold it tightly and sew near to the cord with small running stitches.

Place the raw edges of the piping to the raw edges of the seam or hem and tack the three thicknesses.

Hems. — Finished with piping are turned on to the right side.

Sew the piping to the raw edge of the hem with small running stitches, then fold the turnings under so that the piping is at the edge of the fold and press them. Turn the main hem up and tack it. Stitch firmly but invisibly with running stitch and an occasional back

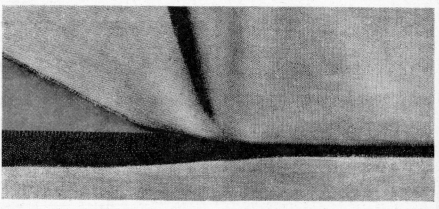

A plain piping inserted into a seam. The piping strip is folded in half, right side outside. The raw edges of the binding are placed level with the seam edges and the stitching is made through the four thicknesses. Press the turnings to one side at the back.

stitch along the fold of the hem and through the piping, just inside the cord. If preferred, a line of machine stitching can be made.

A false hem with piping is joined to the garment like a seam, a piping is sewn to the garment, slipped between the facing edges and machine stitched. **Seams.**—Place the second side of the seam level with the first, right sides together, and the piping between, sew with firm stitches close to the cord, or just inside the fold for a plain piping.

A flat seam may be finished in the same way as a hem by turning under the edge of the second side, placing it over the raw edge of the piping and machining along the fold. The raw edges can then be finished with over-sewing.

Edges.—When the edges of the piping have been placed to the edges of the garment, on the right side, stitch the two together with neat running stitches. Make a small hem on to the wrong side so that the piping is at the folded edge. Stitch the raw edges down with catch stitch which does not show on the right side. Neaten the wrong side with a facing, hemming the fold close to the cord and slip stitching the other edge, on which a hem has been made.

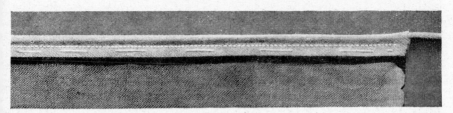

Cord piping. The piping strip is folded over the cord and stitched closely. The edges are then tacked to one edge of the seam or hem, ready for joining together.

Piping a false hem. The edge to which the binding has been tacked is slipped between the two sides of the false hem, which have already been turned under. These are tacked and the machine stitches are made through all four thicknesses, close to the cord.

BINDING

This type of finish is used in a decorative way on the edges of sleeves, necks, pockets and the openings of garments. It can also be employed for the finishing of hem edges when the skirt is rather short as no turnings on the garment are required. A binding that is contrasting in colour or a striped or check binding gives added interest and is a neat way of finishing a plain style garment.

Straight Binding.—Is cut on the straight grain of the fabric and is used only for straight cut edges, it cannot be used on curves as it will not lie flat. Corners must be mitred, see page 208.

Cut the binding strip twice the width of the finished binding plus turnings.

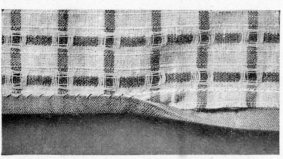

Straight binding on a straight edge. The binding is sewn to the right side, then turned to the wrong side and hemmed.

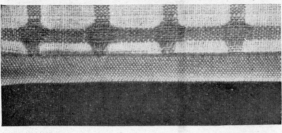

At the top, a straight binding sewn with machining on the right side; one edge is first sewn to the wrong side of the garment. At the bottom, a straight binding, showing the right side, without machine stitching.

Place one edge of the strip to the raw edge of the garment, right sides together, and sew with back stitch or machine stitching, keeping the binding uppermost when machining. Press the binding strip flat over the stitching and turn it on to the wrong side. Make a small hem on the edge and hem this to the previous line of sewing, or just above it. The binding must be kept uniform in width throughout.

A straight binding can be finished with a line of machine stitching on the right side giving it rather a pleasant finish. This method is not suitable for use on thick fabrics. Cut the binding strip four times the width the finished binding is to be, plus half an inch for turnings. Fold the strip into two lengthwise, right side outside, and press the fold. Place the two raw edges of the binding to the edge of the garment, on the wrong side, and sew with back stitch or machine stitching. Press the binding flat over the stitching and turn it on to the right side. Tack the folded edge down so that it covers the first line of sewing and then make a line of machining close to the fold.

Bias Binding.—Can be used for curves, scallops and all kinds of edges. It is not quite so clumsy as a straight binding.

Cutting on the Bias.—Needs to be handled with care, if the strip is not on the true bias the binding will pull in an ugly way. Take a piece of material the edges of which are cut on the straight grain. Fold

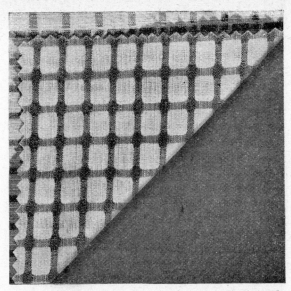

To find a true bias when cutting bias binding, the material is folded diagonally across the straight grain.

one corner over so that straight grain crosses straight grain. Cut along the fold to get the bias and then cut strips from this edge to get the binding.

Joining Bias Strips.—The ends of the strips should be cut on the grain of the fabric. Place them together, right sides inside, so that the bias edges form a right angle. The corners of the strips should protrude at each side of the strip. Make a line of stitching parallel with the straight edge. The sewing should be made between the two points where the bias edges cross each other. Press the seams open and cut off the points. When

The join in a bias-cut strip lies diagonally across the binding. The small points each side are snipped off.

joining stripes, checks and patterned materials take care to match the design.

Place one edge of the binding to the edge of the garment, right sides together, and sew lightly. If light materials are being used it is better to make a line of running stitch with an occasional back stitch. Do not stretch the binding but let it lie flat on the garment, otherwise the garment will pucker. Press

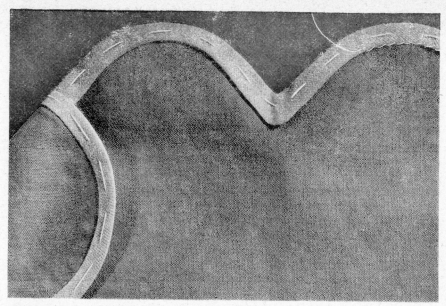

Binding scallops. The binding strip must be cut on the bias. Ease the binding round the curves and stretch it at the corners. A small pleat or dart is made at each corner.

the binding over the stitching, turn it on to the wrong side and hem it down lightly just above the first line of sewing.

At corners make a tiny pleat, which will taper to nothing at the point and form a pleat on the wrong side.

Binding Scallops.—Bias binding must be used for this to get a neat result.

Sew the binding to the edge of the scallops as previously described, but ease the bias edge round the curve of the scallop to avoid pulling, and stretch it at the inside corners to prevent bulkiness. Fold the binding into a tiny pleat at each point to make it lie flat. When turning the binding over in the normal way, see that it is absolutely flat without pulling or fulness.

MITREING CORNERS

Whenever a binding, hem or facing turns a corner a mitre must be made.

Facing.—Sew the facing and garment edge together, right sides inside, all round the edge. Fold the facing at the corners making a diagonal crease from the point of the corner and stitch along this crease. Then cut away the surplus material, open out the turnings and press the seam. Snip off the point at the tip of the corner. Turn the facing on to the wrong side, make a tiny hem and slip stitch it down.

A hem is mitred in the same way.

Binding.—When sewing the first side of the binding to the garment make a tiny dart at the corner, stitch this while sewing round the corner. A matching dart is made in the wrong side of the binding. This dart should be large enough to make the binding quite flat, and it should taper off to nothing at the corner.

Lace.—Fold the corner in the same way as a facing, sew the seam on the right side with tiny oversewing stitches, then cut the turnings close to the stitching on the wrong side of the join.

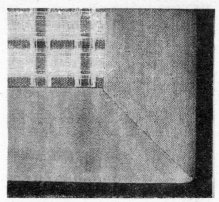

Mitred corner in a facing. A diagonal crease is made from the corner giving the sewing line for the seam. The material is trimmed close to the stitching and the seam is pressed.

Mitred corner in a binding. A dart is arranged in the binding at the corner when the first line of stitching is made, a similar dart is made in the reverse side when it is turned over.

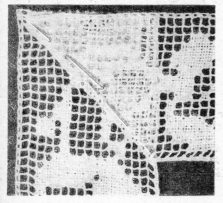

Mitred corner in lace. The lace is folded diagonally from the corner and the seam thus made is sewn with oversewing. The turnings are cut close to the stitching at the back.

TUCKS

Tucks serve the double purpose of adding interest to a garment and introducing fulness where required.

They may be made on the sewing machine, see page 29.

Pin Tucks.—Are arranged in groups, tucks being parallel with each other.

It is a good plan to have a cardboard gauge similar to the one on page 174 which will help to keep the width of each tuck uniform and the distance between straight.

The first notch in the guide is made near to one end; this indicates the first line of stitching, the second indicates the fold of the tuck and the third the second line of stitching. To indicate the position of the tucks first make a tacking line on the grain of the fabric where the first one will appear. Place the end of the gauge to this line of tacking and make chalk marks or insert pins at each notch. Then make

Pin tucks. Arranged in decorative groups.

Inverted tucks. Are the reverse to pin tucks.

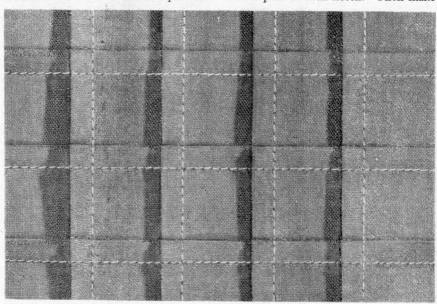

Cross tucks. All the tucks are made in one direction first. They must be parallel and an equal distance apart. The cross tucks are then made the same size as the first set.

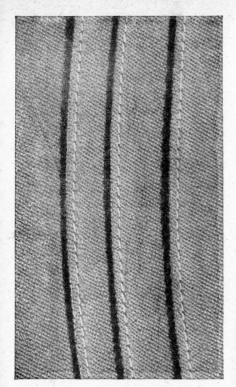

PLEATS

There are three kinds of pleats—inverted, box and knife pleats. When calculating the material required for these allow three times the width the skirt is to be when finished.

Inverted Pleats.—Give the appearance of a single seam line; they are in fact the reverse of box pleats.

Mark the fold of each pleat with a line of tacking stitches made on the grain of the fabric. Measure each pleat carefully, allowing half the width of the pleat each side of the centre panel. For instance if the pleat is to be four inches wide make two tacking lines this distance apart, then a tacking line each side

Curved tucks. Are pin tucks made on a curved line. They need careful stitching.

more tacking lines to replace the pins and repeat this procedure until all the tucks have been marked.

Fold along the appropriate tacking line and pin through the two stitching lines. Sew the tucks neatly with tiny running stitches.

Inverted Tucks.—Are pin tucks used on the reverse side.

Curved Tucks.—The method of making these is similar to pin tucks but great care will be needed as they will be slightly on the bias of the material.

Cross Tucks.—Are purely decorative and make attractive trimmings for children's frocks and cotton blouses.

The same care in measuring the width of these tucks is needed. Having made all the tucks in one direction press them and make the cross tucks similarly.

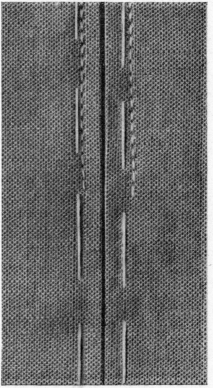

Inverted pleat. The two folds are brought together on the right side to form a pleat.

Box pleats. Can be made singly or in numbers. The material is folded on to the wrong side with the folds meeting in the centre. They should be uniform in size.

Knife pleats. Are flat pleats with a single edge. All the pleats face one way and are uniform in size. The reverse side is exactly the same as the right side.

of these, two inches away. With the right side of the garment uppermost make a fold along the two outer lines of tacking and tack the fold. Bring these two folds together in the centre of the pleat, folding along the inner tacking lines, and tack again. Make a line of machine stitching along the upper part of the inner folds to hold the pleat. Press well on both sides.

Box Pleats.—The reverse to inverted pleats and made in the same way. When a series of pleats is made the right and wrong sides will look alike.

Knife Pleats.—Are similar to half a box pleat. First decide the width the pleat is to be then make tacking lines this distance apart to indicate the folds. There will be three lines of tacking to each pleat. Lay the material flat on the table right sides uppermost.

Take the third line of tacking from the end and make a fold along this for the front of the pleat. Place the fold to the first tacking, thus making another fold the reverse way on the centre tacking. Repeat this procedure throughout.

When making a skirt that is pleated from the waist the pleats must be radiated to fit the smaller measurement. Calculate the difference between the waist and the hip size, divide this by the number

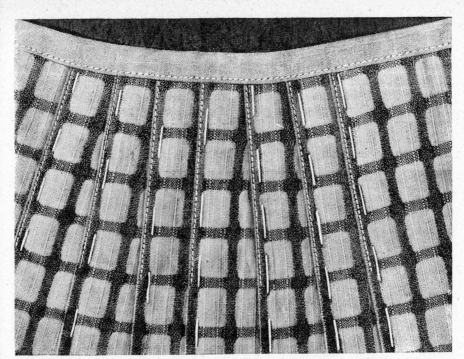

Radiating knife pleats. Are used in a pleated skirt. To make the waist line fit, each pleat is wrapped over more. The width of the pleats will be greater than at the hip line.

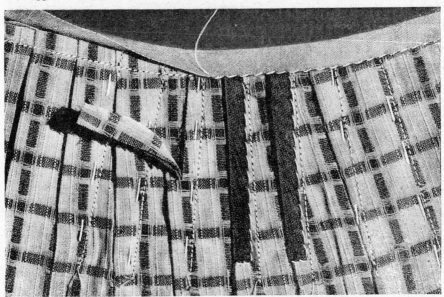

The extra wrapover of radiating pleats is trimmed away on the wrong side and bound with thin bias binding. This prevents bulk and makes the pleats hang well from the waist.

of pleats to get amount which each pleat has to be wrapped over. Do this on the right side and make quite sure that the front edge is kept on the grain of the fabric. At the back, cut the surplus away and bind the raw edges. Machine stitch the edge of the pleats at the top.

Accordion pleats and sunray pleats are made by machine, professionally.

Hemming Pleats.—The hem on a pleated skirt must be made before the pleats are pressed. Seams joining pleats should be made if possible at inner folds. The seam edges are pressed to one side but where the hem appears they must be opened out. Cut through the turnings at the top of the hem, up to the sewing, open the lower part of the seam and press it.

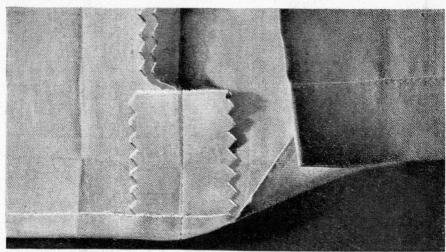

Hemming pleats. The turnings of a seam joining pleats are cut at the hem edge as far as the stitching line. The seam is then opened and pressed flat where the hem of the garment occurs.

Make the hem on a pleated garment before the pleats are pressed so that the creases of the double thickness are correct. A seam which joins material for pleating lies along a fold.

GODETS

A godet is a flared section inserted into the skirt to give extra fulness in a decorative way.

Pointed Godet.—Is a cone-shaped piece of material let into a straight slit.

First draw the shape of the godet on a piece of paper. Draw a perpendicular the length the godet is to be, then decide the width of the widest part of the godet. Measure half this length each side of the perpendicular line, at the base. Then measure the godet length, from the top point of the centre line to the end of the base line, this point being slightly above the base line. Join the two side points just made with a curve, which passes through the bottom of the centre line. Allow turnings.

Cut a straight slit in the skirt the length of the godet and insert the extra piece with a plain seam. Make a line of machine stitching on the right side.

Shaped Godet.—Any shape designed to suit the garment may be used. Cut a piece of paper the size and shape of the godet. Mark this shape on the garment with tacking stitches. To make the pattern for the godet slit the paper up and spread it out in the same way as making a flare, see page 216.

Cut turnings on the godet and inside the skirt inset. Turn under the edges of the skirt and press, place the godet under and make a lapped seam, page 168.

The loose edge of a godet should have a narrow hem or binding to finish.

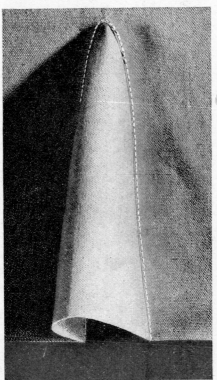 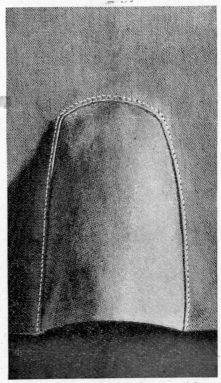

Godets. A section of material cut as a flare and inserted into a skirt to give extra fulness. The godet may be cut to any shape. Cut a slit in the garment or the shape of the godet.

FLARES

To make the pattern for a flare or frill take a piece of paper, the length of the top edge by the depth. Slit the paper from the bottom edge almost to the top, at frequent intervals. Place the strip on a second piece of paper and open out the slits, making sure that the top edge is quite flat, pin it in this position and cut the under paper to match.

Finish the lower edge with binding, or a narrow hem. Sew the top edge of a frill, with the hem on a straight line.

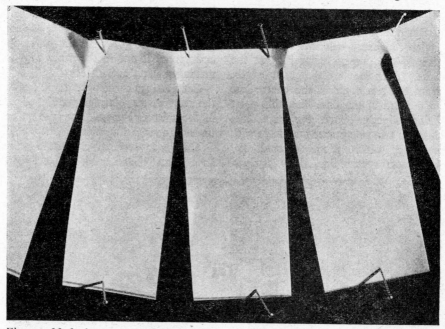

Flares. Made from a straight piece of paper cut from the bottom, almost to the top, at regular intervals. The paper is spread out to make a flare the width needed.

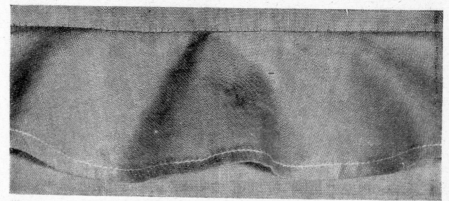

The top edge of a flare is curved but when this is applied to a garment it is sewn along a straight line. In this way the fulness and fluting of the frill is obtained.

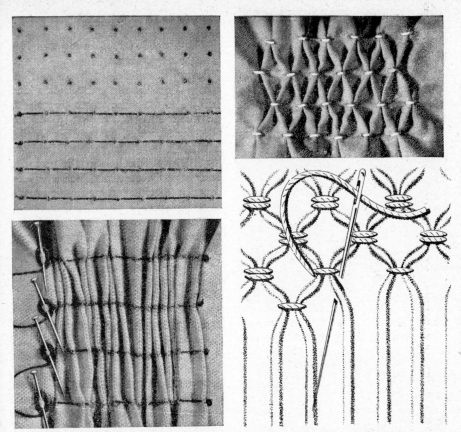

Smocking. Is worked on a series of dots as shown at the top left. Gathering threads are then inserted, making a tiny stitch into each dot, left centre. The material is drawn up into pleats, bottom left. Honeycomb stitch, worked on pleats, right.

SMOCKING

Not only is this type of work very attractive but it is a means of introducing fulness into children's frocks, smocks and muslin blouses. The stitch shown here is honeycomb.

Regularity is the basis of perfect smocking. First mark the material with a series of dots, three-eighths of an inch to half an inch apart. The lines of dots both upright and across should be on the grain of the fabric. Allow three times the amount of material as the width of the smocking is to be when finished.

Now insert the gathering threads, picking up a little of the fabric over each dot. Draw up the threads, stroking the material into tiny pleats. Wind the loose end of each thread on a pin. **The Stitch.**—Join the thread to the first pleat on the top gathering, at the left-hand side. Make a back stitch over the first two pleats; slip the needle down the second pleat to the second row of gathering; make a back stitch over the second and third pleat; slip the needle back to the first row and so on. The next row of stitches is made into the second and third gathering.

GATHERS

Gathers. *Drawn up to correct size, on a stout thread, ready for the stroking.*

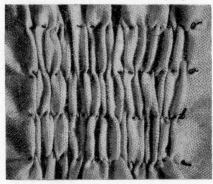

The needle point is pressed between each stitch, stroking them into tiny pleats.

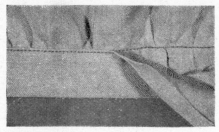

Ruching. *Several rows of gathers worked parallel with each other, are decorative.*

The simplest way of introducing fulness into a garment.

When calculating the amount of material needed for gathers allow one and a half times the length they are to be when finished.

Make a line of fly running parallel with the edge of the garment, see page 157. This stitching should be perfectly straight; a thread of the fabric may be drawn as a guide and the running made into this space.

Draw up the gathering thread and secure it firmly by winding the end round a pin.

Stroking Gathers.—Do not have the thread drawn too tightly.

Hold the gathers in the left hand, between the thumb and first finger. Stroke the gathers with the point of the needle, flat against the material. Starting from the right, form each stitch into a tiny pleat. Press each pleat between the thumb and finger. Fasten off the thread securely with back stitches.

Ruching.—Is a decorative form of gathering used for the yokes of blouses and children's frocks. Several rows of gathers are made one under the other. They must be absolutely straight and parallel. Fly running is used in the same way as for ordinary gathering. It is not possible to stroke these gathers into pleats but neaten them by pressing the needle point between each stitch.

Setting into Band.—Cut the band on the straight grain of the fabric, twice the width the finished band is to be, plus half an inch for turnings. Place one edge of this to the edge of the garment, right side of facing to the wrong side of the garment, and sew the two together. Turn the band on to the right side, make a small hem on the edge and machine stitch it down.

Setting gathers into band. *The band is applied to the right side then turned over.*

When applying a band to gathers that have been stroked the method is slightly different. Both edges of the band are turned under and pressed. One edge is placed over the gathers on the right side, flat; the fold is sewn with hemming stitches, making one stitch into each tiny pleat. Turn the band on to the wrong side and sew with hemming in the same way.

Gathered Frill.—Needs a length of material half as long again as the frill when finished, and as wide as the frill plus turnings. If this strip is cut on the bias of the material it will flute more when finished.

Make a single line of fly running along the top edge, and neaten the bottom edge with a tiny hem or binding. Draw the gathering thread to the size required and fasten off securely with back stitch. The fulness must be evenly distributed.

Divide the frill into four equal parts with pins or creases, divide the garment similarly and match these points.

A frill on an edge is joined with a plain seam, the turnings are turned under and neatened with a facing.

When applying a frill flat on to a garment turn under the top edge before gathering, tack it along a straight line and then sew with machine stitches.

Shell Gathering.—Take a bias strip twice the finished width and fold both edges towards each other to meet in the centre. Press the folds. Then insert a gathering thread diagonally from edge to edge. Draw up this thread so that scalloped edges are formed, and fasten it off securely.

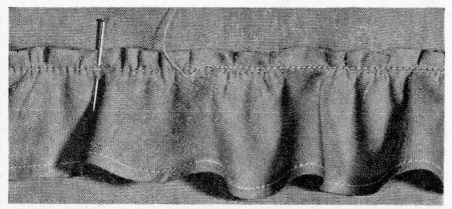

Gathered frill. The top edge of the frill is turned under whilst the gathering thread is inserted. When it is drawn up to the correct length it is sewn to the garment.

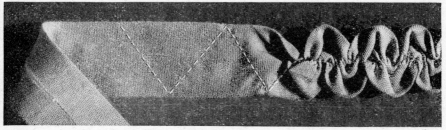

Shelling. A strip of bias-cut material, folded into two, is gathered with a thread inserted in a chevron line, from edge to edge. When drawn up this gives a shell effect.

POCKETS

The position of the pockets should be carefully marked on the garment when it is being cut out. Thread marking is the best method as it is more permanent than pins or chalk. Check the position for accuracy.

Bound Pockets.—The position of the pocket slit is marked with a single line of tacking. Cut a piece of garment material twice the depth of the finished pocket, plus one inch, and one and a half inches wider than the pocket slit. Place this piece, right side to garment right side, with the top edge one inch above the tacking line, and with the centre to the centre point of the line. Tack the pocket piece firmly in position.

Make a line of stitching half an inch each side of the tacking and across the ends, starting in the centre of one side. This sewing must be absolutely straight and an equal distance from the tacking.

Cut along the centre line to within quarter of an inch of each end, then make a V-shaped cut into the corners. Press with a warm iron.

Pull the pocket piece through to the wrong side and open it out flat, making tiny inverted pleats at each end of the slit, so that the binding is quite flat and just meeting in the centre. Tack it down and press.

Make invisible stitches on the right side, through the seam of binding.

Fold the pocket in half and stitch the two sides together. Neaten with overcasting, see page 154, or pinking.

The ends of the slot may be strengthened and neatened with bar tacks or arrowheads, see page 164.

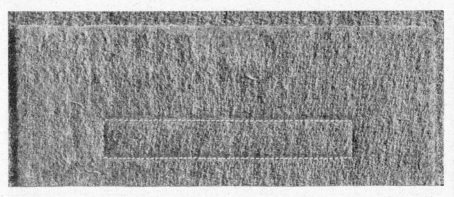

Bound pocket. First step. A rectangle of machine stitching is made all round the pocket slit, after the square binding piece has been tacked in place on the garment.

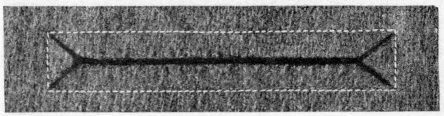

Second step. Cut the slit down the centre of the sewn rectangle, making triangular cuts at each end, snicking right into each corner, almost to the stitching.

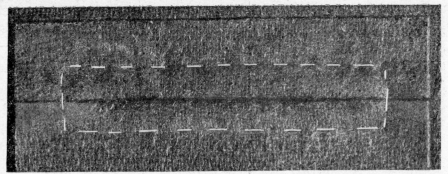

Third step. Push the binding through to the wrong side, pulling it so that the bound edge is even in width and flat, with the slit edges meeting exactly at the centre.

Fourth step. The pocket piece is folded into two and the edges are sewn together all round the binding piece and at each side. The edges are neatened with pinking or overcasting.

The finished pocket. Note how the binding lies flat, and that it is absolutely even for the full length both sides. The neat, square ends are obtained by the inverted pleats.

Welt pocket. The welt and one piece of the lining are tacked with the edges to the pocket slit line. The second piece of lining is tacked and sewn to the other side.

The slit is cut along the tacking and the pocket pieces are pulled through to the wrong side. The seams are pressed and the edges of the pocket linings joined and neatened with a small hem, overcasting or binding.

The welt. After the seam has been well pressed, lift the welt to cover the pocket slit on the right side. Small invisible stitches are made through each end of the welt.

Welt Pocket.—Take a strip of material twice the width of the welt, plus half an inch for turnings, and as long as the pocket slit with turnings added. Fold this strip into two lengthwise, right sides inside, and make a plain seam at each end. Turn right sides out, tack the unstitched edges together, and press.

Place the raw edges of the welt to the tacking which marks the pocket slit, with the welt piece below the line.

Cut two pieces of lining material the size of the pocket, plus one and a half inches on the width. Place the raw edges of one piece to the welt edges, allowing the lining to extend three-quarters of an inch each end. The edge of the second lining piece is placed above the tacking, meeting the welt edges, and extending each side. Tack firmly.

Now stitch through the welt and lining one-eighth of an inch above and below the tacking.

Cut along the tacking line between the pocket pieces, for the exact length of the welt.

Pull both the pocket squares through to the wrong side. The welt stands up and covers the top seam. Stitch both ends firmly with invisible sewing. Press well.

Sew round the pocket edges and neaten.

Slot Pocket.—Similar in appearance to a bound pocket but the method of working is different.

Take a piece of bias cut material, two and a half inches wide by the length of the slit, plus one and a half inches.

Make a line of tacking along the centre of the facing, the length of the pocket slit. Place this over the tacked line on the garment, which marks the position of the pocket. Tack the two together well. Make a rectangle of tacking round the slot and cut along the centre line as in a bound pocket.

Pull the bias strip through to the wrong side, and pull it so that the binding is flat and meeting in the centre of the slit. Pull into tiny inverted pleats at each end. Tack. Sew through the seam of the binding with invisible stitches. Press well.

Now take a piece of lining or garment material as wide as the bias facing piece and long enough to form two sides of the pocket, less the width of the facing. Herringbone stitch one end of this to the lower edge of the facing. Fold the piece into two and sew the other edge to the top of the facing. Stitch down the sides to form the pocket. Neaten all the edges with overcasting or binding and press well.

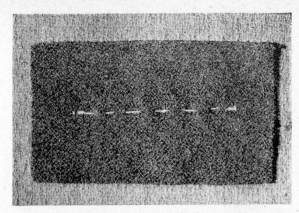

Slot pocket. The facing piece is tacked on to the garment with the tacking matched to the line of the pocket. The facing piece may be a contrasting colour or texture.

When a rectangle of stitching has been made round the slit and the slit has been cut, the facing piece is pulled to the wrong side and formed into pleats at each end.

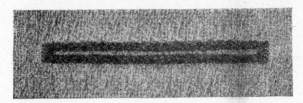

The finished pocket on the right side is rather like a bound buttonhole. The bound edges should be very neat and even, and the ends of the slit should be square.

Patch Pocket.—Decide on the size and shape of the pocket and cut a paper pattern. Place this pattern on the garment and mark round with tacking. The top edge of the patch can be finished in one of several ways. A contrasting facing, cut into decorative shapes, and turned on to the right side with the edge machine stitched, is most attractive. A matching binding or one of a contrasting shade is pleasing on a frock pocket. Rows of machine stitching, made parallel to each other give a tailored finish. This stitching may be continued all round the pocket. For something plain there is the simple hem.

Allow turnings all round.

Make a small hem along the sides and bottom of the pocket, tack it down and press. Place the pocket in position on the garment and tack it firmly. Sew it in place with firm slip stitches or a line of machine stitching close to the folded edge. Press well.

Flap Pocket.—The flap should be designed in size and shape to suit the garment. Make a paper pattern and then cut it in garment fabric and lining material, allowing turnings all round. Sew the fabric and lining together, along the two sides and across the bottom edge, right sides facing. Turn right sides out and press.

Make a single tacked line on the garment, the width of the flap, to mark the pocket top.

Patch pocket. Is sewn on to the right side of the garment. The one shown here is trimmed with rows of machine stitching.

Flap pocket. The pocket itself is on the wrong side of the garment and the slot is covered by a small flap. The flap is lined with lining material which is thinner and lighter in weight than the garment fabric. This picture shows the flap when it is finished.

The pocket and flap are sewn with the edges to the top edge of the slit and the second pocket piece is sewn with one edge to the bottom of the slit. The slit is then cut.

Cut two pieces for the pocket, one garment fabric and one lining, one and a half inches wider than the flap by the depth.

Place the flap, fabric side down, above the tacked line, raw edges touching it, and lay the garment pocket piece over this: the pocket lining is placed under the tacked line. Sew round the slit and cut it as for a welt pocket. Push the pocket piece to the back. Stitch round the three sides and neaten. Herringbone the raw edges of the flap lightly to the garment, and stitch round the ends of the slit for security. Press well.

The seams are pressed and the pocket pieces are pulled through to the wrong side. They are then joined together all round and the raw edges are neatened with pinking, overcast stitch or simple binding.

BELTS AND BUCKLES

Two curtain rings, covered with silk buttonhole stitch and tied together with ribbon, make a pretty fastening.

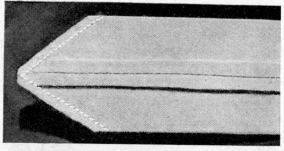

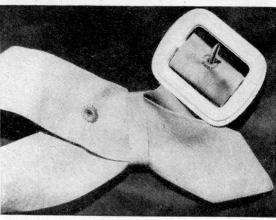

A tailored belt is made in double material with the seam down the centre on the wrong side. The loose end is shaped and has an eyelet hole for fastening.

Belts can be made in several ways to match the garment or to introduce a note of interest. Buckles can be hand made, too.

Ring Buckle.—An attractive way of fastening a belt for a child's frock.

With stout twisted embroidery silk work buttonhole stitch over two curtain rings. Stitch one end of the belt to each ring and tie them together with a ribbon bow.

Straight Belt.—Made in double fabric. Cut a length of material on the straight grain of the fabric, twice the width of the belt and long enough to cover the waist measurement, plus the fold over the buckle and the front wrap.

Fold the belt into four along the length and mark each fold with thread marks. Now place the two long raw edges together, right sides inside, matching the thread marks at the edges. Stitch the two sides together to make a tube. Flatten the tube with the seam down the centre of the belt. Open the seam and press it and the folds at each side.

Stitch across one end of the belt to make the shape desired for the loose end, pointed, rounded or straight. Cut away surplus turnings and then turn the tube inside out. This may be done with an unsharpened pencil pushing against the stitched end, or with a needle and double thread secured firmly to the turnings. The needle, eye first, is pushed into the tube and pulled through.

Pull out the points of the sewn end with a pin, turn in the edges of the other end and stitch. Press well.

The Buckle.—The length of the centre bar should equal the width of the belt. The end of the belt is wrapped over this bar and stitched. If the buckle has a prong make an eyelet hole in the centre of the belt for it to pass through. Make eyelet holes at the other end of the belt for fastening, or, with a plain buckle sew on press fasteners.

Picot-edged Belt.—Make in a single material. Cut the material the length and width required, and work picot edging down each side as described on page 30. Turn under the raw edge and lightly slip stitch it to the belt. Gather the ends to the width desired and neaten with binding. Pass one end over the buckle bar and sew it. Sew press fasteners for fastening.

Fabric Buckle.—Is made from stout cardboard cut to the right shape, and covered with bias-cut strips of material folded double and wound round.

Ribbon Belt.—Cut the ribbon in lengths as required and join them edge to edge. Finish with a bow and press fasteners.

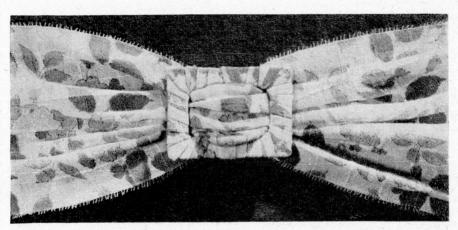

The edges of a single thickness belt are finished with picot edging. The buckle is made of cardboard wrapped with bias-cut strips of fabric which is folded along the length.

Ribbon belt. Two or more colours of ribbon are joined together in a decorative way to make a belt the width required. The ribbon is cut the correct length before joining. The belt is fastened with press fasteners and finished with a bow made up of all the shades of ribbon.

COLLARS

A badly shaped or misfitting collar will ruin the appearance of a garment however well made or well cut it might be.

It is well worth while to cut a collar in soft material such as mull and fit this carefully until it is correct, modelling it to the desired shape with darts for extra fulness. To increase the size slit the pattern and open the slits as necessary. Always adjust the length at the seam in the centre back. When all the necessary alterations have been made cut a second pattern in mull and check the fitting; use this second pattern when cutting the material.

Remember, when fixing a collar, the centre point must be placed to the centre back of the neck, and the ends of the collar must meet at the centre front, or be an equal distance apart.

Collars may be sewn on to the garment or they may be made detachable. In the latter case the neck edge is finished with a bias band, but the method of cutting the pattern is always the same.

A collar usually sits better if it is made in double material, but it is permissible to have single material and bind the edge with bias binding or a rolled hem and lace edging.

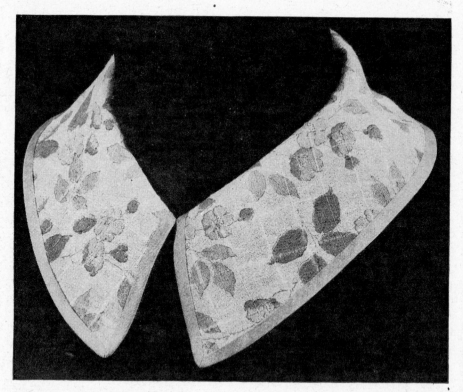

Flat collar. The collar illustrated is made in single thickness material, the edges are bound with a contrasting binding. It can be made to fix into the garment permanently or to be removed for washing purposes. This is an advantage in a collar trimming a dark frock.

Flat Collar.—This type of collar is sometimes called a Peter Pan collar. It may be made in a double thickness of material, or singly with a bound edge. The collar can be sewn into the neck of the garment permanently or made removable to allow for washing.

To cut a pattern for a flat collar place the shoulder seam of the back bodice to the shoulder seam of the front bodice.

Draw the shape of the half-collar on the blocks, making the inside line to fit the shape of the neck. The collars may be made round or pointed to suit the style of the garment.

Place a sheet of paper under the block patterns and draw round the neck line. With the tracing wheel trace over the outline of the collar. Carbon paper, placed between the pattern and the sheet of paper, can be used to trace the outlines instead of the tracing wheel. Cut out the collar pattern from the tracing. Fit the pattern, and make any adjustments necessary, see page 145, before cutting it out in the garment material.

There is one point to remember when drawing these patterns; place the centre line of the front bodice to the straight edge of the paper. This will cause the centre back to be slightly off the straight.

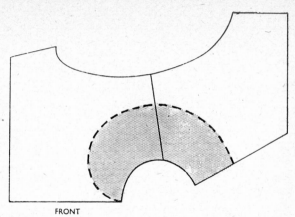

FRONT

A flat collar, points rounded, for a high-fitting neck.

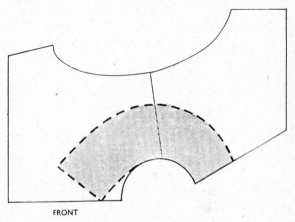

FRONT

The collar is cut to the shape of a V at the neck edge.

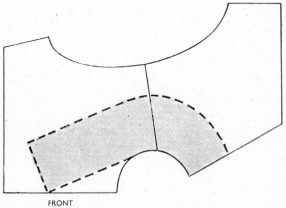

FRONT

When the neck has a low V the collar is extended to fit.

229

Cutting the Collar: place the centre back of the collar pattern to the fold in the material, which must be on the straight grain of the fabric. For a double-thickness collar cut turnings all round, for a bound collar only allow for turnings on the neck edge.

Double Collar.—Cut out two pieces of material exactly from the pattern. Place the two pieces together, right sides inside, and make a line of stitching along the two ends and round the outside edge. Care must be taken to avoid stretching these edges during the sewing. If they are pinned together and then tacked it will prevent them slipping and being stretched whilst the final sewing is being made.

Cut the turnings close to the stitching and trim off the corners diagonally. Press the seams open.

Turn the collar right sides out, pull out all the corners with a pin, carefully, and make a line of tacking round the seam edge. The seam should be at the very edge of the collar. Press well on the wrong side. The collar may be neatened and finished with a line of machine stitching close to and parallel with the seamed edge.

Bound Collar.—Cut this out in single thickness material and bind the ends and the outer edge with bias binding as described on page 207. The binding may be of the same material as the collar or in a contrasting shade or pattern, stripes or checks.

Fixing Collar to Neck: lay the neck edge of the collar to the neck edge of the garment, wrong side of collar to the right side of bodice. Match the centre back of the two neck edges, and pin the ends of the collar in position at the front neck, with the ends meeting exactly. Pin the collar to the neck at frequent intervals, taking care not to stretch either edge. They should fit exactly. Tack firmly in place of the pins.

When finally sewing the collar to the garment include a length of bias binding, in a matching shade, at the same time. The edge of the binding is placed to the neck edge on the collar side; the right side of the binding to the right side of the collar. Make the stitches through the three thicknesses taking care not to stretch the binding or the neck edges, or to have one tighter than the other. Fold the binding over the raw edges and sew neatly.

Press the binding flat, away from the collar, over the sewing line, at the same time pressing the turnings of the collar and neck flat against the garment. These turnings should be snicked at regular intervals to enable them to lie quite flat. Turn the edge of the binding under and slip stitch the fold to the garment.

Detachable Collar.—This is made in the same way as a fixed collar as far as finishing the neck edge. Take a length of net, cut on the bias, about one and a half inches wide. Bind the neck edge with this bias strip, as described on page 207. When binding the neck edge of a double collar, first tack the two edges together to prevent them from slipping.

When fixing this collar into the neck care must be taken to match the centre backs, as with a permanent collar.

Straight Collar.—Draw the pattern in the following way: Make a line A—B the length of half neck measurement. Mark a point D, one inch above B. Join D to the centre of line A—B with a gradual curve. This forms the neck line. Draw a line A—C, the width of the collar, at right angles to A. Measure the front width from D and make a point E. Join C to E with a line curving gradually and parallel with A—D. The line C—E should be extended at the outer edge to make the point of the collar the length required. Join D to E.

A collar fitting to the neck, made in double thickness material from the straight collar pattern. The outer edge is finished with a line of machining.

For a collar with a rounded point draw a good circle at E as shown in the Diagram.

Cut out the collar in material after the pattern has been made, fitted and adjusted where necessary. Make it up in the same way as for a flat collar.

Any trimming should be applied to the top pieces of the collar before joining the two sides together.

Sew the collar to the neck in the way described for a flat collar.

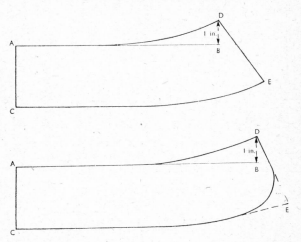

The straight collar pattern with a variation of corners.

A roll collar can be made long or short to suit the style.

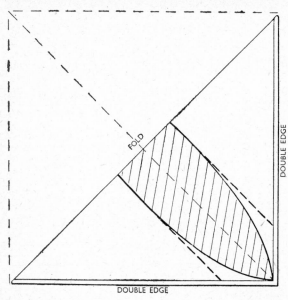

FOLD

DOUBLE EDGE

DOUBLE EDGE

The roll collar pattern cut from a square folded diagonally.

Roll Collar.—This should be cut on the bias of the material and made double.

Cut the pattern from a square of paper. The diagonal of this square is the outside length of the finished collar. Fold the paper diagonally both ways, making a cross in the centre. Fold the paper along one crease and draw the collar pattern each side of the right-angular crease.

Measure the depth of the collar, about four inches, along the fold. These two points are joined to the opposite corner of the square to form the neck edge of the pattern. Make a good shape and a gradual curve.

To make a collar with pointed ends, as shown in the illustration, draw straight lines each side of and parallel with the crease at right angles to the diagonal fold. Follow the dotted lines on Diagram. Fold a square of material in the same way as the paper. Place the pattern to the fold, in the centre, and cut round the edges.

Match the centre back of neck to the centre of collar, and fix one collar edge evenly into the neck, right sides facing. Sew the two together, trim off the turnings, press the seams. Turn under the edges of the second side of the collar and sew the fold neatly to the turnings.

Step Collar.—Draw a rectangle, A, B, C and D. The length should be half the length of full neck measurement by the depth of the collar, about three inches. Two squares equal one inch on Diagram.

Measure two-thirds of the line A—B along this line and make a point E. Measure quarter of an inch along B—D and from this point mark F, quarter of an inch inside the line. Then make H along this line half an inch from D. G is halfway between C and D. Join G to H and E to F with a gradual curve. Rule a line between F and H.

This type of collar is, as a rule, made in double material. The top piece is cut with the centre back placed to the fold on the grain of fabric. The underside has the centre back placed on the bias, the two sides will have to be cut separately and joined in the centre back. Allow turnings on line A—C. Press this seam.

Place the neck edge of the under collar C—H, to the neck of the garment, right sides together, matching the centre backs. Arrange the collar into the neck so that the two ends reach the centre front line on each side, after the seam has been made. Press the seam.

Sew the facings to the front, right sides facing. Trim off the turnings close to the sewing. Turn right sides out and press. The loose part of the facing is lightly sewn to the turnings of the collar seam. Now sew the top sides of the collar with right side to the underside, making a seam along the outer edge and at the two ends. Trim the

A step collar showing how it is joined to the revers.

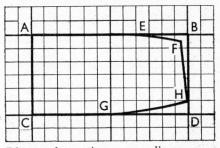

Diagram for cutting a step collar pattern.

turnings close and turn right sides out. Pull out the seam and the corners, tack the edges and press. The neck edge is turned under and hemmed to the back neck, and slip stitched to the facings.

The edges of the collar and facing may be finished with a line of machine stitching close to the seam.

If the collar is made in single material bind the edges with matching or contrasting bias-cut binding, see page 207.

233

Sleeves need as much care in the making, setting into the armhole and fitting as the whole of the garment. There are a few points which apply to all sleeves, whatever the style. The straight grain of the fabric must hang in a straight line from the shoulder, down the centre of the sleeve.

Any extra fulness at the armhole should be arranged at the top of the sleeve rather than underneath.

Darts at Head of Sleeve.—For the pattern of a darted sleeve cut an extra two inches on to the top of the armhole curve. These darts give a built-up squared shoulder effect. If a more built-up shoulder is desired then extra length can be added to the armhole curve.

Take up the extra material into the darts to make the sleeve fit the armhole. The dart itself tapers off to nothing at the normal armhole line.

Seam-to-Seam Sleeve.—This type of sleeve is used generally for an elbow length style. It will hang better if made with a built-up shoulder line and to fit the arm at the lower edge which is finished with a facing or binding.

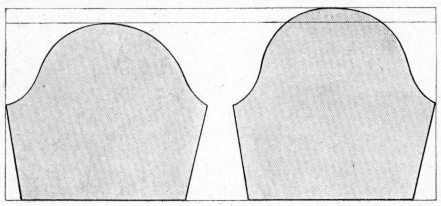

To make a sleeve with darts at the head, giving a built-up shoulder line, the sleeve pattern is re-drawn with additional length, according to the size of the darts.

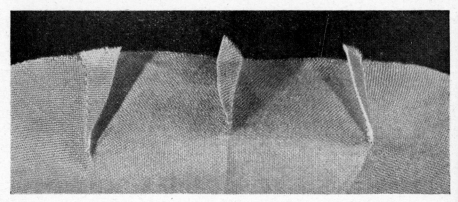

The darts in the head of the sleeve are tapered off to nothing at the normal sleeve line. Extra material is added in this same way when the sleeve top is to be gathered or pleated.

This pattern can be used for a long or three-quarter sleeve, but extra length must be allowed on the back edge of the sleeve seam which is taken up at the elbow in gathers or darts, as shown on page 138, to give elbow room.

When inserting the sleeve into the armhole the seam is matched to the side seam.

Tight-fitting Sleeve.—This is a one-piece sleeve with a second seam from the elbow to the wrist, as described on page 83.

This sleeve may be made with a built-up shoulder, with pleats, darts or gathers, or quite plain without extra fulness of any kind.

When inserting the sleeve into the armhole the seam is placed towards the front of the side seam at a point which is found in the way shown on page 84.

The wrist edge of this sleeve may be finished with—a straight edge, neatened with facing or binding, a narrow cuff or cut in a curve or point. In the latter case the point should lie in a straight line with the centre of the sleeve.

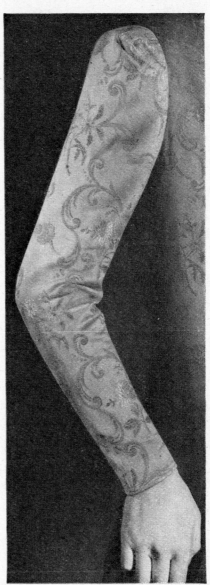

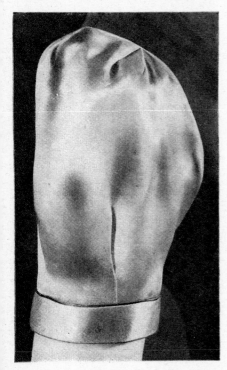

A short sleeve with darts at the shoulders and pleats at the cuff, finished with piped facing. Tight-fitting, long sleeve with darts at the shoulder and a half seam from elbow to cuff edge.

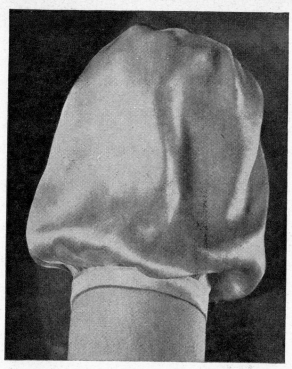

in the normal way, matching sleeve seam to side seam.

If the puff sleeve is not lined, as is sometimes the case in garments which have to be laundered, the binding round the lower edge must be made to fit the arm exactly. If it is made as tight as this it will keep the sleeve in a correct puff.

Elbow Sleeve.—Can be made from the seam-to-seam pattern or by using the one-piece sleeve pattern.

The shoulder can be plain, darted, gathered or pleated, but the sleeve hangs in a straight line from the shoulder.

The lower edge can be finished with a cuff, facing or binding. The finished edge should reach to just

A short puff sleeve gathered at the shoulder and cuff. The bottom of the sleeve is bound with bias binding. The length reaches to halfway between shoulder and elbow.

Puff Sleeve.—For this type of sleeve use the seam-to-seam pattern described on page 84. The sleeve should be lined to prevent it falling down the arm.

The lining is cut to the exact size of the sleeve pattern. The sleeve itself is cut with extra length at the top armhole edge, as for a darted shoulder, page 234, and with more width round the lower edge. The latter is obtained by slitting the pattern in the centre and opening it out into a dart. Allow an extra inch on the length for the fall over of the puff. The extra fulness is taken up into gathers.

To make: sew the seams of sleeve and lining, gather the lower edge and the armhole edge to fit the lining and sew the two together. Bind the sleeve edge and insert the sleeve into the armhole

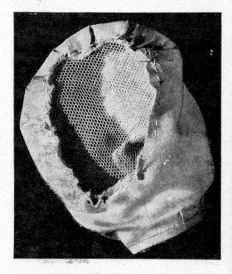

A puff sleeve is lined with a tight lining to prevent the sleeve falling down the arm.

236

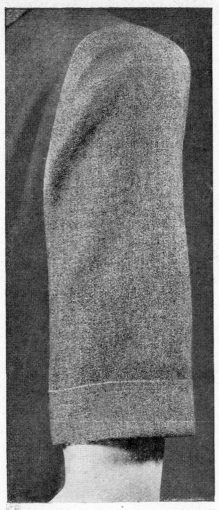

An elbow-length sleeve with straight cuff.

above the crook of the arm to prevent creasing.

Two-Piece Sleeve.—A plain tailored sleeve made from the pattern on page 72. It is set into the armhole with the seam to the front of the side seam as explained on page 83. The shoulder may be built up and widened with darts as described on page 234, but the sleeve must always hang straight from the shoulder. Finish with a tailored cuff, as shown on page 242.

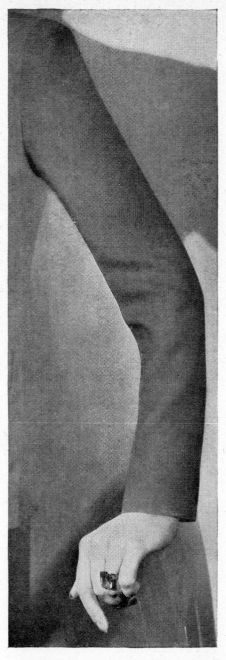

A two-piece coat sleeve with built-up shoulder and plain cuff. This sleeve is tailored in design and suitable for coats. Note the straight hang from the shoulder.

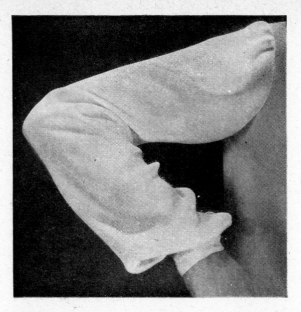

The bishop sleeve is cut with plenty of fulness at the cuff and with additional length so that the sleeve falls over the hand. The shoulder extension is gathered into the armhole.

straight lines. Trace these two lines, the neck line, the armhole edges and the two sleeve seams on to the paper and cut along the traced line to make the sleeve pattern.

It will be necessary, to get room for movement at the shoulder, to insert a gusset into the underarm at sleeve and side seam join. Make the gusset three inches square. Alternatively the join must be curved as for a magyar sleeve, see Diagram page 240.

To get a built-up shoulder effect allow more width at the neck edge by dividing the blocks at the shoulder seam. This ful-

Bishop Sleeve.—The one-piece sleeve pattern or the seam-to-seam sleeve is used for this style, as explained on page 73. The sleeve is cut with added fulness at the cuff which is gathered into a straight band fitting the wrist. It is permissible to allow extra material at the top of the sleeve which is gathered into the armhole seam. If a very full sleeve is wanted, then cut one or two inches extra on the length.

Raglan Sleeve.—The pattern of this sleeve is cut with the aid of the bodice blocks, and the seam to seam sleeve.

Place the shoulder seams of the front and back bodice blocks together and then place the sleeve pattern in position over the armhole, see page 240, pin to a spare sheet of paper. Then measuring from the shoulder line mark A at one-sixth of front neck size and B at one-third of back neck size. Join A to the front armhole edge and B to the back armhole edge with

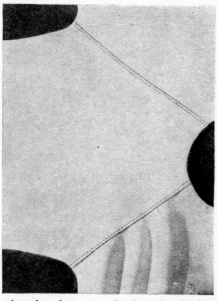

A raglan sleeve extends along the shoulder to the neck, the armhole curve and seam being omitted. Note the gathers in the front bodice to give fulness over the bust

238

ness is taken up in a dart on the shoulder line and padding is inserted, see sleeve pattern, page 240.

The bodice patterns are cut from the part of the pattern left from cutting the sleeve.

When this sleeve is used for a larger figure the extra fulness over the bust must be introduced. An extra one and a half inches is cut on to the front bodice at the side seam. The bodice is then gathered and fitted into the sleeve.

Magyar Sleeve.—Is similar in style and appearance to a raglan but simpler to cut.

The front bodice block is used to make this pattern, see page 240. Place the front line to a straight edge. Draw a line at right angles to this from the top point of the shoulder. This should be the length of the sleeve plus the width of the shoulder. Measure the width of the sleeve. Mark quarter width of bodice at the bottom of centre line, join the sleeve to bodice with a curve for the underarm. Mark the neck the size and shape desired. Try to avoid having a seam at the shoulder, which is ugly.

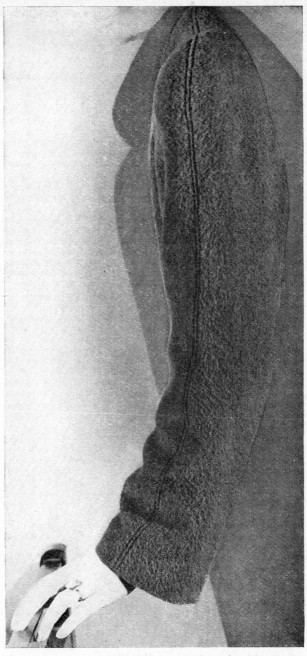

This raglan sleeve, which is for a coat, is made with a centre seam shaped to give a built-up shoulder, which is padded. This seam can be omitted and the sleeve made plain. See the diagram of the raglan sleeve pattern.

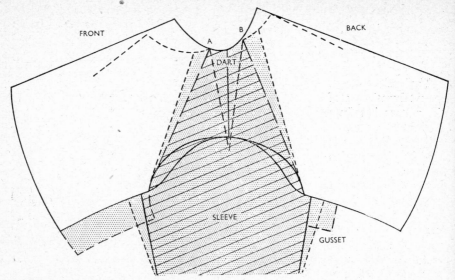

FRONT   A   B   BACK

DART

SLEEVE

GUSSET

Bodice blocks combined with seam-to-seam sleeve for raglan sleeve pattern. Dotted lines indicate darted sleeve, dashed lines sleeve without dart. Note the gusset in armhole.

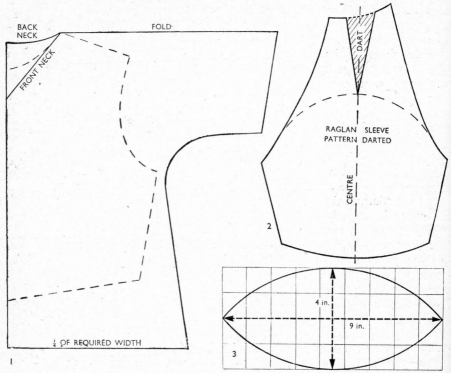

BACK NECK   FOLD

FRONT NECK

RAGLAN SLEEVE
PATTERN DARTED

DART

CENTRE

2

¼ OF REQUIRED WIDTH

1

4 in.

9 in.

3

(1) A magyar sleeve pattern cut from the front bodice block pattern. (2) The raglan sleeve pattern with a dart. (3) The pattern for shoulder padding made in cotton wool.

SHOULDERS

The padding used in sleeves and shoulders should be carefully chosen to suit the type of garment being made. A thick bulky padding made of wadding is not suitable for garments that have to be laundered, and flimsy stiffening will not suit heavy materials.

Muslin Stiffening.—For filmy blouses and tub frocks. Cut a piece of double organdie or stiff muslin to the shape of the sleeve top, when darts and gathers have been made, and four inches wide when doubled. Insert this into the armhole at the same time as the sleeve so that it lies under the darts or gathers and holds them out.

Woven Stiffening.—This is made of whalebone and is bought by the yard. It is sewn to the sleeve seam after the sleeve has been inserted into the armhole. Use it with light-weight fabrics that do not need laundering.

Thin Padding.—Is stronger than a muslin padding, but not so bulky as a wadding padding. It will launder well.

Cut an oval-shaped piece of garment fabric, nine inches by four inches, pointed at both ends, as shown in the Diagram on page 240. Cut a stiff muslin shape the same but quarter of an inch smaller all round. Lay this in the centre of the garment piece and turn over the quarter-inch turnings and tack them down. Sew the two together with crossed lines of machining, about one inch apart. Fold the shape into two lengthwise and sew to the sleeve seam.

Wool Padding.—Is a thick padding and will give a squared shoulder effect.

Cut a triangular shape in lining material, with each side four inches long, plus turnings. Turn under the edges of two sides and sew them together. Pad the shape evenly with wadding. Turn under and sew the edges at the base of the triangle.

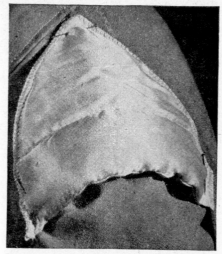

The padding extends to the ends of the sleeve darts. The apex is sewn to shoulder seam and the corners of the base to armhole.

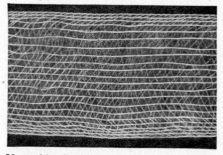

Very thin shoulder stiffening made of fine whalebone. It can be bought by the yard.

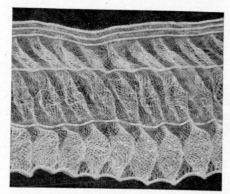

Shoulder stiffening made of fine whalebone and elastic for use with thin materials.

The material for a tailored cuff on a coat sleeve is cut on to the sleeve. The back seam is left unstitched for the depth of the cuff plus turnings, and hemmed.

The cuff hem is turned on to the wrong side of the sleeve and lightly caught to the garment. The wrong side is neatened with a lining, which is hemmed to the cuff.

The slit of the cuff on the right side is a continuation of the sleeve seam. This can be finished with three or four buttons, sewn through all thicknesses to close the opening.

CUFFS

All sleeves need a finish of one kind or another and there is nothing nicer than a plain tailored cuff. The type of finish used depends on the style of the sleeve.

Coat Cuff.—Is not a cuff in the form of a turn up as one generally imagines a cuff to be. It is, however, the most usual way to finish a two-piece sleeve especially when a tailored finish is desired.

When cutting the sleeve add an extra inch to the back seam both on the upper sleeve and the under sleeve. This should extend for about five inches from the cuff edge, before the turnings have been made. Stitch this seam as far as the wider portion and the second seam for the full length. At the end of the back seam snip the turnings of the under sleeve almost to the seam join and let the cuff turnings lie flat under the upper sleeve. Make a narrow turning on this edge and tack it. Tack the extension on the upper sleeve, making the fold a continuation of the seam.

Turn up the cuff to the required depth and catch stitch, see page 155, the turnings thus made to the garment, making sure the stitches do not show on the right side.

The lining is cut in the same way as the sleeve, leaving the cuff edge of the back seam unstitched to correspond with the sleeve. The edges are turned under and hemmed lightly to the turnings to neaten the raw edges. The edge of the lining should reach to within half or one inch of the wrist line.

Neatly slip stitch the folds at the edges of the opening to form the wrap over and fasten the two together with three or four buttons.

Hand-worked buttonholes may be made in the wrap over if desired, see page 200, with buttons sewn to match.

Straight Cuff.—For a shirt blouse or bishop sleeve. This style of cuff should be made to fit the wrist fairly tightly, in a double thickness of material.

A lapped opening made into the sleeve end, page 182, or a sleeve opening, page 186, is needed.

Cut a straight piece of material the width of the cuff, plus one inch for turnings, and the length round the wrist plus sufficient for turnings and wrap over, about two inches. Fold the cuff piece in half lengthways, right side inside, and stitch along the ends. Turn the cuff right side out and pull the corners out carefully with a pin. Press the seams and the crease of the fold.

Gather the edge of the sleeve and arrange the gathers evenly. Place one edge of the cuff to the gathered edge, right sides together. Pin the two very carefully, keeping the gathers evenly spaced. Tack along the pin line and then finally sew with machining or back stitch. Hem the second folded edge to turnings on the wrong side of the sleeve.

Fasten the cuff with press fasteners or buttons and buttonholes.

Pointed Cuff.—For the edge of an elbow length sleeve. The point of the cuff is placed in the centre

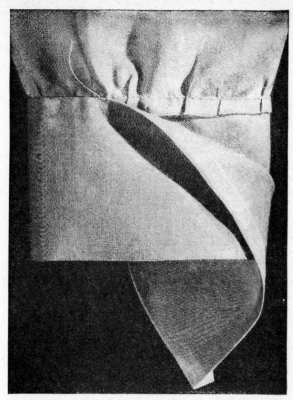

A straight cuff is sewn first on the sleeve right side, then folded in half and hemmed to the turnings.

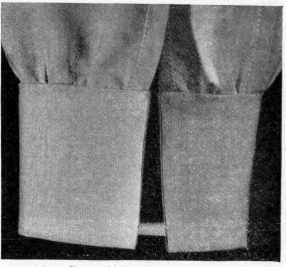

A small seam finishes both ends of the cuff.

243

of the sleeve on a line straight from the middle of the shoulder.

To make the pattern cut a triangle with the distance between the apex and the base the required height of the cuff at the point.

The triangle base is extended each side to the width of the sleeve. The sides are half the depth of the point.

Make the cuff double, sewing the top edges together. Finish the cuff edge with binding as for a loose collar, page 207, or hem the turned under edges inside the sleeve hem. Trim with lace or other decoration.

Turned-back Cuff.—Is made and attached in the same way as a straight cuff, but it is cut double the width to allow for the turn back. The turn-back edge may be cut straight or pointed.

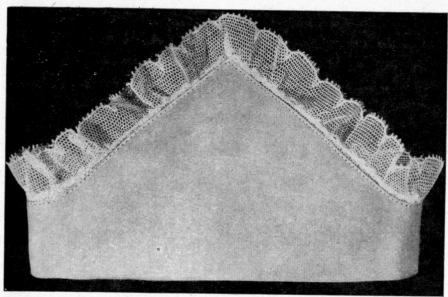

A pointed cuff for a short sleeve, made double and trimmed with gathered lace edging.

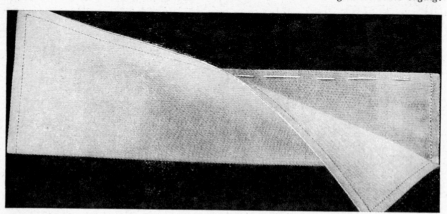

A turn-back cuff for blouse or shirt sleeve. The cuff is cut twice the width it is to be when finished. Make the cuff and finish the edge with machining before sewing to sleeve.

LININGS

It is always advisable to line coats and jackets as they will hang better and wear longer. There is no more work involved as, with a lined garment, it is not necessary to neaten the seams. Unless the material used is very loosely woven then the raw edges can be lightly oversewn to prevent fraying. A lining helps a coat to slip on more easily and prevents it from clinging to the dress underneath, causing uncomfortable dragging and pulling.

The garment pattern can be used for cutting the lining, omitting any extra turnings or other form of decoration which has been allowed for. Allow extra material down the centre back of the lining to give an easy fit and prevent pulling. This extra is formed into a small pleat in the centre back at the neck. Omit the section where there is facing.

Tack up the lining seams and all the darts and fit it in the same way as fitting the garment itself. The lining should always be on the loose side, never tight. Then sew the seams lightly and insert it into the coat, after pressing.

Match the seams of the lining to the seams of the garment. Tack the lining shoulder seam to the garment shoulder seam and tack the armhole turnings

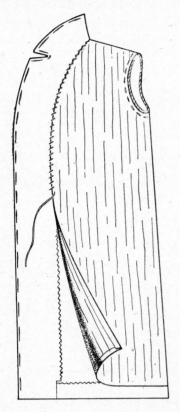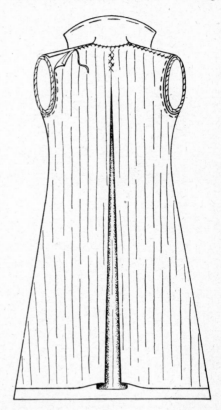

Linings should fit easily in the garment. The front edges are hemmed to the facings and there is a small pleat down the centre back of the lining to give play and prevent pulling.

together, making quite sure that the lining is not too tight. Make the pleat in the centre back at the neck and slip stitch it for about two inches. Turn under the neck edge and the edges of the two fronts and tack them. When the lining is fitted into the garment in this way it is a good plan to turn it inside out and fit to the figure, checking up every detail, see page 149.

Then sew the lining into place. Hem along the neck and front edges. The bottom edge of a short coat is turned under and slip stitched to the garment hem. In a long coat a normal hem is made and lightly sewn. This should be shorter than the coat itself, but long enough to cover the top edge of the coat hem.

Half linings in long coats should be hemmed and left free and the seams showing below the lining should be neatened with binding, see page 206.

Sleeves.—Sew the seams of the sleeve lining, which has been cut from the same pattern as the garment. Press the seams.

Turn the sleeve inside out and slip the lining over it, with the right side outside. Turn under the cuff edge and slip stitch it to the sleeve cuff, about one inch above the wrist line. Turn under the armhole edge and hem it firmly to the coat lining, making sure that the hang of the sleeve is correct. It is a good plan to turn the coat inside out and slip it on the figure when fixing the armhole of the sleeve lining; this will prevent it from becoming twisted.

Interlinings.—An asset to a garment as they provide extra warmth and give additional weight to light materials. With this addition the finished garment will set and hang better.

Soft flannel should be used for the interlining which is cut from the garment pattern. Unlike the main lining, which is loose, it should fit the coat

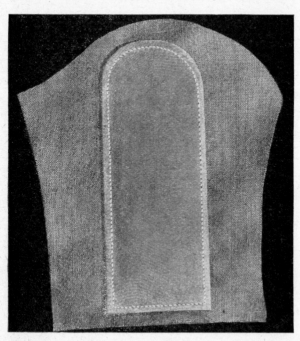

A sleeve interlining is sewn to the lining material, down the centre of the sleeve. The lining itself is sewn to the turnings at the cuff edge and to the coat lining armhole.

exactly. Omit the part where the facings occur.

Place the garment, before inserting the sleeves, on to the figure or dress form, wrong side outside. Slip the lining, right side out, over it. Lap the back over the front at the seams, trimming the single turnings down as narrow as possible to avoid bulk. Tack the seams. Trim away any surplus at the armhole and neck edges and tack the lining to the garment. Then fasten the lining to the facings with tacking stitches.

Remove the garment from the figure and herringbone stitch the front edges and neck to the facings and sew the overlapped seams with herringbone. Leave the bottom edge free. Then insert the lining.

Sleeve interlining.—It is advisable to line the top part of the sleeve only, otherwise it may become bulky and interfere with the hang. Cut a rectangular piece of flannel as long as the sleeve, without turnings, and half the width. Round off the corners of the end which is to be placed to the head of the sleeve. Mark the centre of the lining lengthways with a tacked line and place this line along the centre of the sleeve lining, on the wrong side, from the shoulder to the wrist. Keep the ends of the interlining well inside the fitting line on the lining. Sew the flannel strip to the lining and then make up and insert the sleeve into the garment as previously described.

Interlinings should be made as flat as possible and without any bulk, or the whole appearance of the finished garment will be ruined.

Linings should be of shiny material and loosely fitting so the coat will slip on easily and not pull in any way when worn.

The interlining should be made to fit the coat exactly.
The fronts are herringboned and the seams made flat.

This attractive shirt-waister frock is smart for all occasions. The pleated skirt gives a slimming line with ample room for walking, and the bodice flatters the larger figure.

MAKING UP

ORIGINAL GARMENTS

All the detailed steps in the making of a garment—designing, cutting, fitting, sewing and finishing—have been described in the foregoing chapters.

In this section of the book these details are massed together into the making of finished garments. Simple designs, which the most inexperienced beginner cannot fail to make into something that is smart and wearable, have been carefully chosen.

SHIRT-STYLE DRESS

With Pleated Bodice and Skirt

There should be a simple classic dress in every woman's wardrobe, and this one, if made in firm, lightweight woollen material, is a good standby. The flattering yoke and fulness of the pleated bodice and the slimming lines of the skirt are kind to the fuller figure, as well as flattering to the young and slim. The skirt is panelled and slightly flared at the back, and this, in addition to the well-designed pleated panel on the front, gives an attractive swing and allows for freedom of movement.

The four-button front opening and the straight-cut sleeve are easy and comfortable to wear.

An unpatterned material in a neutral shade is the best choice, a smart colour note can then be introduced in the buttons and belt, and a contrasting loose collar with matching cuffs may be added for more gaiety and variation.

This pattern is so designed that the bodice can be adapted to make an attractive blouse; extra length will be needed at the waist. If the skirt is made with a petersham it can be worn separately.

The back bodice is gathered slightly to give comfort and ease of movement. The panelled skirt has a slight flare.

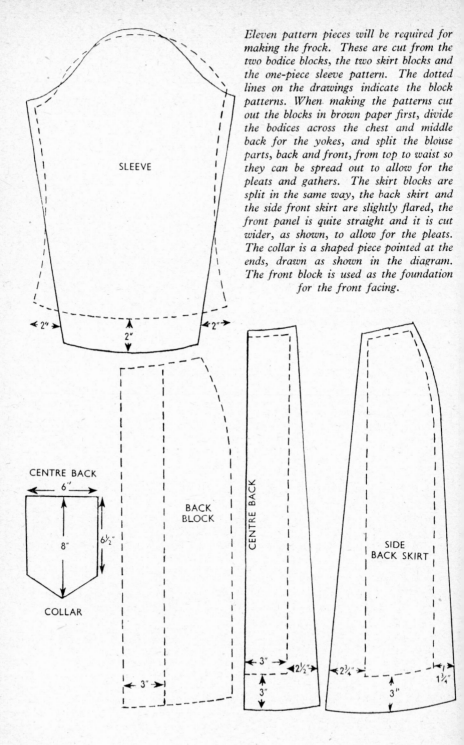

SLEEVE

← 2" →   ↕ 2"   ← 2" →

CENTRE BACK
← 6" →

COLLAR

8"   6½"

BACK
BLOCK

CENTRE BACK

SIDE
BACK SKIRT

← 3" →

← 3" →   ← 2½" →   ← 2¾" →   1¾"

↕ 3"   ↕ 3"

Eleven pattern pieces will be required for making the frock. These are cut from the two bodice blocks, the two skirt blocks and the one-piece sleeve pattern. The dotted lines on the drawings indicate the block patterns. When making the patterns cut out the blocks in brown paper first, divide the bodices across the chest and middle back for the yokes, and split the blouse parts, back and front, from top to waist so they can be spread out to allow for the pleats and gathers. The skirt blocks are split in the same way, the back skirt and the side front skirt are slightly flared, the front panel is quite straight and it is cut wider, as shown, to allow for the pleats. The collar is a shaped piece pointed at the ends, drawn as shown in the diagram. The front block is used as the foundation for the front facing.

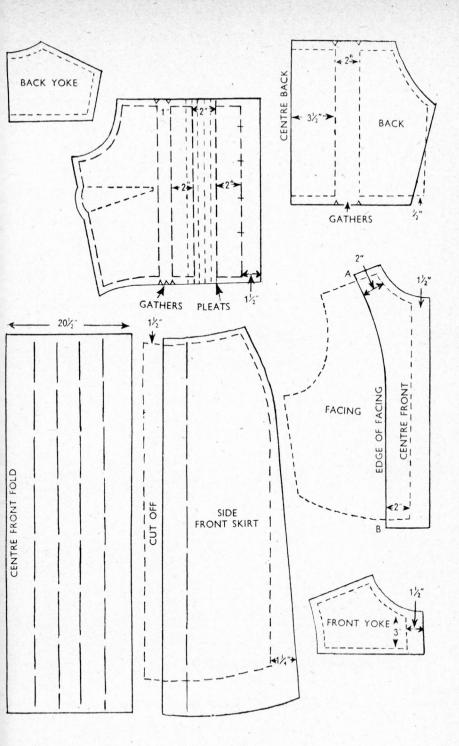

BACK YOKE

CENTRE BACK

BACK

2"

3½"

GATHERS

½"

1"

2"

2"

2"

GATHERS   PLEATS   1½"

A   2"   1½"

FACING

EDGE OF FACING

CENTRE FRONT

2"

B

20½"   1½"

CENTRE FRONT FOLD

CUT OFF

SIDE
FRONT SKIRT

1¾"

FRONT YOKE   1½"

3"

The Skirt.—The pattern for the centre front panel is a straight piece, the half pattern measures twenty and a half inches across and is the length required. Mark the folds of the pleats as indicated by the dotted lines; the under section of the two outer pleats are cut on to the side front of the skirt.

Side Front: make a pattern of the front block, page 70, and cut off a strip from the centre front one and a half inches wide. Re-draw the side seam, add half an inch for turnings on the hip and one and three-quarter inches at the hem. Re-draw the waist curve, adding half an inch for turnings, and add three inches to the length for the hem-turning. Mark the position of the fold edge of the outer pleat.

The Back: cut a back block pattern, page 70, and draw a line three inches away from and parallel to the centre back. Divide the pattern in two along this line. Place the centre back piece on a sheet of paper with the centre back to the edge of the paper, re-draw the other edge, adding half an inch for turnings at the waist and two and a half inches to the width at the hem, add half an inch to the waist line for turnings and three inches to the length for the hem.

Side Back: place the side back pattern on a separate sheet of paper, widen the

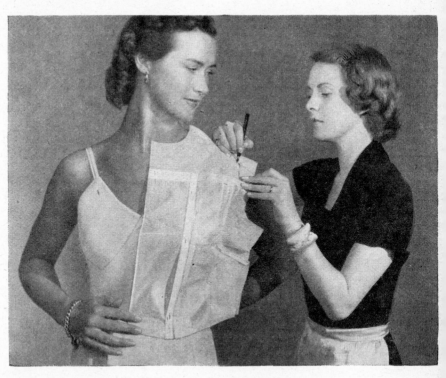

The blouse part of the bodice pattern is pleated and eased, where the gathers occur, into the yoke. Here you see the shoulder, which is too wide, being marked to the correct width. Note how the centre front is correctly placed, this is most essential.

hem one and three-quarter inches at the side seam edge and two and three-quarter inches at the other edge, re-draw both these seams, allowing half an inch at the waist for turnings. Re-draw the waist, adding half an inch for turnings, and add three inches to the length for the hem, as Diagram.

The Bodice.—This is cut with a yoke back and front, there are double pleats and slight gathers at either side of the front and gathers make the fulness in the back.

The Front: Yoke: cut a front bodice using the block pattern with a side-seam dart, number 5 on page 77. Measure three inches down from the centre front neck and cut straight across the block, dividing the pattern into the yoke and blouse portion. Place the yoke pattern on a piece of paper and re-cut, adding half an inch for turnings at neck, shoulder and armhole, and one and a half inches at the centre front for the wrap.

Blouse Part of Front: take the lower part of the block pattern and divide it twice down the length, one cut is made two inches in from the centre front and another is made two inches away from the first cut.

Lay these pieces on another sheet

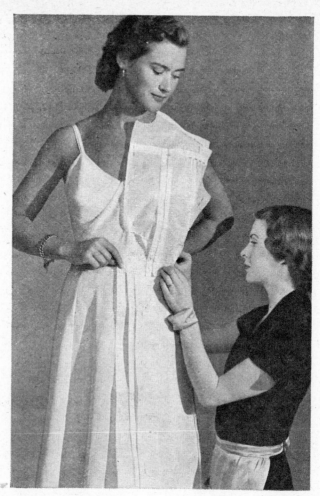

When the bodice has been fitted correctly the skirt is pinned to it and the alterations required are marked in the same way.

of paper, leaving two inches between the first cut for the knife pleats, and one inch at the second cut for the gathers.

Add half an inch to the top, waist, armhole and side seam for turnings, and add one and a half inches to the centre front for the wrap. Mark the position of the side dart, the pleats, the gathers and the buttonholes, and put in fitting notches at the seams and straight grain indicators.

The Front Facing: place the front block pattern on a piece of paper, add one and a half inches to the centre front for the wrap-over, half an inch to the neck and along two inches of the shoulder line to A, and half an inch at the waist along two inches of the lower edge to B.

Join A to B with a good curve and cut out the pattern.

The Back: Yoke: cut a back block, as the one on page 69, cut straight across for the yoke four and a half inches below the back neck, re-draw this yoke pattern with half-inch turnings at the shoulder, neck, armhole and lower edge. *Blouse Part of Back:* divide the lower part of the block in two lengthways,

three and a half inches from the centre back. Lay the pieces on paper, adding two inches at the cut for the gathers, and re-draw the side seam, taking it in half an inch at the waist and adding half an inch at the armhole end for turnings. Add half an inch to the top, lower edge and armhole for turnings. Mark the position of the gathers, and put in fitting notches at the seams to correspond with the front.

The Collar: a straight piece is used for the collar with the ends shaped in a point. The half collar is eight inches long (into the point) with the sides six and a half inches long. It is six inches wide, see Diagram.

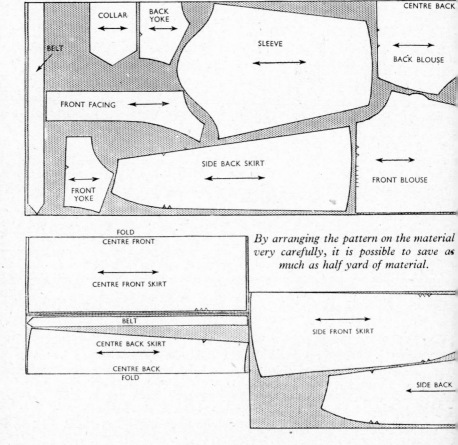

By arranging the pattern on the material very carefully, it is possible to save as much as half yard of material.

The Sleeve: this is based on the seam-to-seam sleeve, as described on page 84, but the head of the sleeve is re-drawn to an even shape both sides, and the wrist is made narrower by two inches each side, as in the Diagram. The seams are straight. Add two inches to the length for the cuff hem.

The Belt: cut a strip two and a half inches wide and long enough to go round the waist, plus turnings and wrap-over, as described on page 226.

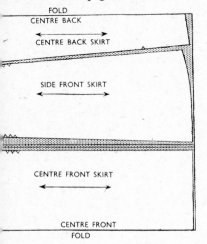

FITTING, CUTTING and MAKING

You will now have eleven pieces in the pattern, the centre front and side front skirt, centre back and side-back skirt, the front yokes and the front bodice blouse, the back yoke and the back bodice blouse, the front facing, the sleeve and the collar.

Cut out the patterns carefully and pin them together, taking up the correct turnings. Make the pleats on the bodice blouse and ease the gathered part into the yoke, matching the notches. Fit the bodice on to the figure without inserting the sleeves and make any alterations necessary. Arrange the pleats on the skirt, then pin this to the bodice and fit it in the same way. Finally, fit the sleeve pattern, separately.

Unpin the patterns and correct to the adjustments made, if necessary recut the pattern. Check the fitting notches, the straight grain lines, the folds of the pleats, the position of the gathers.

These diagrams show in two ways how the patterns can be laid out on the fabric, above on fifty-four-inch-wide material, below on thirty-six-inch-wide material. It may even be necessary to cut some of the patterns in single material, in which case second paper patterns should be made. At all times, when laying out patterns on the fabric, care should be taken to place the "fold" edges to the material folds, and the straight-grain line of the patterns must be placed on the grain of the fabric, as shown by the arrows in the diagrams. The right and wrong "way" of the material, if any, has to be noted, too.

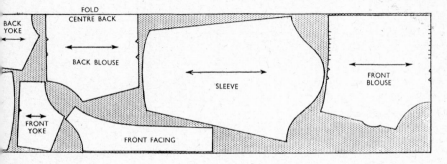

Cutting.—Lay the pattern on the material as economically as possible. The Diagrams show two different layouts, one on fifty-four-inch material and one on thirty-six-inch-wide material. The skirt back, blouse back, back yoke and collar should all be placed to a fold of the material. Cut the sleeve, front waist and front yoke on double material if possible; in any case, make sure that you have one sleeve, one front and one yoke for the right, and one of each for the left of the garment. It is sometimes more economical to re-fold the material for part of the pattern, as the Diagrams show. Mark the position of the pleats, darts, buttons and buttonholes, gathers and notches with tailor's tacks.

Making.—*The Bodice:* (1) Make and tack the pleats on each blouse front. Tack the dart at the side seam. Insert gathering threads to take up the fulness at yoke and waist edges on both front and back bodice, then fit the blouse parts into the yokes. Tack the shoulder and side seams.

(2) Fit the bodice on and make any adjustments necessary. Check the position of the buttons and buttonholes.

(3) Untack the yoke from the blouse and the side seams. Stitch the pleats along the under fold and press them away from the opening.

(4) Tack the bodice to the yoke again and stitch this seam, press the turnings up towards the yoke. Stitch the under-arm darts, slit them open and press. Stitch shoulder seams. Join the side seams, leaving five inches for the opening on the left side. Press. If bound buttonholes are to be used make them now, as described on page 202, and press them.

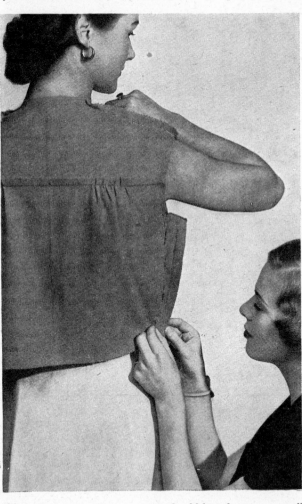

When fitting the side seams care should be taken not to pull the garment too tightly. There should be enough room to allow for ease of movement, without pulling across the back.

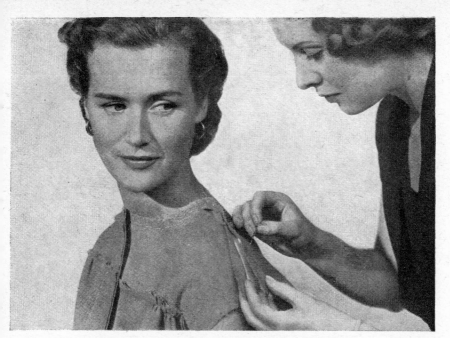

The shoulders need very careful fitting. If the first tacking is incorrect, whip it out and refit. The shoulder line should be slightly to the back rather than the front.

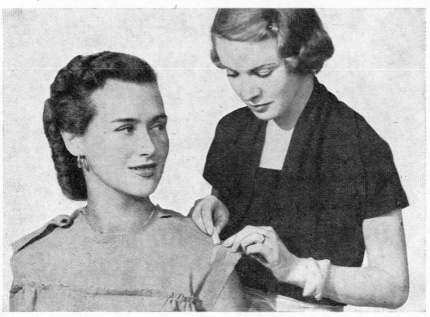

When the shoulder and the bodice are correctly fitted the sleeve line is marked at the armholes with tailor's chalk. This should be just over the bone of the shoulder.

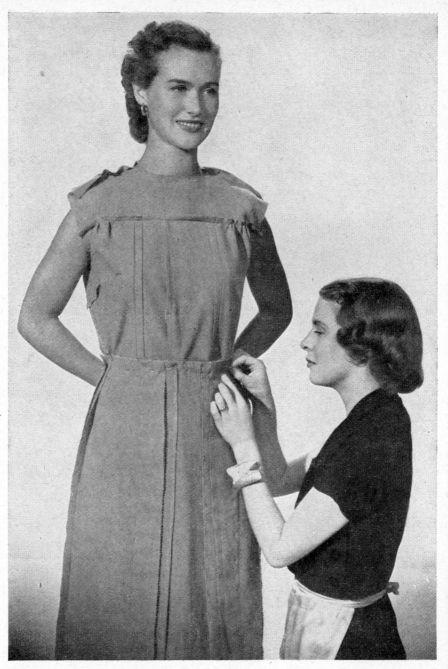

When the bodice has been fitted correctly the skirt is joined to it, with the pleats made and tacked, and the bodice gathered correctly. The seams of the skirt are then adjusted to give a comfortable fit. The hang of the skirt should be checked at the same time.

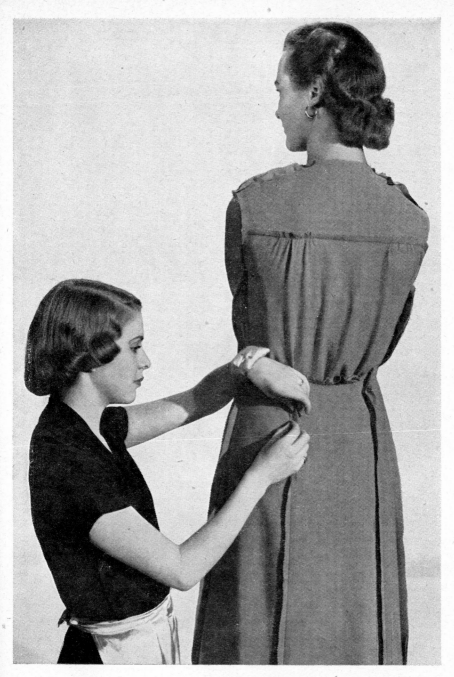

The waist seam is fitted at this stage, too. It is sometimes necessary to make a small dart, from the waist downwards, at each side of the front. This is done when all the fulness cannot be taken into the side seams. The position of the waist should be checked.

All seams are stitched neatly and firmly without puckering.

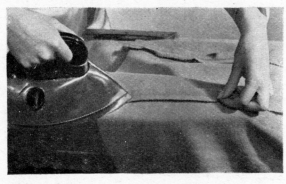

The iron should be in use constantly throughout the making of the garment and all seams should be pressed well.

(5) Stitch the facings to the fronts, right sides together, and continue the seam along the neck edge to make the rever. Finish the loose edges of the facing with a small hem sewn with running.

The Skirt: (6) Seam the centre front piece to the side front. Press the seams flat towards the centre.

(7) Make the two knife pleats on each side of the front, thus forming a box-pleat panel down the centre, then tack the pleats well.

(8) Tack the centre back to the two side back pieces, then join the back to the front, tacking the side seams and leaving an opening of six inches at the left side of the waist for the placket.

Tack the bodice on to the skirt.

(9) Try on the bodice and skirt and make any alterations that may be necessary.

(10) Unpick the skirt from the bodice and stitch the pleats for thirteen inches down from the waist, sewing half an inch away from the fold, press them well.

Sew the seams and press them open.

(11) Join the skirt to the bodice, matching centres and side seams, adjust the gathers on both sides of the back and front bodice to fit the waist, then stitch.

Press the seam, complete the side opening, mak'ng it in the way explained on page 178.

The Sleeves: (12) Pin up and tack the seams, then fit the sleeve on the arm, making sure that it fits the armhole.

Stitch the seams and press them open.

(13) Fix the sleeves into the armholes with the seams to the side seams of the bodice and make sure the top point of the armhole curve is at the centre of the shoulder, so that the sleeve hangs quite straight with the grain down the centre. Any slight fulness round the top of the shoulder can be shrunk away afterwards by means of a hot iron and a damp cloth.

Stitch the sleeve into the armhole and press the seam well.

(14) Fit the frock on again and turn up the sleeve to the correct length at the wrist line, leaving it long enough to allow for the elbow bend. Finish the cuff with a braid hem.

The Collar: (15) Stitch the ends of the collar, making sure that it is the correct length for the neck, then press the seams and attach it to the neck and revers, as explained on page 233.

Neaten the bound buttonholes with the facing, turning in the edges of the

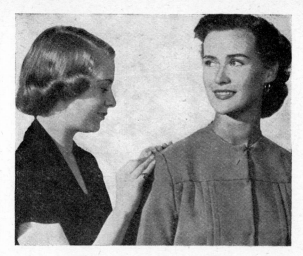

The sleeve is fitted into the armhole with the garment on the figure and the shoulder pads in place.

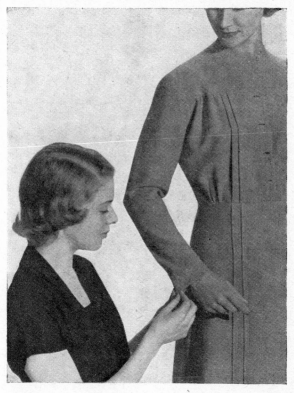

When the sleeve has been stitched in correctly, the cuff is turned up to a suitable length, just below the wrist bone.

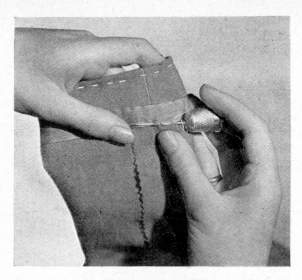

The cuff edge is neatened with a braided hem; this should be sewn with very neat slip stitches on to the sleeve.

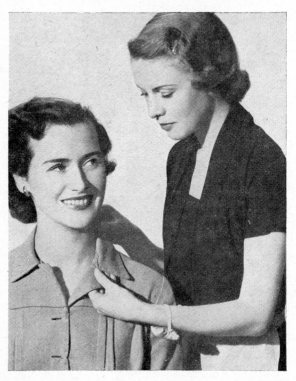

When fitting the collar into the neck is the time to make sure that the corner, where it joins the lapel, is neat and flat.

slit, and hemming them down neatly.

(16) If you prefer to have worked buttonholes these should be made now; to get the spacing and position correct, lay the frock flat on the table, measure the distance between the buttonholes and insert pins at the correct points.

(17) Using the hem guide or a yard stick, chalk the edge of the hem at the correct length. Turn the hem under along these marks and pin at regular intervals, then check carefully to see that the hem is even all the way round.

(18) Lay the dress on the table and tack the hem, if necessary making small darts to dispose of extra fulness; these darts should be pressed carefully before the hem is stitched, for this method see page 175.

The seams at each side of the front, which are on the underfold of the pleats, should be snicked just above the hem, and pressed open before the hem is made, as shown on page 214.

Finish the hem with braid and slip stitching, then press well using a damp cloth.

(19) Slip the frock on and wrap over the front correctly. Mark the edge of the wrap-over, insert two pins, at right-angles to each other, in each button-

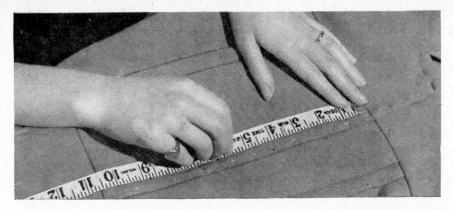

When marking the position of the buttonholes, the dress is laid flat on the table, with the fronts correct. The position of the buttonholes is measured and a pin is inserted at each.

The correct length of the hem is marked with the aid of the hem guide.

The hem is turned up and pinned. It is advisable to check for straightness.

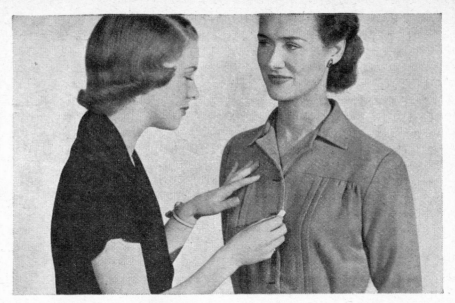

With the dress slipped on and wrapped over correctly, the edge is marked with chalk.

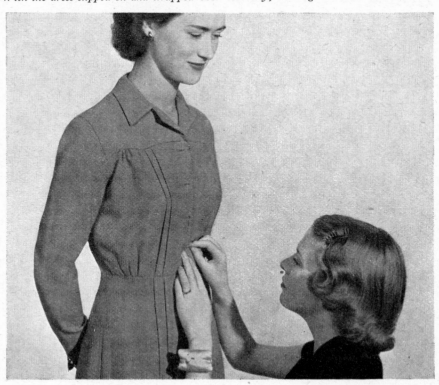

Two pins are inserted into each buttonhole, to mark the position of the buttons.

hole, to mark the position of the buttons.

(20) Neaten all the edges by making a small hem sewn with running stitch; on thicker materials, pinking or the oversewing method of neatening can be used.

Sew the buttons to the front bodice, remove all tacks and give the frock a final pressing.

Make a narrow waist belt from the straight piece of material, as shown on page 226. Sew on a buckle and make eyelet holes for fastening. A belt always looks better and stays in the correct position over the waist-line seam, if loops are sewn to the side seams for it to pass through. Make these in the same way as a loop fastening, page 196, but sew each end into the side seam, with the loop lying flat on the join.

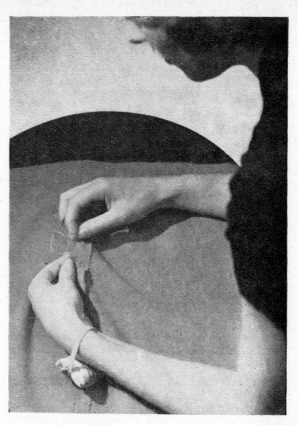

All the seams should be neatened with a tiny hem, or some other method suitable for the material being used.

SEMI-TAILORED SUIT

Made in fine woollen material, this suit will be smart for the cooler days of summer or under a coat in the winter. It would be equally attractive and useful if made in a heavy linen fabric.

The coat is designed with becoming straight lines, the single-breasted fastening reaching right up to the neck. The straight-cut skirt has a plain back and a wrap-over front which allows for freedom of movement, but still retains the smart slim-fitting line. Worn with the blouse shown on page 273, it would be attractive for casual occasions.

Choose a firm material with plenty of weight so that it will keep its shape and not ride up, fine woollen, or heavy linens are the best.

THE COAT

The Pattern.—The following pattern pieces will be required: front, back, two-piece sleeve and a flat collar. The front facing is cut in one with the coat front.

The Front: draw a bodice block pattern, with shoulder dart, number 3 described on page 77, but close the waist dart for

The jacket is tight-fitting with a darted back and flattering, high-button front. The wide pleat at one side of the front skirt adds width to the straight cut.

half its width only, thus making a narrower shoulder dart. Place this on a piece of paper, leaving additional paper below the waist line and at the centre front. Draw a line half an inch away from the neck, shoulder and armhole lines. Shape the side seam, as shown in the Diagram, and draw in the bottom edge of the coat six inches below and parallel to the block pattern. Add one inch to the centre front for the wrap-over. To get the extension for the facing, which is cut on to the front, fold the paper back along the line of the wrap-over and trace round the neck and along the shoulder for two inches. Join this point, with a gradual curve, to the hem line.

Mark the position of buttons and buttonholes and of the waist darts.

The Back: the block pattern, described on page 69, is used for this. Add half an inch for turnings at neck, shoulder and armhole, shape side seam to match the front and add six inches extra length below the waist, as shown in the Diagram. Mark the position of the darts.

The Sleeve: the two-piece sleeve pattern, page 71, is used for this. Half-inch turnings will be needed at the top and on the seams, and two inches is added at the wrist for the hem.

Shoulder Pads: these are made from triangular-shaped pieces of material the size required for the pad. Cut two pieces for each shoulder, and for details of making see page 241.

The Collar: the flat collar pattern with rounded corners, shown at the top of page 229, is used. It is cut in double-

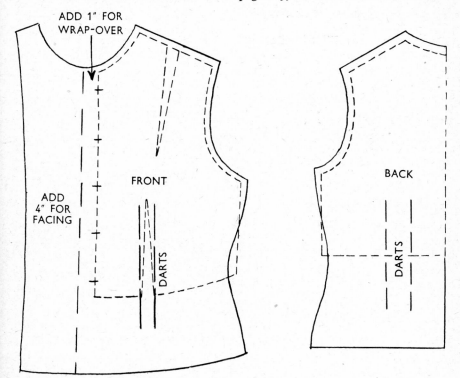

The front bodice block with shoulder dart, slightly modified, and the back bodice are the foundation patterns of the jacket. The wrap-over is added to the centre front piece.

thickness material and made up as described on page 230. Allow for narrow turnings all round the pattern when cutting out.

Cutting.—Arrange the pattern pieces on the material as economically as possible, placing the centre back and centre collar to a fold. Cut two fronts, two upper and under sleeves, two collars, one back (double) and shoulder pads.

When placing the patterns on the material make sure that the straight grains run vertically and horizontally across each piece. The top of the sleeve should be straight with the grain of the material, as shown in the drawing on page 116. If the patterns are not properly placed the garment will not hang correctly.

When working with a material that has a definite "up and down" make quite sure that all the pieces are matched correctly. Before removing the pattern mark with tailor's tacks the position

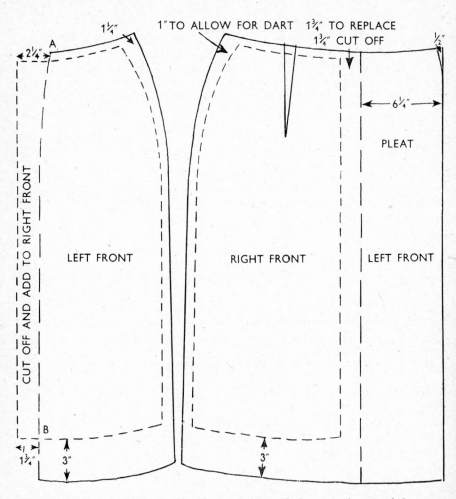

The skirt is based on the simple skirt block. An extra block pattern is cut and then recut, as shown above, to give the narrow left front, and the width for the pleat.

of the darts, buttons and buttonholes, and the edge of the front wrap-over.

Making.—Turn under the front facings along the wrap line, matching the curves at the neckline, and tack in position. Tack the shoulder darts of each front and the waist darts of the fronts and back. Tack the shoulder and side seams.

Fit the coat on the figure, inserting the shoulder pads and wrapping the front over correctly. When you are quite satisfied that the coat fits perfectly

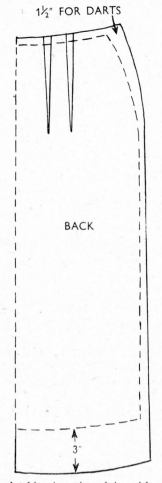

The back skirt is quite plain with two darts each side at the waist.

and that all the necessary alterations have been made, check the position of the buttonholes. Untack the front facings on the right front and make five bound buttonholes, as explained on page 202. Stitch the darts, tapering the shoulder darts to nothing at the point and running the waist darts off to nothing at both ends, above and below the waist. Stitch the seams, making plain seams, as described on page 166. Cut the darts down the centre, press them open and press all the seams and buttonholes. Turn back the right front wrap-over again and tack it in position. Complete the buttonholes.

Make the collar, as explained on page 230; if thick material is being used for the suit, a thinner lining should face the under side of the collar. Pin it to the coat with the centre to centre-back neck, and with the underside of the collar against the right side of the coat, tack it in place and fit. Stitch the two together, then snick the seam and press it against the inside of the neck. Neaten the seam with a strip of bias binding.

Fit the coat again. Turn up the hem to the correct length, tack and press, and neaten with a braided hem, as described on page 175.

Tack up both sleeves, easing any slight fulness at the elbow. Fit them into the armholes with the dress on the figure and with the shoulder pads in place, at the same time mark the sewing position in the armholes correctly. Stitch and press the seams, and shrink away any easing by means of a damp cloth.

Fix the sleeves into the armholes, easing any fulness round the top of the sleeve. Fit again, then stitch and press well, shrinking away the easing, as described on page 112.

Insert the shoulder pads and try on the coat again, turn up the sleeve at the wrist and finish it with a braided hem, sewing with slip stitch. Press well.

If the coat is to be lined, then it will not be necessary to neaten the seams. Make the lining and insert it, as explained on page 245.

The seams of a coat without lining should be carefully neatened with binding, as described on page 167.

Mark the position of the buttons with the garment on the figure. Sew on the buttons. Press the coat again.

THE SKIRT

The Pattern.—There are three pattern pieces in the skirt: the back, the right front and the left front. These are based on the front and back block patterns.

The Right Front: place the front block on a sheet of paper, leaving additional length at hem, and width at centre front. Draw the pattern, as shown in the Diagram. Add one and three-quarter inches to the centre front to replace the one and three-quarter inches cut off the left front, and add a further six and a quarter inches for the pleat, shape the top of this extension for the waist dart. Add one inch to the side waist for the dart and half an inch for side-seam darts. Add about three inches to the length, for the hem.

The Left Front: place the front block pattern on a piece of paper, leaving additional length at the hem. Measure two and a quarter inches in from the centre front at the waist and mark this A. Measure one and three-quarter inches in at the lower edge at centre front and mark this B. Add one and a quarter inches at side waist for the dart, half an inch above waist line and at the side seam for turnings and three inches to the length for the hem. Remove the block and join A to B, shaping the line at the waist to allow for hip curve, see Diagram. Cut out the pattern.

The Back: the back skirt pattern, described on page 70, is used for this,

half an inch is added at the waist and the side seams, and three inches is added to the skirt length for the hem.

The Belt: the strip needed for this will be the waist measurement plus extra for fastening, and twice the required width plus turnings.

Cutting.—Lay the pattern pieces on the material as economically as possible. The centre back should be placed to a fold, but the right front and the left front must be cut separately.

Making.—Tack the back darts and the dart on the right front, tapering them off to a point at the hip line. Stitch two fronts together, leaving about eight inches unstitched at the hem line, these loose edges are finished with a narrow binding. Make the pleat and tack it well. Tack up the side seams, leaving an opening at the left side for the placket. Fit the skirt, pinning it on to the waist band and make any adjustments necessary, making sure that the pleat hangs correctly. Then stitch the darts, slit them open and press. Stitch the pleat three-quarters of the way down from the waist and one inch in from the fold, then press it well. Stitch the side seams and press them open. Make the placket as described on page 184 or, if a zip-fastener is to be used, page 194.

Stitch the petersham to the waist and fit the skirt once more. If there are no adjustments to be made, mark the edge of the placket and position of fastenings.

Turn up the hem, as described on page 174, keeping the seam inside edges of the pleat quite flat.

Make a straight belt as described on page 226 and catch it to the waist. Neaten the hem with braid and slip-stitch to the garment as described on page 175, then press well.

Sew on the hooks and eyes and press fasteners, see page 192. Neaten the seams with pinking, overcasting or binding. Then press the skirt again.

MAGYAR BLOUSE
With Shawl Collar and Front Fastening

This blouse, cut in magyar style, is smart for all occasions and can be worn with a plain tailored skirt or under a suit. The shoulder seam shapes the cap sleeve, and the shawl collar, cut in one with the front, fits snugly at the neck.

The Pattern.—There are five pieces in the pattern, front, back, front facing and two sleeve facings. The bodice blocks are the foundation patterns.

The Front: place the front block pattern on a single sheet of paper, arranging centre front three inches in from the right-hand edge of the paper and with lower edge five inches up from the bottom of the paper, as can be seen in Diagram. This will give sufficient width to allow for the front wrap, collar and shoulder dart and sufficient length to tuck into the skirt. Draw the pattern, using the block as a guide. The shoulder seam, drawn parallel to the block and half an inch away from it, is eleven inches long, plus one inch at the neck edge for the dart. The sleeve is eight inches wide with the edge drawn in a slight curve to a point two and a half inches from the block at the side seam. The collar is added to the front and is drawn as shown. The extension from the shoulder seam is half the back neck measurement plus half an inch for turnings, roughly two and a half inches. The centre back of the collar is three and a half inches wide and the outer edge is drawn in a good curve to five and a half inches below the block neck, into the line of the wrap-over, which is one and a half inches wide at centre front. Extend the wrap-over to the bottom edge, which is drawn parallel to the block and five inches below it. Join the sleeve to the bottom edge, making a good curve for sleeve and side seam.

Front Facing: draw a second front pattern from the first and mark off the facings as shown by the dotted line, then cut out round this and the front edge, as shown in the Diagram.

Sleeve Facing: this can also be cut from the second front pattern. It is a shaped piece one and a quarter inches wide.

The Back: place the back block pattern on a single sheet of paper with the centre back to the left-hand edge and the bottom edge five inches up from the lower edge of the paper, as shown in the Diagram. Draw the shoulder seam eleven inches long plus half an inch at the neck for turnings, so that it matches the front. Make the sleeve curve seven inches long, taking it to three inches from the side of block, and draw in the side and sleeve seam to match the front. The bottom edge of the back is straight and five inches away from the block. Draw in the neck curve half an inch away from the block. Use the sleeve edge for drawing the pattern of the back sleeve facing.

Half-inch turnings have been allowed on all the measurements for this pattern.

Mark the position of buttons and buttonholes, and the darts. Cut out the pieces, pin together and try them on, making any necessary alterations.

Cutting.—Arrange the pattern pieces on the material as economically as possible, placing the centre back to the fold of the material. Have one front for the right and one for the left, and a facing for each front. You will need two facing pieces for each sleeve.

Making.—*The Back:* make two seven-inch darts, each one three inches away from the centre back; the darts are made at right-angles to the lower edge and should be half an inch wide at the

271

waist, tapering to a point top and bottom. After stitching, press them flat with the folds towards the centre.

The Front: clip diagonally, for half an inch, into the turnings at the inner corner of each shoulder and the collar. Make and tack the darts, which lie at right-angles to the shoulder seams, from the clipped inner corners and along each side of the neck line; these should be half an inch wide and seven inches deep, tapering to a point. Stitch the back seam of the collar and press it open. Tack the shoulder seams and tack the collar into the back neck. When you are quite sure the fit is correct, stitch the shoulders, sew the darts and the neck seam, stitching right round in one operation. Press the darts towards the front, snick the neck seam and press it up into the collar.

The Facing: stitch the centre back collar seam and press it open. Clip diagonally into the turnings at the corners as on the front. Arrange the facing on the blouse carefully, right sides together, and with centre back seams matching.

Tack and stitch round the edge, snick and press the seam. Make a small seam with the facing and the bottom of the blouse and turn right side out. Tack through the seam at the edge of the facing and press. Turn under the neck edge of the facing and hem it neatly over the turnings on the blouse. Neaten the inside edges of the facing with a small hem and catch them to the shoulder seams.

Join the side seams and neaten these and the shoulder seams. Join the facing for each sleeve, place it round the edge of the sleeve right sides facing, tack, stitch, snick the turnings and press the seams. Turn right side out, tack through the seam and press it, turn under and stitch the inside edge, loosely, to the blouse. Finish the bottom of the blouse with a small hem.

Check and mark the position of the buttonholes and make three hand-worked buttonholes, as described on page 200, at right-angles to the front. Sew on the buttons and give the blouse a final press on the wrong side.

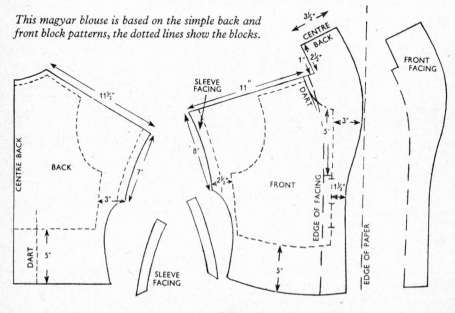

This magyar blouse is based on the simple back and front block patterns, the dotted lines show the blocks.

A simple magyar-style blouse will prove a good standby for many smart occasions. It has little cap sleeves, a snugly fitting roll collar cut in one with the front, and it fastens with three small buttons and buttonholes. The original was made in white piqué.

Soft gathers in the bodice, a V-neck and pin tucks at the waist line make this sleeveless nightie tailored in fit yet comfy to wear. The simplicity of style makes for easy laundering. Floral printed lawn was chosen for the original garment, with bias binding in a shade to tone with the flower sprays. Other soft materials, silk or rayon will be suitable.

274

LINGERIE

SOME USEFUL PATTERNS

The main principles of dressmaking apply to lingerie as much as to any other garment. There is, however, one point to remember—whereas outer garments are smarter and more professional if the main sewing is done by machine, lingerie is more dainty and harder wearing if sewn by hand.

All the seams must be neatened to prevent fraying with constant laundering. The turnings should be as narrow as possible.

BIAS-CUT NIGHTDRESS

The bodice is gathered under the bust to give fulness, and pin tucks are made at the waist.

The Pattern.—Cut from the block patterns described on pages 69 and 70. *The Front:* place the bodice and skirt blocks level at the waist, keeping the centre front straight. Mark the waist and armhole levels. Draw the neckline from one inch along the shoulder to point C at the armhole level. Draw the side seam narrowing the waist and continuing in a slanting line to the skirt hem, making it fifteen inches wider. Extend this line to obtain the full

length of the nightdress and re-draw the hem line. Make a gradual curve from C to one and a half inches above the waist level at D. Cut along line C—D. *The Back:* is cut from the back bodice and the skirt blocks in the same way as

The back skirt is pointed at the waist line to match the front but the bodice is left plain, without gathers. Note the groups of pin tucks at the waist line.

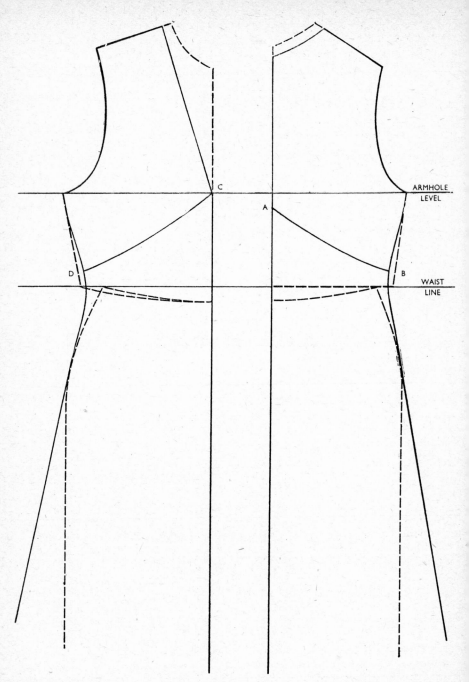

The nightdress pattern is cut from the back and front bodice and skirt blocks, allowing extra width on the front bodice for the gathers, and dividing back and front for the V-shape. Additional material is added to the skirt hem to make the nightdress the correct length.

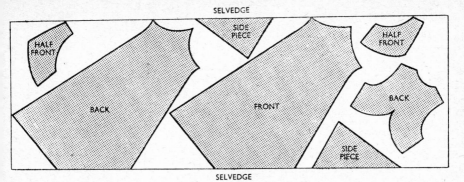

As the nightdress is cut on the bias it is more satisfactory if the material is opened out single when cutting the pattern. Make a full-size pattern of each piece and arrange them on the fabric as shown. The centre of each section of the pattern should be on the bias.

the front. Re-draw the neck line one inch inside the normal neck. Draw the curve of the bodice with a line A—B, one and a half inches above the waist to one and a half inches below the armhole level at the centre front. Draw the side seams and hem edges as for the front. Cut along line A—B when cutting out the pattern.

Cutting.—As this pattern is cut on the bias, make all pieces full width and arrange them on single fabric, as in the Diagram on this page. Allow turnings.

Making.—It may be necessary to add material to each side of the skirt hem edge. Join these pieces accurately first. Press the seams and neaten them.

Make the pin tucks at the waist, as on page 210, back and front. Bind the

points with bias binding, see page 207. Gather the bodice edge to fit the points. It is not necessary to gather the back bodice.

Place the point of the skirt over the lower edge of the bodice and tack them together. Tack the side and shoulder seams and fit the nightdress.

Turn under the lower edge of the bodice on to the right side and hem it neatly to the binding, then slip stitch the right side of the binding to enclose the turnings. Sew the shoulder and side seams, making a placket on the left side, as described on page 179. Neaten the seams and press them. Bind the armholes and the neck with bias binding to match the points. Finish the bottom edge with a small hem. Press well.

LONG-SLEEVED NIGHTDRESS

The bodice is gathered into a yoke at the shoulders and fastened down the front to the waist. The skirt is quite straight.

The Pattern.—Is cut from the block patterns on pages 69 and 70.

The Yoke: lay the front and back bodice pattern on a spare piece of paper with the shoulder seams touching. Draw the yoke so that it extends half an inch to

the back of the shoulder line and two inches to the front. Trace along these two lines, the armhole and neck.

The Front: place the bodice level with the waist of the skirt, centre front lines continuous. Re-draw the shoulder line to match the yoke, two inches below the shoulder seam. Extend this line one inch at the armhole edge and re-draw armhole, as Diagram, page 278.

Add two inches to the centre front for the full length. Make a continuous side seam and add to the hem for the length required.
The Back: is linked with the skirt in the same way as the front. The shoulder is re-drawn to match the yoke, half an inch below the seam line.

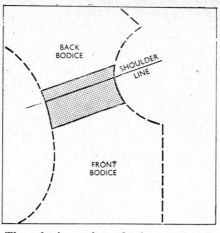

BACK BODICE

SHOULDER LINE

FRONT BODICE

The yoke is cut from the front and back bodice blocks, shoulder lines together.

The Collar: is a flat collar as described on page 229.
The Sleeve: is a bishop sleeve, see page 238, with a lengthened armhole, page 234.
The Cuff: is straight as on page 243.
The Belt: is a straight piece, see page 226.
Cutting.— Place the centre back to

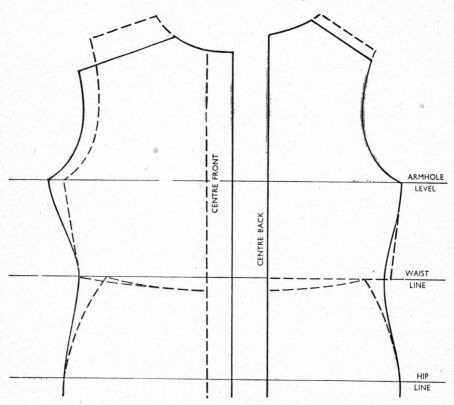

CENTRE FRONT

CENTRE BACK

ARMHOLE LEVEL

WAIST LINE

HIP LINE

The shoulder seam of the front bodice is widened at the armhole, below the yoke, to allow for the gathers. More width is allowed on the centre front for the wrapover. The back bodice block is unaltered, except for the yoke allowance.

A cosy nightie for cooler weather. The long full sleeves and the gathered bodice allow ample room for comfort, combined with style. Use satin or soft woollen material for making.

a fold, and cut the collar and yoke double. Allow turnings all round. **Making.**—Ruche the front bodice to fit yoke, page 218. Join the two together and pin the back bodice to the yoke. Neaten on the wrong side with the second yoke piece. Join the side seams. Turn under the centre fronts for one inch and sew them. Make the buttonholes, page 200, on the right front. Join the fronts below the waist. Make the collar and insert it into the neck as on page 229. Gather the sleeves to fit the armhole, make and insert them, as shown on page 238. Hem the edge of the garment, neaten the seams and sew on the buttons. Make the belt and press the garment well.

It is fun to have sets of lingerie all matching, so this simple princess slip has been designed with fitting features similar to the sleeveless nightdress. The back and front are exactly alike, with groups of pin tucks at the waist for snug fitting. The edges are bound with self-coloured bias binding to tone with the pattern on the material.

PRINCESS SLIP

The front and back of this slip are both alike. The pattern is one straight piece, shaped at the waist with groups of pin tucks. The top edge can be shaped and have shoulder straps, or a built-up shoulder may be made, if preferred. The skirt is slightly flared to give width at the hem line.

The Pattern.—The bodice and skirt blocks, described on pages 69 and 70, are used.

The Front: place the bodice and skirt blocks level with each other at the waist line. Mark the armhole level, middle chest, waist line and hip line.

Divide the shoulder line into two at point A and measure one-third of front bust measurement along armhole level, from centre front, mark B. Join A to B with a straight line. Measure two inches down from the middle chest line, along A—B and mark C. Make a point D on the centre front line, two inches above armhole level. Join D to C with a gradual curve and join C to the side seam with a similar curve.

Draw a continuous side seam line, curving in at the waist. Make the seam straight from the hip line, widening the skirt at the hem three or four inches.

Slit the skirt from the hem to the hip line and open out the slit to make a slight flare. Mark the position of the tucks at the waist line.

The Built-up Shoulder: this is drawn in the same way as the V-shaped top, but the point D is joined to the shoulder seam with a gradual curve, to make the neck line, at a point one inch away from line A—B. Draw along the shoulder line for one inch the other side of A—B, and draw a curve for the armhole from this point to one inch below the armhole level at the side seam.

The Back: is made in exactly the same way as the front pattern, but the back bodice and skirt blocks are used.

Cutting.—Place the centre front and centre back lines to a fold. Cut turnings all round.

Making.—Make the tucks at the waist line, as described on page 210. They should extend to well below the waist and just below the bust.

Join the side seams, making a side opening, see page 178, on the left seam, and bind the top and hem edges with bias binding as described on page 207. Sew on the shoulder straps, neaten the seams and press the whole garment.

CAMIKNICKERS

This is a slim-fitting garment cut on the bias in four panels. The centre front and back seams are shaped, as are the side seams, to give a neat fitting line to the waist. With the bias cut it is not necessary to make a side opening as there is enough stretch to slip the garment over the shoulders or hips.

The same pattern can be adapted to make a princess slip, by lengthening below the knicker hem line, or to make french knickers by cutting the pattern at the skirt waist. Sketches showing

the pattern used in this way are given on page 286.

The Pattern.—Is cut from the bodice and skirt blocks shown on pages 69 and 70.

The Front: place the bodice and skirt blocks together at the waist line, with the centre front line continuous. Mark the armhole level, the waist line and the hip line.

Draw in the side seam, shaping the waist, and flaring it out from the hips in a straight line to the hem. This

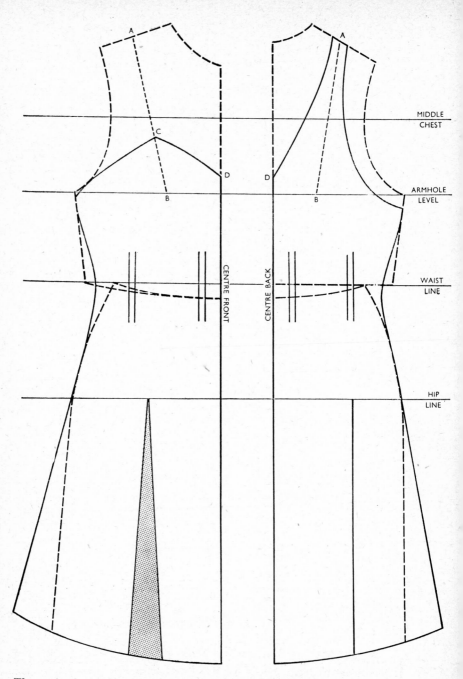

The petticoat can be made with shoulder straps, as the one illustrated, or with built-up shoulders, as seen in the right-hand diagram. In the latter case cut the back neck slightly higher than the front. The bodice and skirt blocks are the foundation of both styles.

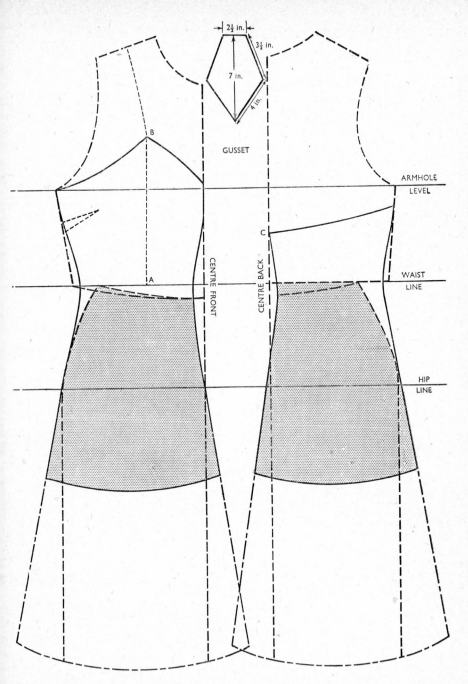

2½ in.

3½ in.

7 in.

4 in.

GUSSET

B

ARMHOLE
LEVEL

CENTRE FRONT

CENTRE BACK

C

A

WAIST
LINE

HIP
LINE

This camiknicker pattern is designed in such a way that it can be adapted for use as a princess slip, by cutting longer, or as french knickers, shaded portion below waist. It is cut in four sections from the block patterns, well shaped at the waist for slim fitting.

line should extend to five or six inches beyond the normal seam at the hem line of the skirt.

Mark a point A at a distance halfway between the centre front and the side seam, at waist. Draw a line from A to B, parallel with the centre front and reaching three or four inches above the armhole level. The length of this line depends on the size of the bust. The line from B to the centre of the shoulder seam gives the line for the shoulder strap.

Shape the centre front line to match the side seam, curving in at the waist and flaring out at the hem edge. The width at the hip line must correspond with that of the skirt block.

Measure the length of the knicker from the waist line, and draw in the hem line to correspond with the line of the skirt hem. *The Back:* is slightly different from the front as the top edge is cut low in a curve and not V-shaped.

Place the bodice block to the skirt with the waist lines level and shape the side seam as for the front. Mark a point C on the centre back line, halfway between the waist line and the armhole level. Join this, with a gradual curve to the side seam, one inch below the armhole level. Shape the centre back to match the side seam line and draw in the edge of the knicker leg, to match the front.

The Petticoat Pattern. —Is drawn in exactly the same way as the cami-knickers, but the full skirt length is retained.

The French Knicker Pattern.—The skirt block only is needed for this. Flare out the side seams in the same way as for the camiknickers but cut along the waist line and follow the normal side seam line above the hip.

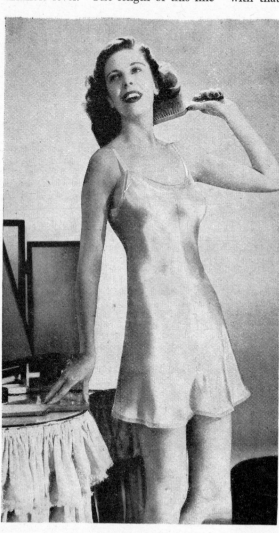

The front bodice is cut in points at the top and finished with net edging, which also trims the leg edges. The centre seams and bias cut make for slim fitting.

Cutting.—Make another pattern of the front panel and one to match the back. Having the complete pattern in this way will help in the arranging of the pieces on the material. The straight line down the middle of each pattern piece is placed on the bias of the fabric. Allow turnings all round and make sure that one front and one back are for the right side and one for the left.

Making.—The cami-knickers and slip are both made in the same way.

Join the side seams, and centre front and back, taking care not to stretch them. A dart is made in the front bodice, just below the armhole level. This will make the side seam fit the back and give shape to the bust. The length of the dart will vary and should be carefully fitted. This type of garment, when cut on the bias, needs gentle handling during the fitting; it must not be pulled too tightly.

Leave four inches of the centre seams, in the cami-knickers, unstitched at the hem edge, back and front, and insert the gusset into the seam.

The Gusset: take a strip of material fourteen inches long and ten inches wide. Make a line of tacking down the centre of the length. Fold the strip in two across the width. Measure one and a quarter inches each side of the tacking at the fold. Then measure three inches down from the fold and at this point two and a half inches

each side of the tacking. From this point to the two and a half inch line at the fold is three and a half inches, and to the tacked line at the end of the strip four inches. Cut along these two lines and make the second side the same. Cut two pieces of material exactly the same, one for the lining.

The four-inch line of the gusset is

The back of the camiknickers is cut in two panels, like the front, but with a straight edge at the top. The legs are slightly flared for comfy fulness.

joined to the seam back and front and the fold is slit. Neaten the gusset with the second piece and sew buttons and make buttonholes at the centre.

Make a tiny hem or facing along the top edges and the skirt hem, see pages 174 and 177. Then oversew net edging or narrow lace to the edge of the hem; this may be quite plain or frilled, to suit individual tastes.

Sew shoulder straps to the points on the fronts and correspondingly to the back of the camiknickers and the slip.

Neaten all seams and press well.

The French Knickers: join the side seams and make darts in the back to get a good fit at the waist line. Make a placket at the left side, see page 183, and finish the waist edge with a facing, as described on page 177.

Insert a gusset into the centre seam at the lower edge to make the legs, as for a camiknicker, but do not slit the fold of the gusset. Neaten the hem edges of the legs with a tiny hem and lace as described for the slip.

Make buttonholes and sew buttons on the placket of the french knickers.

A petticoat and french knickers made from the camiknicker pattern.

BRASSIERE

This brassiere is cut on the straight and moulded to the shape of the bust. The front is cut in a V and the back is straight with elastic in the centre.

The Pattern.—Front and back bodice blocks on pages 69 and 70 are used.

Place the two patterns together with side seams touching. Mark the middle chest, armhole level and a line midway between armhole and waist line.

Divide the shoulder seams into two at A and measure four inches from the centre front along the armhole level to B. Join A to B and continue the line, parallel with centre front, to C.

Measuring along middle chest, mark E one inch from A—B towards armhole, and D one and a half inches towards centre front. Similarly, measuring along midway line mark G one and a half inches from A—C towards side seams, and F one inch towards centre. Join D to F with a curve through B, and E to G with a corresponding curve which touches D—F at B.

From D draw a line to centre front, half an inch above armhole level. Following line of armhole, join E to the centre back, one inch above midway line. The shaded portion in the diagram indicates elastic.

Cutting.—Place the centre front to a fold and allow turnings all round.

Making.—Join the curves E—G and D—F with a plain seam. Make two tiny pleats across the centre front. Fit the brassiere. Finish the lower edge with a facing, bind top edge, or make a small hem and add lace. Sew on shoulder straps and press fasteners at centre back.

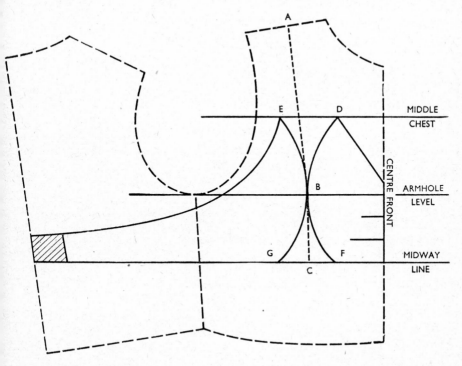

The front and back bodice blocks are placed side seams together for the foundation.

Tailored in design, without bulk of any kind, for wear under a fitting frock.

Pattern.—Draw two rectangles with A—B the length of the leg plus one inch, and A—C quarter waist measurement plus seven inches.

The Front: drawn in one rectangle. From A measure along A—C one quarter of the waist measurement plus half an inch, to allow for the dart. E is three-quarters of an inch below this point. Join A to E with a gradual curve, and mark the position of the dart three and a half inches from the centre front. Measure the length of the leg from A along A—B. From D measure three and a half inches along D—C and mark F, and measure two inches along B—D and mark G. Join G to F with a curve, and draw a line from B to G. Join E to F with a slanting line. *The Back:* is drawn in the second

rectangle. The leg part is same as the front except for the top. From C measure quarter waist plus one inch along C—A and mark H. Mark the position of the darts three and a half inches apart and three and a half inches from the centre front. Join H to F.

Cutting.—Two front and two back pieces. Allow turnings on all edges.

Cut two three-inch squares for gusset.

Making.—Make the darts, see page 178.

Join the centre front and back seams and the side seams, leaving left side open at the waist for a placket. Insert the gusset, placing a point to each seam, and join the leg seams. Neaten the gusset with the facing piece. Make the placket as on page 183. Finish the waist line with a faced hem, see page 177. The leg edges are finished with bias binding, page 207. Sew on buttons and make button holes on the placket.

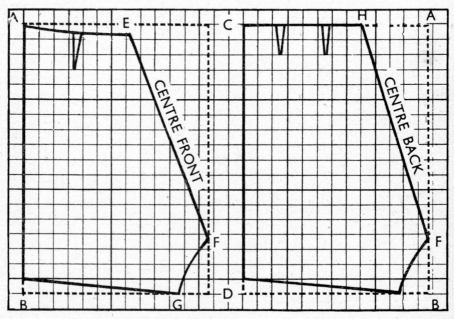

The knicker pattern is drawn in rectangles, one for the front and one for the back, both patterns being similar with slight variations at the waist. The leg can be made any width.

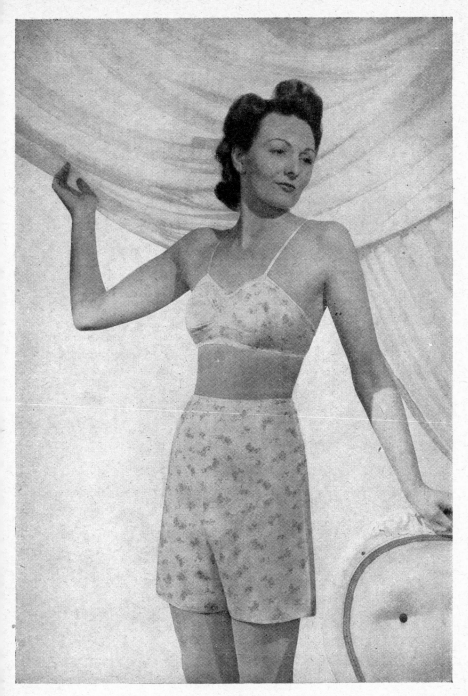

The knickers are tailored in style and can be made to complete the set of straight cut princess slip and sleeveless nightdress. The back waist line is darted, for slim fitting.

The woman who can ply her needle skilfully is able to replace the family's clothes when necessary. The life of children's garments is short either through the child growing quickly or through constant hard wear and tear and frequent laundering.

CHILDREN'S WEAR

FOR ALL AGES

Clothes for children are more easily made than adults' garments. The seams are not so long and the fitting is easier, but the same careful attention must be paid to detail.

The boy's suit consists of a shirt, trousers and a blazer. The skirt for the girl is pleated and can be worn with the shirt and the blazer.

BLAZER

This garment can be made for any aged child but it is most suitable for a ten to twelve year old.

First take the measurement as described in the Measurement Chapter, page 53.

The Pattern.—Make a block pattern, using the measurements just taken, as explained on page 69.

The Front.—Place the block pattern on a spare sheet of paper, leaving plenty of space at the side seams, centre front and hem.

Shoulder: re-draw the shoulder line, one inch from the block. Make the neck edge slightly smaller to counteract this extra length. Widen shoulder half an inch at armhole.

A tailored and useful blazer for schoolboy or girl.

The Armhole: is re-drawn with a curve starting at the end of the new shoulder line, which deepens the armhole by half an inch. Add two inches to the side seam at the armhole and continue the curve in an upward line to meet the new seam line one and a half inches above the armhole curve at C. The second side of the curve should match the one already made on the front of the side seams.

The Neck: re-draw the neck curve half an inch inside the normal line. Add two inches to the centre front line for the wrap-over.

Add to the length of the blazer, as necessary, about six inches, below the waist line. The hem line of the coat is quite straight and should be one and a half inches wider at D than the width of the front at C. Join C to D.

The Back.—Draw this from the back block pattern to match the front.

The Shoulder: add half an inch to the shoulder line and half an inch to the armhole edge.

Re-draw the side seams one inch inside the normal line and extend it to meet the armhole curve at A.

Lengthen the coat to match the front and curve the side seam gradually to meet the hem line at B.

The Sleeve: is made from the two-piece sleeve pattern described on page 72.

The Collar: is a step collar made in the way shown on page 233.

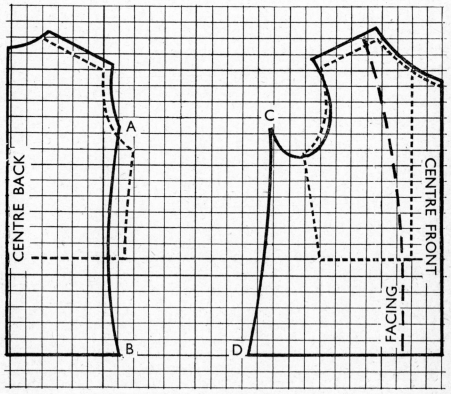

A foundation block pattern is made and used for making the blazer pattern. Extra width is cut on to the centre front for the wrap-over and the back pattern is made narrower.

The Facings: are cut from the centre part of the front pattern, making them one inch wide at the shoulder seam and three inches wide at the hem edge.

Cutting.—Place centre back to a fold. Cut two sleeves, two fronts and facings, one for the right side and one for the left. The collar should be made double. Three square pieces will also be needed for the patch pockets; allow for a one-inch hem at the top edge and narrow turnings on the three remaining sides.

Cut turnings as required on the rest of the garment.

Making.—Tack shoulder and side seams and fit the blazer, remembering that it should not fit tightly. Sew the seams and press them. Stitch the facings to the fronts, placing the right side of the facing to the right sides of the front and sewing all round. Trim the seams quite narrow, press them. Turn the facings to the wrong side, and tack them down.

Sew the two sides of the collar together and stitch into the neck as described on page 233.

Make the sleeve and fit it, then finish the seams and when pressed hem the cuff edge as described on page 242. Fit the sleeve into the armhole and stitch it.

Hem the lower edge. Neaten the facings and catch them to the shoulder seam and to the coat hem. Make three buttonholes on the left front, as described on page 200. Make the pockets and sew them in place.

If the blazer is to be lined, then make the lining and insert it as explained on page 245, using the blazer pattern. If unlined the seams will have to be neatened with binding, see page 167.

THE TROUSERS

The trousers are short and can be made in material matching the blazer or in flannel for wear with the shirt and a school blazer.

Measurements required.—Round waist, hip measurement, length of leg at the side, length of fork.

The Pattern.—A block pattern will have to be drawn, using the measurements given above.

Front: draw a rectangle quarter hip measurement plus three inches, by outside leg length. Mark the top line A—B and the opposite line C—D, see Diagrams on page 296.

From B measure three and a half inches along A—B and mark E, and from B measure along B—D for the length of fork and mark F. Join E to F, making the line straight to the hip level and curving it gradually for the fork. G is one inch from D along C—D. Join F to G for leg curve.

The Back: draw a rectangle, A, B, C and D, as for the front and the same size, marking points E and F to match the front.

Add the pocket facing to the line A—C, making it one inch wide and six and a half inches deep, as J—H.

From E measure one inch on the outside of A—B and half an inch towards B for K. Join H to K with a straight line. From a point half an inch below F measure three and a half inches outside the line B—D and mark this L. Join L to K with a curved line for the fork to match the front leg. Extend the line C—D one inch at D, and at half an inch below this point make M. Join M to L for the leg curve. C is joined to M for the bottom of the leg.

The Fly Piece: is cut from the front leg pattern. Draw the line of the front fork, E—F, and two inches along the leg curve, F—D. Draw a second line

Trousers cut on tailored lines for a schoolboy. They can be made to measure to fit any child. The shirt is made in cotton poplin or soft flannel.

parallel to E—F and two inches away from it.

The Pocket: the straight side is nine inches long for the depth and the top edge is four inches wide. The side edge slants outwards towards the base and the corner is curved, see Diagram on page 296.

Cutting.—Have the leg seam level with the selvedge grain of the fabric. Cut two fronts and two backs, one for the right and one for the left. Cut two fly pieces in garment material and three in strong lining fabric. Cut two pockets in lining. Allow turnings all round.

Making.—Line one fly piece and sew it to the right front so that it lies under the overlap as the under-part of the fly. Line the second fly piece and make buttonholes about two to two and a half inches apart, as described on page 200. Then line the edge of the left front with the third lining piece. Tack the buttonhole fly piece to the left front, linings facing. Stitch it neatly to the trousers round the outer curve and catch the edges together between the buttonholes. The buttonholes should be left free so that the buttons lie between the two edges.

Join the outside leg seams below the pocket facing and join the inside leg seams. Press them open. Join the centre back seam, continuing along the front crotch seam as far as the fly.

Fit the trousers and make darts or pleats where necessary at the back waist.

The Pockets: sew the lower edges together leaving the opening unstitched. Turn under the pocket edge of the front trouser and tack it, hem the pocket to this neatly. The facing is sewn to the other edge of the pocket.

The waist edge is turned under and faced with lining as on page 177.

The crotch is neatened and strengthened with a patch of lining material.

Hem the legs of the trousers with a plain hem. Sew the buttons on the right front fly, to match the buttonholes, and give the trousers a final press.

SKIRT

The pleats in this skirt give plenty of fulness round the hem, keeping a streamlined effect.

It is not necessary to cut a pattern for this skirt as it is made from a straight piece of material with a band at the waist.

There are six box pleats, three at the front and three at the back. To calculate the amount of fabric needed in the width multiply the hip measurement by

The straight-cut pleated skirt, made on a belt or calico bodice, is ideal for a schoolgirl of any age. The blouse is made in the same way as the boy's shirt.

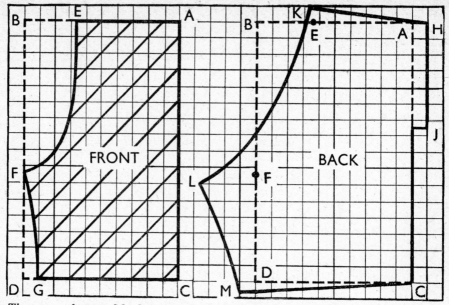

The trouser front and back patterns are cut separately in two rectangles of equal size.

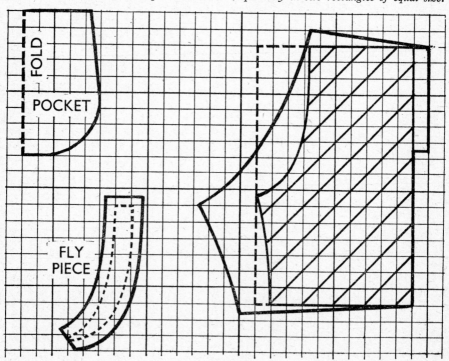

Place the front pattern over the back, matching up the various points. Make sure they are both right for size. The pocket facing is cut on to the back pattern at the side.

three. The selvedge grain of the material must run straight from the waist to the hem. Allow for one and a half inch turnings at the hem line and smaller turnings at the waist.

To get the width of the box pleats divide the material into six with tacking lines. Then divide each section into two. Five of these lines represent one pleat, see Diagram, page 299. C represents the centre line of the box pleat, B and D the edges of the pleat and A and E the folds on the wrong side of the garment.

Fold the pleats carefully, starting at the right side. Mark the lines A, B, C, D and E. Make a fold at A and one at E and place these two, edge to edge, at C on the wrong side, creasing along B and D. Pin all the pleats as they are made in the material, then tack them well for the full length. Keep the material flat on the table.

Make any necessary joins in the material before arranging the pleats. These seam edges should be pressed to one side and where possible they should be at the inside fold of a pleat.

Joining the Side Seam.—If the material is calculated correctly one section will be left after the pleats are made; this edge is joined to edge A of the first pleat. Leave a few inches unstitched for the placket.

Stitching the Pleats.—Make a line of machining at each edge of every pleat, sewing three or four inches down from the waist line. The edge of the pleat which covers the placket should be sewn singly and not to the garment.

Bind the placket opening with bias binding, as described on page 207.

Finish the waist with a straight belt applied in the same way as a straight binding shown on page 206.

If preferred the skirt can be attached to a calico bodice made from the block pattern. The neck and armholes should be cut a little lower than in the block and bound with bias binding.

Hem the skirt as on page 214, and press it before completing the pleats.

Finally press all the pleats very well both sides as described on page 105. Sew fastenings to the placket, page 192.

THE SHIRT

The making of a shirt is described as if for a boy but it is equally suitable for a girl. For a boy the left front wraps over the right and for a girl it is the reverse way. When making the shirt for a girl it can be cut shorter and the hem finished with a heading and elastic. This style is necessary if the skirt has a bodice.

The Pattern.—Front and back bodice block, made as shown on page 69, is used. The sleeve and collar are drafted as shown in the Diagram on page 299.
The Yoke: draw this from the shoulder of the front and back bodice blocks, by placing the shoulder seams together, as described for the nightdress on page 278. Keep the centre of the back

straight and cut across to the armhole at a line three inches below the neck line. Cut the front parallel with the shoulder and one inch away from it.
The Front: the block pattern less the inch cut off for the yoke at the shoulder. Add three-quarters of an inch to centre front for wrap-over and seven inches below waist, widen at hips for girl.
The Back: the lower part of the back block, left after cutting the yoke, is used for the back pattern. Add two inches to centre back width for pleat and nine inches below the waist for the lap.
The Sleeve: is drawn as shown in the Diagram on page 299. Draw a rectangle with A—B equal to the armhole measurement and A—C the longest

measurement of the sleeve length. Mark the four corners A, B, C and D. Measure two inches along A—C from A and mark G. From C measure along A—C for one and a half inches and mark H. Measuring from A mark E at a point half plus one inch of A—B.

F is six inches from D along D—C. Join B to F with a straight line. Three and a half inches along this line mark J and draw the curve for the head of the sleeve from J to G through E.

The Collar: is a stand and fall collar as shown on the opposite page.

The Stand: draw a rectangle with A—B half neck measurement and A—C one and a half inches. G is half an inch from B along A—B. E is half an inch from A along A—C. Join G to E with a curve. Halfway between B and D is F. Join F to G with a straight line and F to C—D with a curve.

The Fall: draw another rectangle with A—B half neck measurement plus one and a half inches. A—C is three inches. E is half an inch from A, G half an inch from C along A—C and F is one and a quarter inches from B along A—B. Join F to E and G to D with a curve, F to D with a straight line.

Cuffs: straight cuffs, as on page 243.

Cutting.—Place the centre front and back lines to a fold in the material. Cut four yoke patterns, placing the shoulder line to the straight grain of the material, see Diagram. Place the front edge of the sleeve to the selvedge grain as in the Diagram and cut two. The centre lines of both collar pieces are placed to the fold. Cut two pieces of each. Allow turnings all round.

Making.—Cut the front opening the length required, about nine inches. The slit should be made a quarter of an inch one side of the centre front, to the left for a boy and on the right for a girl. Make a narrow hem on the under side.

The Facing: is a straight piece three and a half inches wide and as long as the front opening plus one and a half inches. Join one edge of this, with right side of facing to wrong side of shirt, to the front opening, neck edges level. Fold the facing on to the right side along the seams and press. Make a pleat at the bottom of the opening. The centre of the facing corresponds with the under hem. Turn under the edge of the one and a half inch surplus and the second edge of the facing and machine stitch the edge.

Join the yokes at the centre back and press the seams. Make a box pleat in the centre back of the shirt, see page 212, and join to the yoke with the centre of the pleat to the seam. Then sew the front yoke to the front shirt. Neaten on the wrong side with the second piece, turning under the edges and hemming them to the turnings.

The Collar: sew the two fall pieces together at the ends and along G—D, press the seams, turn right sides out and machine stitch round the edges. Stitch the two stand pieces together at the ends, press and turn right side out. Join E—F of the fall to E—G of the stand, inserting the fall in between the edges of the stand. Then fasten the edge C—F of the stand to the neck, sewing it first on the right side of the garment and then on the wrong.

All the seams on a shirt should be run and fell seams, as on page 169.

Make an opening in the sleeve at the wrist, see page 186, and make a straight cuff attaching it as described on page 243. Join the sleeves to the armholes, then sew up the sleeve side seams in one continuous line, leaving three inches at the hem edge unstitched.

Hem the lower edges of the shirt. Make buttonholes on the facing, see page 200, and sew buttons to correspond.

A gusset, page 316, may be inserted into the sleeve and side openings.

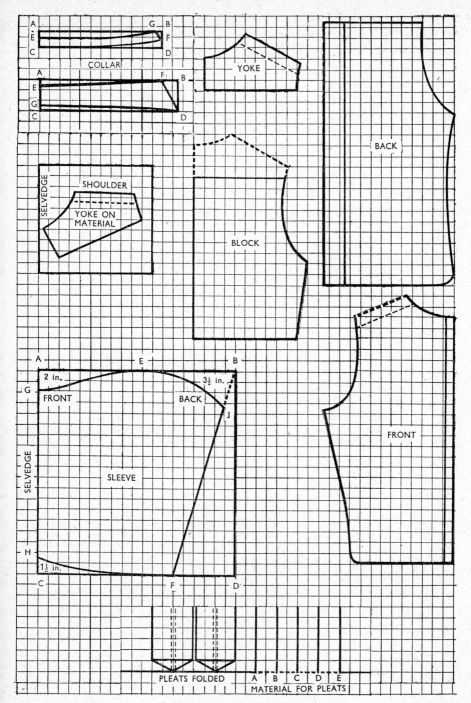

The shirt pattern, yoke and collar. The sleeve pattern. Pleats for the girl's skirt.

SCHOOL KNICKERS

This design is suitable for a tiny toddler or an older girl, right up to teen age. It is very quickly and easily made as there are only two seams to be joined. **The Pattern.**—Is drawn in the way shown in the Diagram on this page.

Draw a rectangle with the line A—B equal to the quarter waist measurement plus four inches. A—C equals half waist size plus two inches.

From A measure along A—C one inch and mark E. F is two inches from B along A—B. Join E to F with a gradual curve. Measuring from B along B—D make G two-thirds of the length of this line. Make H two-thirds of the length of C—D from D. Join H to G for the leg curve and join F to G with a straight line.

Cut one pattern for the front with waist line E—F and one for back leaving waist as A—F.

The Gusset: this piece is used for strengthening the crotch between the legs. It is cut from the knicker pattern as indicated by the diagonal line on the Diagram. J is made one-third of the leg curve from H, and K is six inches from C along A—C. Join J to K.

Cutting.—To avoid a seam at the crotch fold the material into two widthways and place the line C—H to this fold. The centre front and centre backs must also be put to a fold. Allow turnings all round. The lines C—K and C—H of the gusset pattern are also placed to

Schoolgirl knickers, simple to make and easy to launder, can be made for all sizes.

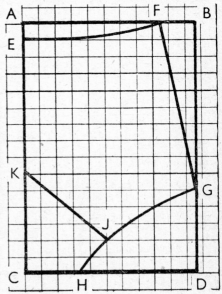

The knickers are cut from a square or oblong of material folded into four.

300

folds in the material. Cut a square for a patch pocket if required.

Making.—Make all seams french seams, page 170. Make a hem at the waist and insert elastic, making buttonholes for the ends to pass through as described on page 200. Tack the gusset piece in place, fitting it carefully. Turn under the edges and hem or machine stitch them. Bind the leg edges with bias binding as explained on page 207. Make the pocket and sew it to the right leg.

To make knickers for wear with party frocks, when thinner material is used, the leg edges can be finished with a small hem and lace or frilled fabric.

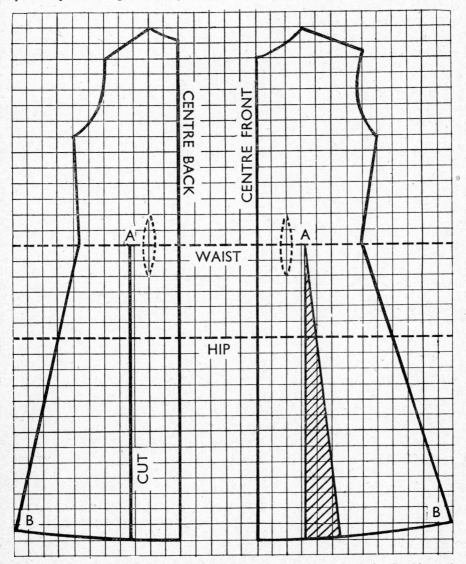

The teen age frock is cut as a simple block pattern. A slit is made in the skirt and opened out to give a slightly flared effect. Make the pattern to the correct measurements.

TEEN-AGE FROCK

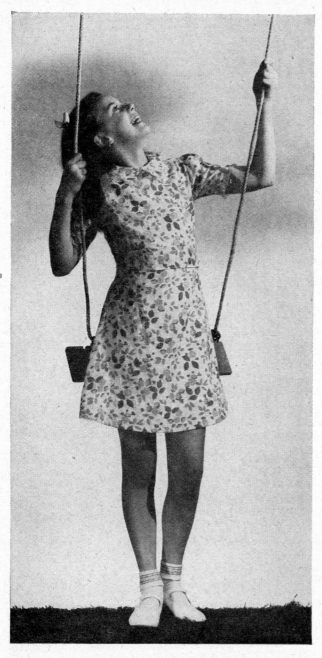

The waist line of this simple frock is darted for a good fit. The skirt is slightly flared to give width at the hem.

Made in crisp printed cotton this is a charming summer frock for the younger teen age. The slight flare in the skirt gives the necessary fulness at the hem line. But the simple straight lines make laundering easy.

The Pattern.—Is drawn as shown on page 301. Make a front and back bodice block pattern in the way described on page 69.

Place these patterns on a spare sheet of paper with ample room below the waist and draw the pattern for the skirt. Continue the centre front line from the waist for the length to the bottom of the skirt. At the hem line make a point B, at right angles from the centre line and half the waist measurement plus four inches away from it. Measure the skirt length at the side seam, from the waist to B. Join B to the centre line, for the bottom edge, with a gradual curve.

Make a slit in the pattern for the flare. This should be parallel to the centre line and about three inches away from it. Cut from the hem line to A at the waist line. Open the slit for about two inches at the hem, and insert a length of paper to complete the flare. Mark the position of the waist darts.

The Sleeve: is cut from the one piece sleeve pattern shown on page 74, with an extended head as page 234.

The Collar: is a flat collar, as the one described on page 229, cut into two separate halves.

The Belt: a long sash belt, made double.

Cutting.—Place the centre back and the centre front to a fold. Cut two sleeves, one for each arm. Make the collar double. Allow turnings all round.

Making.—Tack the side and shoulder seams and fit the garment, making the darts at the waist line, see page 178. Sew the darts and the seams, leaving an opening at the left side for the placket, which is finished in the way described on page 179.

Cut a three-inch opening at the back neck and finish it in the way described on page 183.

The Collar: make this as described on page 230 for a double collar, but making each half quite separately. Attach it to the neck in the way explained with a division at the centre front as well as the centre back. Finish the edges by oversewing narrow lace edging, which has already been gathered, to the seam.

Fit and sew the sleeves, making gathers at the head of the sleeve and tucks or pleats at the bottom edge; fit the sleeve to the arm. Insert it into the armhole and add stiffening as described on page 241. Face the lower edge of the sleeve and finish with a narrow lace, slightly gathered.

The Belt: is made in the same way as a straight belt, described on page 226. It is caught to each side of the dress at the side seams and ties in a bow at the back like a wide sash.

Turn up the hem to make the length required and slip stitch it, page 156.

Sew the fastenings to the side opening and the neck. Press the frock.

To make a more simple style of frock from this pattern, one that is suitable for school wear or a summer play frock, trimmings of a tailored style are used.

Make the frock as previously described but bind the collar, sleeves and the edge of the belt with contrasting bias binding. Plain material with striped or check binding is most attractive. Make a striped belt to match, with a buckle or button for fastening.

The long sash ties at the back. The sleeve edges and collar are trimmed with lace.

303

FROCK FOR BABY

This little frock is made with a full skirt gathered on to a small yoke, a style very suitable for a baby or toddler.

The original was trimmed with feather stitch and lace round the edge of the yoke, and feather stitch at the hem edge. The sleeve and neck edges were finished with lace edging.

A frock for a toddler can be made from the pattern described for the baby's dress.

There are many attractive ways of decorating the frock, especially for the older child; gingham check with plain contrasting binding, or check binding on plain materials. The skirt and bodice edges can be finished with tiny tucks. Puff sleeves may be made and a small Peter Pan collar to finish the neck.

The Pattern.—*The Yoke:* is cut as shown in the Diagram. For a very small baby the width of each yoke is four and a half inches across the bottom. The centre line is three inches. From the point of the shoulder to the lower edge is four inches. The neck curve is one and a half inches wide. The shoulder line is two inches. The side seam is one inch. Add an extra half inch to the centre back for the opening.

The Skirt: is a straight piece twelve inches deep and three times the width of the yoke, about fifty-four inches.

The Sleeve: is a one-piece sleeve cut in the same way as shown on page 73. The width of the pattern should be made about five and a half inches wide and the top is cut to fit the armhole, allowing extra for gathers.

Cutting.—Place the centre front to a fold and allow turnings all round.

Making.—Join the shoulder and side seams of the yoke with narrow french seams, see page 170. Make narrow hems down the centre back.

Join the skirt seams. If there is only one seam make it down the centre back and leave two or three inches unjoined. When there are two seams make them at the sides and slit the centre back for the opening; finish this opening with a hem as described for a hemmed opening on page 182. Ruche the top edge with about three rows of gathers, page 218, draw up the thread to fit the yoke and space the gathers evenly. Join the skirt and yoke together.

The skirt is gathered into a straight yoke. The pattern of the yoke is shown below.

Face the neck edge, see page 190. Make the sleeve, gather the top and insert it into the armhole. Hem the the skirt, and the edge of the sleeve. Work a row of feather stitch, page 159, on the skirt hem, at the top of the turnings, and work the same stitch round the neck, the sleeve edge and round the bottom of the yoke. Trim the sleeves, neck and yoke with lace which is hemmed along one edge. Neaten the seams, sew buttons to the opening and make loop buttonholes, as described on page 197.

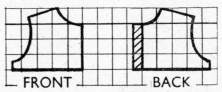

FRONT   BACK

A frock for an older child is made in the same way, but of course it must be cut to the required measurements. As an alternative a puff sleeve can be made, as described on page 236, and a flat collar, see page 229, will make a new neck finish. For trimming, rick-rack braid, instead of lace, is attractive.

These simple pyjamas can be made for boy or girl of any age. The girl wears the right front wrapped over the left and for a boy it is the reverse way. Use soft cotton fabric for the summer and flannel for winter pyjamas. Both these fabrics are easy to launder.

PYJAMAS AND SLEEPING SUIT

The pyjama pattern can be adapted for a boy or a girl; if made for a boy the left front wraps over the right, and for a girl it is the reverse way. The same pattern is altered slightly to make the sleeping suit.

The Pattern.—The coat is the same as the blazer coat shown on page 292, with a different sleeve and collar.

The Collar: is a flat collar as shown on page 229.

The Sleeve: is drafted as the diagram on page 308.

Draw the sleeve pattern on double paper, which is folded lengthways to make a rectangle half the size of the armhole measurement, A—B, by length of sleeve from shoulder to wrist, A—C.

Measure two and a half inches from B along B—D and make E. From C measure along C—D half wrist size and make F. Join E to F with a straight line and A to E with a gradual curve.

The Facings: two and a half inches are added to the centre fronts, over and above the allowance for the wrap over. If the material is not wide enough to allow for this cut two lengths of fabric, three inches wide by the length of the fronts.

The Trousers: are drafted from the trouser pattern already made and described on page 293.

Place the side seams of the front leg and back leg together, allowing the pocket facing to overlap the front. Leave plenty of spare paper below the bottom edge of the trouser leg to get the length for the pyjamas. Extend the waist line one inch at the centre back seam and join this point to the point of the crotch

Adapt the pyjama pattern for a tiny child's sleeping suit.

with a straight line. Make the half leg eight and a half inches wide each side of the side seam line and join the front and back crotch points to each end of this line, drawing a curve to match the trouser leg.

Make a fly piece in the same way as for the trousers.

Cutting.—Place the centre back of the coat pattern to a fold, cut two sleeves, two fronts and facings and two trouser legs. Cut the collar double as described for a flat collar on page 229. Cut the fly piece in double material.

Making.—Use a run and fell seam, see page 169, for all the seams. Join the shoulder seams. Turn back the facings and stitch them down. Make the collar and insert it into the neck as explained on page 229. Insert the sleeve and stitch up the sleeve and side seams. Hem the sleeve edges and the bottom of the coat. Make the buttonholes, page 200, and sew on the buttons. Stitch a patch pocket to the left front, see page 224.

Join the front and back leg seams of the trousers. For a boy sew the fly

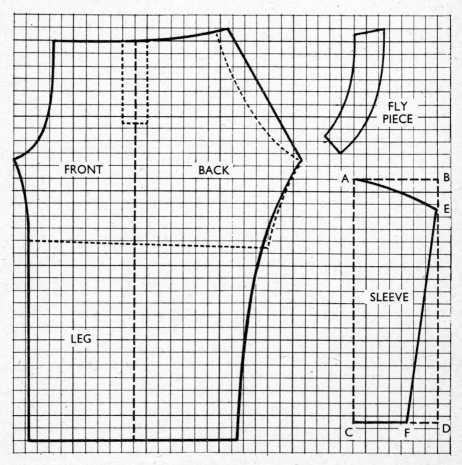

The short trouser pattern is used as the foundation for the pyjama trousers. Re-draw the centre back seams and lengthen leg as required. The coat is cut like the blazer.

piece to the right front and neaten it with the facing piece. Hem the left side. For a girl make a small hem on both sides of the front. Finish the waist line with a hem as a heading and insert tape for tying, or elastic. Hem the bottoms of the legs.

Sleeping Suit.—
Make the pattern from the bodice blocks and pyjama leg. Place them together at the waist, see the Diagram on right. Add two inches at the centre front for the wrap-over. Draw the side seam straight from the armhole and make the ankle five inches wide. Re-draw the front leg seam and add the length of the foot, curving the bottom edge.

Add two inches to the side of the back leg at the waist. Re-draw the centre back leg seam from the bodice to the crotch and re-draw both the lower leg seams to make the ankle five inches wide.

Draw a sole pattern the length of the foot by five inches wide at the straight edge, and curve the toe to match the front.

The sleeve and collar patterns are the same as for the pyjamas.

Make up in the same way as the pyjamas, leaving the centre front open

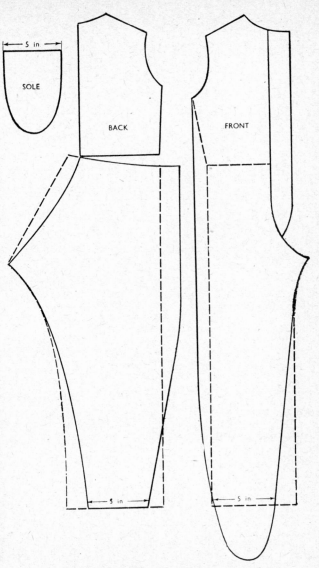

The bodice and trousers combine to make the sleeping suit.

for the extension piece. Face it and make buttonholes. Gather the centre back of the trousers and insert into a band, as page 218. Leave each side open below this band for three inches and make a hemmed opening, see page 182. Make a straight belt for the waist,

MENDING

AND PATCHING

A good darn or patch should be as invisible as it is possible to make it. Make the repair as soon as the worn part is noticed and extend the mend over the whole of the thin area round the hole. The secrets of good repairs are—matching material or sewing thread in colour and texture; neatness, and stitching that is easy and does not pull the garment out of shape.

DARNING

Repair a thin place before it wears into a hole. Work on the wrong side, weaving in and out of the fibres of the fabric, making small stitches. Then weave in and out of the darning thread at right angles. Do not fasten off a darn and never pull the thread tightly. If wool thread is used leave a loop at the ends of the sewing lines to allow for shrinking. A darn can be oval, square or oblong in shape.

Darning a Hole.—If the repair shows, make the darn on the right side. In the foot of a stocking make the darn on the wrong side for comfort.

A simple darn worked over a hole.

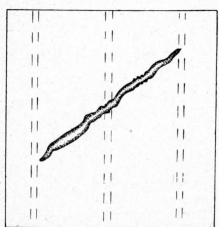

A cross cut is one which breaks the fabric threads across the bias.

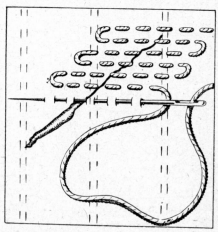

Make the stitches along the straight grain, drawing the cut together.

Weave into the fabric at the sides of the hole wherever it is thin and throw threads straight across the hole until it is completely covered. Then darn under and over these threads as described for a worn place. When darning knitted fabric weave into the warp way of the knitting first, making a stitch into each loop of the fabric weave.

Cross Cut Darn.—When the cut is across the bias of the fabric make darning stitches on the straight grain of the fabric, each time making a stitch into the cut itself so it will be pulled together. Then weave under and over these threads in the reverse direction. Darn beyond the split at each end.

Hedge Tear.—A right-angle tear on the grain of the fabric. First draw the edges of the slit together with fishbone stitch, see page 156. Darn under and over the threads of the fabric across each slit, starting at the end farthest from the corner, and a little beyond the slit. Continue well beyond the slit at the corner. When working the darning over the second slit weave under and over the threads of the first stitches, at the corner, making a neat square and giving extra strength.

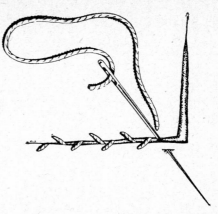

A hedge tear is triangular in shape. Close the cut with fishbone stitch.

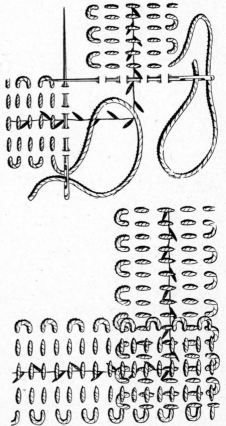

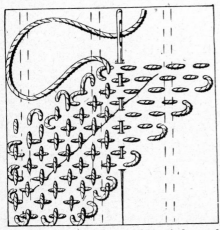

Darn under and over the first stitches and at right angles to them.

Darn up and down across each cut, making double stitching at corner.

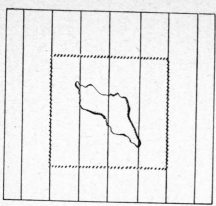

The pattern of the patch must be matched carefully to that of the garment.

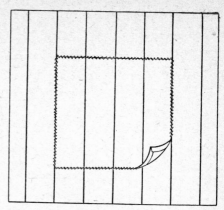

Tack the patch in position on the right side and neatly sew all round.

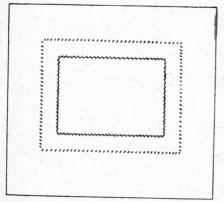

Place the patching piece over the hole on the right side and hem it down.

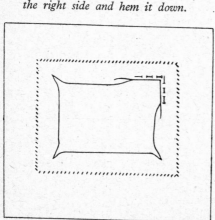

Turn under the raw edges on the wrong side and neatly hem the fold.

PATCHING

When the hole, or the thin part surrounding it, is too large for darning, then it must be patched. Always try to match the patching material to the garment and avoid using new fabric. If the patching piece has not been used before, rinse it through before sewing.

Cotton Patch.—The most simple kind of patch which can be used on any fabric other than woollen. Cut the patch square or rectangular, on the grain of the fabric, to cover the hole and all the thin parts around it; add quarter of an inch for turnings all round.

Make the turnings and tack the patch over the hole, on the right side of the garment, matching the grain of the patch to that of the garment. Hem the patch in place, neatly. Turn to the wrong side and trim the material round the hole down to within quarter of an inch of the hemming stitches. Make a slit halfway to the corners. Trim the patch turnings to half this width. Turn under the edge of the garment all round the hole and neatly hem the fold with stitches that are small on right side.

Print Patch.—When choosing the patching material for this type of patch match the pattern to that of the garment

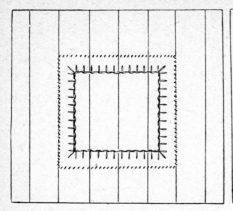

The raw edges on the wrong side are neatened with buttonhole stitch.

Place the patching piece over the hole and sew it with herringbone stitch.

surrounding the hole. If there is no spare garment material available it is sometimes possible to take a piece from the inside of the hem, replacing this with plain material as a cotton patch. If it is not possible to get a square large enough in one piece, then cut two small pieces and join them in the centre, matching the pattern carefully. Cut the patch to the grain of the fabric, making it large enough to cover all the thin parts and adding quarter-inch turnings.

Turn under the edges of the patch and press them. Place the patch in position on the right side of the garment, matching the pattern very carefully. Neatly hem round the edges.

On the wrong side trim the edges to within quarter of an inch of the stitching and buttonhole stitch the turnings.

Flannel Patch.—This is the kind of patch to use when mending woollen fabrics. Cut the patch large enough to cover the hole and all the worn area round it. Place the patching piece over the worn section and tack it. Work herringbone stitch, page 155, round all four sides without making turnings. Turn to the wrong side and trim the garment to within quarter of an inch of the stitching. Then fasten this edge with herringbone stitch.

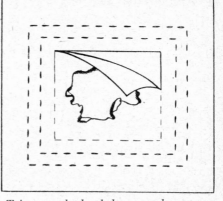

Trim round the hole to make narrow single turnings on the wrong side.

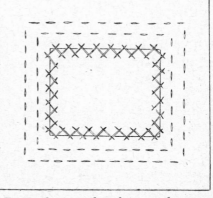

Fasten the raw edges down on the wrong side with neat herringbone stitch.

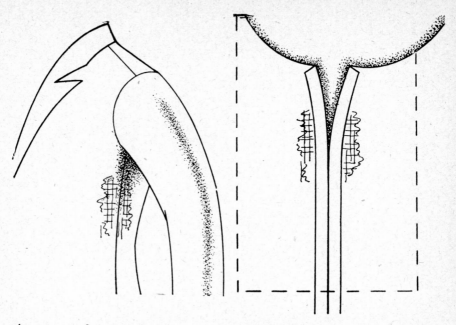

A worn part that occurs at a seam such as the underarm or elbow needs special care. The sleeve is partly removed and the seam unpicked to allow the patch to be inserted. Mark the area to be patched with a line of tacking stitches.

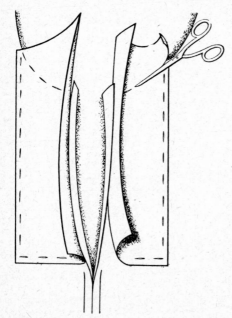

The surplus material is trimmed away carefully to fit the edge of the armhole.

Underarm Patch.—To repair a worn part at the underarm of a garment, or anywhere where a seam occurs, such as the elbow, patching is a little more complicated.

It is necessary first to unpick the seams where the patch is to be placed. Cut a piece of patching material, or two if necessary, large enough to cover the worn parts. Allow the patching pieces to reach the highest point of the armhole at the side of the patch and trim away the surplus, see Diagram. Place the patches on the wrong side of the garment and tack them, then sew them in place with herringbone stitch. Turn to the right side, trim the patch neatly, turn under the edges, after snipping the corners for the width of the turnings, and hem them down very neatly.

Press well and sew up the seams on the original sewing line, insert the sleeve again and replace the lining.

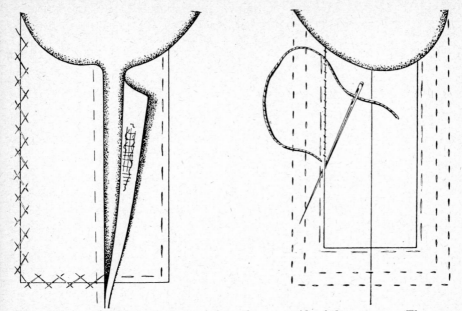

The patch is sewn with herringbone stitch on the wrong side of the garment. The seam is joined again neatly. Then trim round the edge of the hole and hem along the fold. Insert the sleeve into the armhole stitching on the old seam lines.

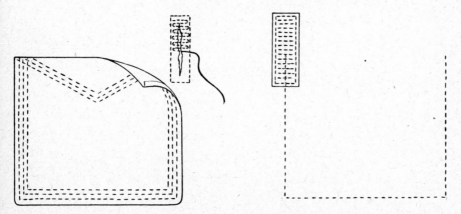

The pocket is unpicked over the tear and a piece of fabric is sewn to the wrong side.

As in all other patches the grain and pattern of the patching piece must be matched to those of the garment.

This method of patching is not used when leather is applied to elbows; then the patch covers the seams completely. **Torn Pocket.**—Needs special treatment. Unpick the corner of the pocket where it is torn. Tack a piece of tape or straight cut material at the back of the tear. Then make neat small darning stitches across the tear and through the patch, on the right side. Remove the tacks from the patch and press it well. Then stitch the pocket back in place where it was originally sewn.

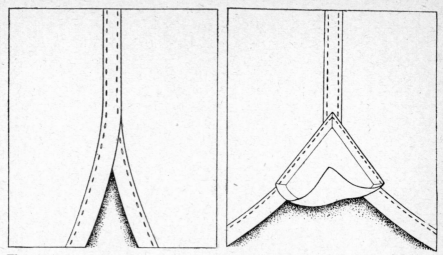

The opening is hemmed and two sides of the square gusset are turned under and sewn to it. Mitre the corners of the patch and trim off surplus turnings.

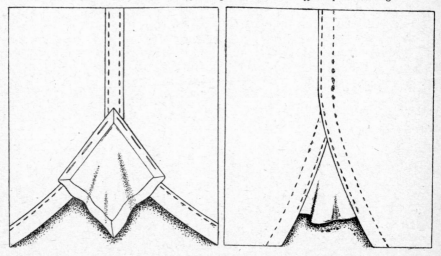

The gusset is folded across the centre and the first half is neatened with the second.

If material is used for the patch, match the grain of the fabric to that of the garment and turn under the edges. **Inserting a Gusset.**—It is sometimes necessary to insert gussets into the ends of side seams or into sleeve seams at the cuff end. To do this cut a square of material about four inches square. Leave the end of the seam unstitched to allow for the inserting of the gusset.

Sew one side of the gusset to one loose edge of the seam, which has been turned under and sewn with the point to the seam. Then sew the second side on the other loose edge of the seam, see Diagram. Fold the gusset in half from corner to corner and stitch it along both sides to the under-section. Sew the seam edge to the gusset neatly, on the right side. Press the seams well.

316

INDEX

Made and Printed in Great Britain by Odhams (Watford) Ltd. ,Watford
S.352.R1.S